Herbert MARSHALL
a Biography
by Scott O'BRIEN

ALSO BY SCOTT O'BRIEN

Kay Francis—I Can't Wait to be Forgotten (2006)
Classic Images Magazine—"Best Books of 2006" Laura Wagner—"O'Brien has a way with words as he beautifully examines Kay's films. He skillfully uses Kay's own diary to paint a picture of an independent woman ahead of her time."

Virginia Bruce—Under My Skin (2008)
Daeida Magazine—David Ybarra (editor)—*Under My Skin* is a well researched, tactful, and skilled examination into the tragedy of a talented, beautiful and popular figure in film history, desperate to fall in love at any cost. Highly recommended."

Ann Harding—Cinema's Gallant Lady (2010)
San Francisco Gate—Mick LaSalle—"Scott O'Brien has managed to come up with a thick, fact-filled, smart and very readable biography of this enormous talent. Harding deserves to be known, and the public deserves to know her."

Ruth Chatterton—Actress, Aviator, Author (2013)
Huffington Post—Thomas Gladys—"Best Film Books of 2013"

George Brent—Ireland's Gift to Hollywood and its Leading Ladies (2014)
Classic Images Magazine—Laura Wagner—"One of my favorites, Scott O'Brien, has written another excellent biography. O'Brien etches a fascinating portrait. His sources are extensive and, unlike hack writers, O'Brien provides pages of documentation."

Sylvia Sidney—Paid by the Tear (2016)
Sight & Sound—Dan Callahan—"O'Brien has labored to find the surviving people who worked with Sidney. Comments from these co-workers add texture to her story. O'Brien's book provides welcome insight into the jabbing toughness Sidney needed ... to survive in show business as long as she did."

Herbert Marshall: A Biography
© 2018. Scott O'Brien. All rights reserved.

All illustrations are copyright of their respective owners, and are also reproduced here in the spirit of publicity. Whilst we have made every effort to acknowledge specific credits whenever possible, we apologize for any omissions, and will undertake every effort to make any appropriate changes in future editions of this book if necessary.

No part of this book may be reproduced in any form or by any means, electronic, mechanical, digital, photocopying or recording, except for the inclusion in a review, without permission in writing from the publisher.

Published in the USA by:
BearManor Media
P O Box 71426
Albany, Georgia 31708
www.bearmanormedia.com

Printed in the United States of America
ISBN   978-1-62933-261-1 (paperback)

Book & cover design and layout by Dan & Darlene Swanson • www.van-garde.com

Contents

Foreword	(by Kevin Brownlow)	vii
Introduction	*"I was a lady from hell"*	xi
Chapter 1	Trying to Forget	1
Chapter 2	The Right Pub ... at the Right Time	17
Chapter 3	Bart & Edna	39
Chapter 4	Back & Forth Across the Big Pond	63
Chapter 5	Marshall & Swanson	91
Chapter 6	"I'm sick and tired of being a gentleman"	119
Chapter 7	A to Z—*A Woman Rebels*—*Zaza*	145
Chapter 8	Adventure in Transition	169
Chapter 9	Mrs. Marshall and *The Man Called X*	195
Chapter 10	Marshall & Maugham	217
Chapter 11	"What the hell is going on here?"	239
Chapter 12	"Goodness after all is the greatest force in the world"	265
Legacy	*The Marshall Family*	293
	Acknowledgements	303
	Endnotes	307
	Credits	329
	Index	357
	Photo Credits	363
	About the Author	365

Englishmen. Mastermind Hitchcock directing Marshall during the filming of *Foreign Correspondent* (1940) (UA)

Herbert Marshall

– BY KEVIN BROWNLOW

Just imagine that an early, despotic President, obsessed with our sins in the Revolutionary War, succeeded in banning the British from the United States. How would Hollywood have coped? No Chaplin, no Ronald Colman, no Cary Grant – and certainly no Herbert Marshall.

Herbert who?

Perhaps you're too young to have seen him on the screen. In that case, you ought to round up DVDs of the outstanding films in which he appeared – Hitchcock's masterpiece *Foreign Correspondent* (they wouldn't have let Hitchcock in – an *Englishman!*), Lubitsch's masterpiece *Trouble in Paradise,* Sidney Franklin's masterpiece *The Dark Angel* (set in England, oh dear!), Wyler's masterpieces *The Letter* and *The Little Foxes,* both with Bette Davis…

By now you will be a devoted fan of this singular, middle-aged man with the clipped accent, who plays so subtly with your emotions. He was perfect for military roles, but for an ironic reason you will discover in this book, he would seldom be cast in them.

Luckily, he conveyed remarkable sensitivity. In his book on James Stephenson, with whom Marshall appeared in *The Letter*, David Redfern wrote: "[Marshall's] forte was a hard to beat expression of both tenderness and silent suffering when playing a love scene."

Marshall was once asked how it was that he was so magnificent at playing British roles. "I am British," he replied, suggesting that, like so many great artists, he was inarticulate about his own work.

Marshall had a distinctive personality – who could resist that authoritative voice and no-nonsense manner? He didn't immerse himself in a part and become that person, like Alec Guinness. He adapted the part to himself, and what a reassuring, reliable and sensible self that was, appealing not just to women but, as a decorated combat veteran of WW1, to men as well.

Books on film and film actors have flooded the market. But fear not. Scott O'Brien's is not a scissors-and-paste job, nor an academic tome with words you've never heard of. It is well researched with a straightforward approach that does full justice to his admirable subject.

Kevin Brownlow
London, 2018

A contemplative Bart Marshall, rarely opened up about his past

INTRODUCTION
"I was a lady from hell...."

Herbert Marshall (August 1936)

When Portland reporter David Hazen went to Hollywood to interview Herbert Marshall in the summer of 1936, he was in for a surprise. Upon Hazen's arrival, Bart, as his friends called him, sat perusing an issue of *Stage* magazine. He shook Hazen's hand, and the round of questions began. Pointing to the photo of entertainer/composer George M. Cohan on the magazine cover, Marshall smiled, "There's a great old fellow." This brought up the patriotic anthem "Over There"—which had galvanized young men during the Great War, to enlist and fight the Germans. Hazen, who had been a war correspondent in France, knew that Marshall had his share in it, at great cost. Marshall himself didn't parade the fact, nor did he dodge it. "Were you in the war?" Hazen asked.

"Most certainly," Marshall replied, "with *both feet*, as you say in America."

"With what outfit?"

"I was a lady from hell."

"Sir?"

"The London Scottish, a kilted infantry regiment. You remember the Germans dubbed us 'ladies from hell.' That was a very good phrase."

"Wounded?"

"At Arras, early in the first day of the battle."

"Out long?"

"One year in a London Hospital. I was a private when I was wounded, but my papers were going through for a commission."

"Did you get it?"

"They made a hell of a fuss about it."[1]

Hazen walked away impressed by Bart Marshall's candor. The forty-six-year-old actor was very much in demand. He had played opposite Garbo, Dietrich, Shearer, Colbert, Kay Francis, Ann Harding, Sylvia Sidney, Jean Arthur, Ruth Chatterton, and most recently, Katharine Hepburn in *A Woman Rebels*. What Marshall brought to the screen was, in many respects, rooted in the unforeseen consequences of his war experience—which had left thousands of less fortunate comrades, "ladies from hell," dying in the trenches.

WWI (France) - The London Scottish, a.k.a. "The Ladies from Hell"

INTRODUCTION

The underlying compassion, warmth and *connection* that Herbert Marshall registered in his portrayals was often tinged with a random weariness. Understandably, so. He was a man without a leg, being confronted with pretend situations and characters whose résumé of human complaint, in comparison, seemed almost trivial.

Marshall never offered a frank, intimate interview regarding the loss of his leg. He wanted his craft as an *actor* to be the emphasis. His droll remark to David Hazen in 1936, about having "both feet" in the war, was Marshall, being Marshall. It was his way of embracing "what is" and maintaining a sense of humor about something he had no control over. In this respect, he came out ahead. More complicated, was the reality of what he referred to as "phantom pain" from a leg that wasn't there. Alcohol brought relief. And, there's a logical, physiological, medical explanation for that. During Marshall's life, pain management options for amputees were few and far between.

But, we get ahead of ourselves. Let's begin at the beginning. A grandmother and her two spinster daughters were the mentors and nurturers of young Bart Marshall. His parents, Percy and Ethel Marshall were perpetually on tour, in a theatrical world where, as Bart put it, "Greasepaint concealed humiliation and heartache." Nonetheless, Bart Marshall *cared* about these people whose tired faces were illuminated only by footlights.

Mill Lane in Hampstead, London, where Bertie Marshall lived with his grandmother

CHAPTER 1
Trying to Forget

PERCY AND ETHEL

Percy Marshall could make people laugh. In 1878, the eighteen-year-old made his stage debut with London's Roscius Dramatic Club. By the time he tackled the popular farce *Woodcock's Little Game* in West London, critics agreed that Percy, "a really clever actor," should stick to light comedy.[2] He followed their advice. In 1883 he began trouping with the Compton Comedy Co., playing up to fifty characters in standards such as Sheridan's *The School for Scandal*, *The Rivals*, and Goldsmith's *She Stoops to Conquer*. Percy began writing, acting and directing his own one-act plays and musical sketches. His lyrics for the satirical duet "Utterly Utter" were designed for two aesthetic-looking gentlemen to sing, while one flirtatiously offers the other a lily—a takeoff on Oscar Wilde. Townsfolk in the provinces caught the innuendo. It wasn't until he turned thirty that Percy, himself, found time to fall in love. On July 6, 1889, he married a young actress named Ethel May Turner. The newlyweds had something in common: famous fathers.

Percy Falcon Marshall was born in Kensington, England in 1859, to Thomas Falcon Marshall and his wife Amelia. Thomas was considered a versatile painter of portraiture, landscapes, and history. By the time he passed away in 1878, he had exhibited sixty works at the Royal Academy, forty at the British Institute, and was awarded the silver medal by the

Society of Arts. His prolific talent was not confined to his paintbrush and pallet. Thomas and Amelia had eleven children.

Producing a houseful of children was something that Percy Marshall, and his bride Ethel May, avoided. Ethel herself had ten siblings. Ethel was born in Middlesex, in 1868. Her father, Godfrey Wordsworth Turner, was a renowned author, art critic, and columnist for London's *Daily Telegraph*. Godfrey was known for his "straightforward, unsentimental style."[3] While he was pushing his pen and traveling worldwide, his wife Marianne stayed at home raising five sons and six daughters. One offspring, son Leopold, carried on his father's talent as a journalist and drama critic. It was Leopold who would prove to be a lifesaver for his nephew Herbert, the only child of his sister Ethel May.

Nine months into their marriage, Percy and Ethel welcomed their baby boy: Herbert Brough Falcon Marshall. He was born in London on May 23, 1890. "Brough" was after his godfather, Lionel Brough, a leading comic actor in London. Inevitably, the couple began using the diminutive "Bertie" for their son. Parental guidance, however, only went so far. It wasn't long before baby Bertie was on his own. The 1891 census listed ten-month old Herbert residing as a "Visitor" at the home of the widow Eliza Hopkins, a sick nurse. Following their marriage, Percy and Ethel were perpetually busy with various acting companies. The same census listed them as residing in a boarding house in Liverpool. Percy's 1891-92 tour in the farce *The Late Lamented*, lasted forty weeks. In December 1894, the couple sailed to the U.S. for Percy's six-month tour in *The Gaiety Girl*. There was no time to tend to a baby. Besides, Percy and Ethel had their fill of family life while growing up. Fortunately, Ethel's mother and two spinster sisters opened their arms to provide hearth and home for little Bertie Marshall.

In 1895-96, Percy, along with the popular actress Alison Skipworth, toured the U.S. east coast in the witty light opera, *An Artist's Model*. The following year, back in England, he was rated as "the life and the soul" of the rollicking comedy *A Night Out*. One critic noted how audiences thoroughly embraced "the immorality of the plot." Percy kept everyone in stitches, playing to packed houses in Bristol, where his "quiet and quaint style of emphasizing embarrassing situations" was a local favorite.⁴ Meanwhile, in London, one seven-year-old lad wasn't laughing.

Caricature of Percy in *Mrs. Othello* (1893) - Percy in *The Perplexed Husband* (1912)

In the summer of 1936, Herbert Marshall reflected back to his childhood. "My father was responsible for making me dread the theater," he confessed. "My father was a grand actor, better than I can ever dream of being, as a matter of fact. The world never found out how grand he was."⁵ Marshall acknowledged his father's talent, but felt that Percy lacked the drive, or ability to sell himself. Of course, Percy was essentially a character comedian. Instead of world fame and recognition, there were money problems, and plenty of worries. Young Bertie witnessed all this first hand during his vacations from school. Accompanying his parents on tour, he was often tired and cold. All he could see was a drab world filled with discouraged, tired faces—hard-working people who slaved for a few shillings. Greasepaint concealed humiliation and heartache. Marshall added, "I am one actor who never wanted to be an actor. I never postured before the mirror at the age of six, with the ambition to play Hamlet. I had no reason to love the theater. I spent most of my time ... trying to forget."

Marshall was explaining all of this, over a cup of tea, to Gladys Hall, cousin of novelist Faith Baldwin. He pointed out that he was uncomfortable talking about himself. After considerable persistence on her part, he apologetically began to open up. Marshall stepped from behind the actor to reveal personal anecdotes, which was unusual for him. Hall kept glancing at the photographs hung on the wall. One was of Percy and Ethel. She described them as a "pathetic young couple, timid and frightened looking." Next to it, was a photo of the three women who were young Bart's caregivers at the turn of the century. They were Marian Turner, his widowed grandmother, and his two spinster aunts, Margaret and Ellen. It was they who looked after Bertie, while Percy and Ethel toured the provinces. Mrs. Turner lived at 16 Mill Lane in Hampstead, inside London's Borough of Camden. The area was touted for being an intellectual, liberal, artistic community. However, Bertie's grandmother and aunts were gentle and *unworldly*. They loved Bertie, and, as he put it, "worried over his soul."

Aunt Ellen, or "Nellie," was a particular favorite. She made poetry out of everything she read, from advertisements in magazines, to slogans on soap wrappers. She would recite them aloud as if reading verse. It gave her young nephew many a smile. The patience and kindness Bertie received from these women of the Victorian Age reflected into his own personality. Bertie entertained himself by illustrating the people he met. This also allowed him to laugh, and quash his frequent bouts with depression—a lifelong, and protracted battle. His passion for drawing caricatures would never waver. Many years later, Marshall told sportswriter Chip Royal, "I don't know a better way to get a lift, if you are depressed, than to take a pencil or crayon and draw."[6] By that time, Herbert Marshall had also amassed an impressive collection of original cartoon caricatures by British and American artists.

CHAPTER ONE

Marshall recalled that at age twelve, due to his parents profession, he thought himself a shoo-in for the lead in a school play titled *Snicketty Nick*. He learned the lines, but didn't get the role. On opening night, Bart locked his competitor in the school coal bin, then volunteered as an emergency replacement. The grimy competitor showed up for the Third Act.[7] Bertie's enthusiasm for theater was put on hold for a few more years.

Following his early schooling, Bertie and his mother took time out to make what he considered to be a life-changing decision. In 1953, Marshall reflected,

> As a child I was called Bertie. When I became 16 my mother and I took a long walk. We had to do something about that name. We looked up and saw an advertising sign, 'Bartholomew and Company.' That sounded solid. We picked a part of it—Bart—and its stuck ever since.[8]

The newly christened "Bart" enrolled in St. Mary's College in Old Harlow, Essex. He focused on business and accounting. Some sources say he graduated, but Marshall countered this assumption during his talk with Gladys Hall. "When I was about sixteen," he admitted, "I had to leave school entirely—not enough money to go on." At eighteen, Bart's ambitions remained un-ignited, and he took whatever came along: an office boy for a London public accountant. He eventually lost interest in checking over interminable columns of figures that other people had added. It came as no surprise when he was fired—"through sheer incompetence," he admitted. Apparently, there were other such gigs—"I was fired much too often." He also wagged, "It looked as though I was destined to be a successful failure."[9]

Bart returned home to live with his grandmother and aunts. "I was at loose ends, unhappy," he recalled. "Finally came a letter, offering me an assistant managership of a musical comedy company going out on tour. I took the job for the sake of the few shillings in it." He was nineteen at the time.[10] Stories vary, but most likely it was Percy who lined his son up for this position, as the letter was from his friend, theatrical producer Robert Courtneidge. In a few months, Bart Marshall was on the other side of the footlights. He mentioned to Gladys Hall that he played a footman in the operetta *The Arcadians*, which was a noteworthy success for Courtneidge. Marshall also indicated that character actor Eric Blore was in the cast. This would have taken place in October 1910.[11] The fledgling, young actor Herbert Marshall was suddenly nudged toward what he called a *real* turning point in his life.

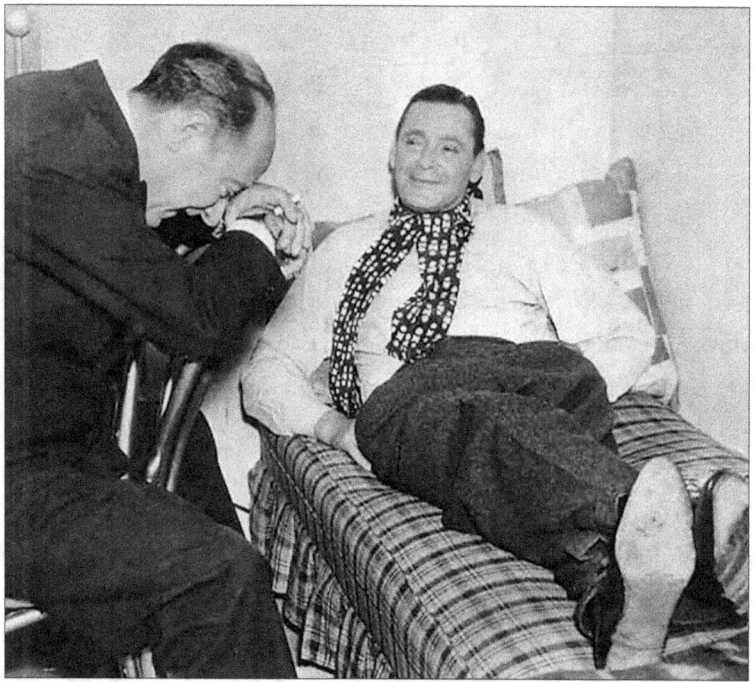

1937 - Candid shot of old pals Eric Blore and Marshall

Marshall's friendship with Eric Blore never faltered. They would team in three Hollywood films during the 1930's and 40's. Bart elaborated on this significant relationship.

> It was Eric Blore who was the turning point in my adult life. It was Eric who opened doors for me. It wasn't that

he did anything concrete for me. Quite simply, by the fact of him being just Eric, he spoke a language I had not been hearing. He was unique ... and his wit was brilliant. His brilliance (which I had the good fortune to recognize) removed me mentally from the genial, but frightfully limited language I was acquiring from other lads. He gave me what I can best describe as a 'flavor' to life. And I, who had never had any real ambitions, any soaring hopes for myself, began to reach out, to stir, as it were, in my sleep. I have Eric to thank for this.[12]

Blore, who was three years older than Marshall, also shared stories of trouping in Australia. Bart began to see himself as an actor. He was not an overnight success by any means. At the Opera House in Buxton, for example, he was handed the part of a footman in a 1911 revival, *The Adventure of Lady Ursula*. He was granted one line, "Madame is served." Actor-manager N. Carter Slaughter also offered Bart and a young Ronald Colman bit parts in various productions.[13] As Marshall's thespian abilities increased over the next two years, he began receiving notices. His first notable success was at London's Princes Theatre (May 12, 1913) in the farce *Brewster's Millions*, in which he played Tommy. *The Era* declared, "The requisite nutty favor is given Tommy Smith by Mr. Herbert Marshall." When a slump came along, Bart took an offer as a dramatic tutor. He later admitted, "It was such a hopeless task trying to teach people to act ... I finally resigned."[14] From that experience he drew the conclusion that acting was a question of instinct, and that success was a matter of luck.

Throughout the Summer of 1914, Marshall was praised across England and Scotland for his "irresistible" and "plucky" performance as Jack, the dimwitted son of a clergyman, in *The Headmaster*. Just as Marshall began to stir interest among audiences, Europe was in the throes of entering what would be known as The Great War.

In August 1914, England declared war on Germany. The British were quite unprepared, and rushed to reorganize what Kaiser Wilhem II described as "a contemptible little army." Half the English forces were already posted overseas to garrison the British Empire. The government pushed the press to support the war. 225,000 men signed up to fight.[15] War related industries multiplied, and women were brought into mainstream employment. Britain also created its first Royal Air Force. It would be over a year before conscription was introduced for men between the ages of 18 and 41. In the meantime, Bart Marshall stayed behind the footlights.

At the outbreak of the Great War, Marshall had aligned himself with veteran actor Cyril Maude, who had played the title role in *The Headmaster*. Marshall's skillful performance playing Maude's nephew in the comedy *Grumpy*, further endeared him to the actor-manager, who had a reputation for being quite particular. Marshall later admitted, "I actually was embarrassed at the tryout."[16] Fortunately, his timidity suited the nephew's character. In the summer of 1915, Maude asked Marshall to accompany him and this troupe of players to the United States. Bart surely must have had some misgivings. The British liner *Lusitania* had been sunk by a German U-Boat that May. Before sailing, Bart worked steadily in London, and for good reason. "I waited til I could put something into my wife's lap," he later recalled, "leave her with enough money to go on for a while."[17]

On August 14, 1915, Bart Marshall had taken a bride, an attractive co-player he had wooed on stage and off. It's no wonder she received accolades for her "powerful portrayal of Portia" in *The Headmaster*. Hilda Lloyd Bosley was a year older than Bart, and went by her stage name, Mollie Maitland.[18] The couple moved in with Bart's parents at 134 Sutton Court in the London district of Chiswick. After two weeks of matrimony, Bart left Mollie behind. The cast of *Grumpy* sailed on the *S.S. New York*, leaving Liverpool on September 1st. It would be another nine months before Bart reunited with his bride. That Fall, Mollie contented herself touring Scotland and England, playing the role of Mrs. MacLaren in *Grumpy*, with Horace Hodges in the title role. Hodges was co-author of the play.

CHAPTER ONE

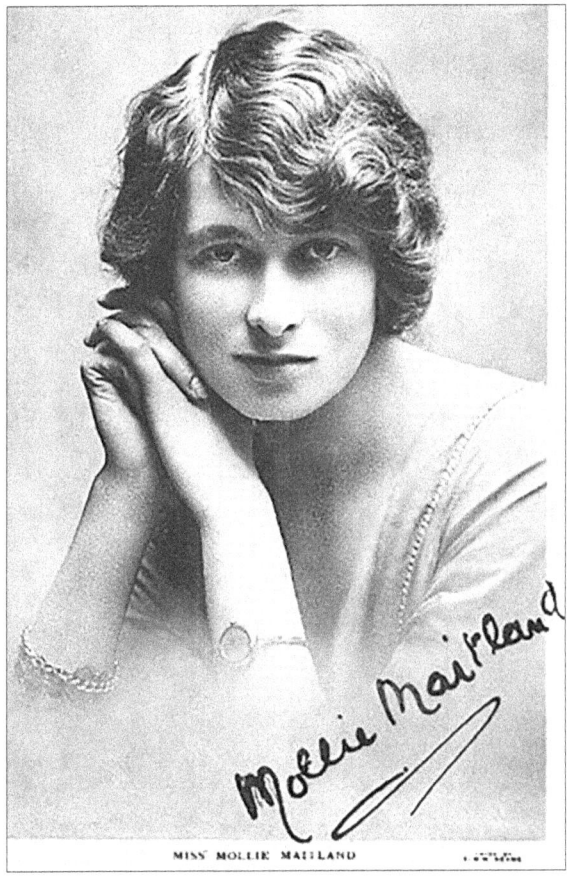

Marshall's first wife, Mollie Maitland, his co-star in *The Headmaster* (1915)

Cyril Maude's company of *Grumpy* was greeted with outbursts of applause as it kicked off its four-week run at Broadway's Empire Theatre. The four-act comedy centered on Grumpy himself, an eccentric, crotchety, retired barrister, who welcomes home his young nephew Ernest (Marshall), just returned from South Africa. Ernest carries with him a sizeable diamond of great value, which is to be placed in the hands of his employer. Another houseguest, Jarvis, is a clever gentleman jewel-thief. He has already stolen the heart of Grumpy's granddaughter, Virginia, with whom Ernest is madly in love. A mix of assault, attempted murder, and mayhem triggered more laughter, until Grumpy (abetted by Scotland Yard) solved the mystery.

1914 - Margot Kelly and Marshall in *Grumpy* (Glasgow Daily Record) - 1915 ad from New York tour

The tour played Buffalo, Niagara Falls, Omaha, Grand Rapids, Boston and other major cities, including His Majesty's Theatre in Montreal. Occasionally, Marshall would be singled out for praise. A critic in Duluth nodded, "Herbert Marshall, as Grumpy's nephew, displays canny discernment in managing a young woman of flirting tendencies."[19] An Ohio review applauded, "Herbert Marshall shared honors with the star." As Cyril Maude was a thirty-year stage veteran, it was indeed a feather in Marshall's cap. While in Cincinnati, Maude celebrated his 700th performance as Grumpy. Three months later, in May, he laid *Grumpy* to rest. Bart and co-star Elsie Mackay (who had played his love interest) sailed home together on the *S.S. Noordam*, arriving in England on May 20, 1916.

Marshall was greeted with open arms by his wife Mollie, as well as those of his King and Country. The newly legislated conscription law demanded that he enlist. As casualties in the Great War increased, recruitment had fallen rapidly. The previous January, mandatory conscription into the army was introduced for the first time in England's history. This initial recruitment was for single men. When Bart arrived home, conscription had been extended to all men between the ages of 18 and 41. He, two male co-players from the U.S. tour of *Grumpy*, and 2,700 other London actors had no choice but to sign up.[20] On June 2, 1916, Herbert Marshall enlisted in the 14th Battalion, London Regiment (also known as the London Scottish). The London Scottish was headquartered in the heart of London in close proximity to West End theatres—a natural destination for young actors "doing their bit" in the war effort.

"While waiting for my summons," recalled Bart, "I kept on with the road show in which I was working [*Grumpy*]. We players crossed the channel to Ireland for an appearance in Dublin. The show was successful and could have remained there another week, but one Sunday I suddenly felt compelled to return to London and get into my uniform. My co-actors tried to persuade me to stay, and ... finally I told them my hunch. Most of them agreed with me that I should obey it, although it meant the disbanding of the company. So we all returned that weekend to England aboard a certain little channel steamer, the same on which we had arrived. The very next Sunday—the day on which we would have returned had we stayed in Dublin—the same channel boat was torpedoed by a German submarine and sank with the loss of every person aboard."²¹

Marshall was mobilized for active service on August 28. His choices, and hunches, were no longer in his hands. He was placed in what was called The 5th Army (or Reserve Army), under the command of General Hubert Gough. In a matter of months, Private Marshall would be sent to the Western Front. No amount of training could have prepared him for what happened next.

H.B.F. Marshall - infantry record; London Scottish during The Great War

Marshall departed for France on January 4, 1917. He joined his unit on February 10. They operated in the Pas-de-Calais region. Two months later, on April 9, British troops attacked German defenses near the French city of Arras (known as the Second Battle of Arras). The aim was to end the war in forty-eight hours.²² Author Mark Lloyd's detailed study, *London Scottish in the Great War* (Pen and Sword, 2000) offers military diary excerpts of what followed. Zero-hour was at 5:30 a.m. It was dark, snowing heavily, and visibility was poor. It wasn't until 11:30 a.m. that the London Scottish received orders to prepare for attack. They advanced in artillery formation over muddy ground and steady shell fire. Despite enemy resistance, losses were considered to be light. Seventeen soldiers were killed and another sixty-six wounded.[23] Herbert Marshall, on that first day, April 9, was the recipient of a snipers bullet into his left knee.[24] Bart was admitted to a military hospital in Abbeville on April 12. His military career came to a halt, and by the time the Battle of Arras was over (May 16), so were the lives of 160,000 British troops.

The prelude to this battle gives an idea as to what Bart and other enlistees were up against. By the eve of the Battle of Arras, front-line trenches collapsed, and barbed-wire defenses were blown to bits. Men were exhausted from trying to maintain troop dug-outs, while subsisting on minimal food rations—two or three days would go by with nothing to eat. Movement was restricted by day to avoid the attention of German reconnaissance aircraft. General Gough had gained a reputation for "heavy losses and complete failure." One Brigadier General wrote into his diary, "General Gough does not care a button about the lives of his men."[25] Many divisions hated transferring into The 5th Army, because of Gough's lack of empathy for the common soldier.[26] Marshall would downplay these hellish conditions, complaining only of "terrific boredom." "There was no drama lying in the trenches," he told one journalist. "I must have felt fear, but I don't remember it. I was too numb to recall any enterprise on my part."[27]

On May 1, 1917, Marshall boarded the hospital steamer *H.S. Jan Breydel*, and returned home to England to recuperate. Wheelchair-bound, then on crutches, he received a reduction in military status to that of "temporary duty." The next step was to try and save his leg. It wasn't healing properly. He spent ten months in a base hospital. "I had plenty of lonely nights to think about the future," said Marshall, "and about mine in particular, which I was afraid was pretty well spiked by the war and by my injury. I was twenty-[six] years old, with three years of theater under my belt and one loving fan, my mother."[28]

Numerous surgical procedures added to Bart's frustration. When all hope was lost, doctors decided to amputate below the hip. Following this, Marshall was finally designated: "No longer physically fit for war service."[29] He had served a total of 1 year, and 350 days. For his loss, Marshall received the Silver War Badge (for those wounded in battle), and the Victory and British War Campaign Medals. He was officially decorated, discharged, depressed, and disabled. He walked with the assistance of canes, which he begrudgingly referred to as "sticks." Years afterward, he remarked, "I got off the train in London station feeling lower than anyone but a German ought to feel."[30]

While his wife Mollie toured Scotland, Marshall, resigned to his status as an invalid, went to stay with his mother's older brother, Leopold, better known as "Uncle Bogey." Bogey, a journalist, editor, lyricist and drama critic, lived in a villa twenty-five miles outside of London. He had lost his first-born son Penrhyn in the war. The twenty-year-old was killed in action in October 1916. Bogey was devastated by the loss. Bart would recall, "I came to know him as man to man—both men desolated." Amidst the nightly threats of air-raids and intermittent sound of explosions, Uncle Bogey and his nephew faced their own emotional battles.

Bart credited his uncle for shaping his world view, and acknowledged later, "He proved to me that a man may face utter desolation without whimpering. By his fine courage and gorgeous sense of humor, which not even grief could crucify, he showed me how a man may know irreparable loss and still inherit the earth."[31] Together, they talked intelligently about books and plays. Despite the circumstances, Bogie had a rich outlook on life. Bart took time to think and read. Needless to say, there were numerous young actors incapacitated by war, who didn't have an Uncle Bogey to encourage the fortitude to move forward with life, passions and careers. Fueled with some semblance of renewal, Bart was now prepared to deal with his physical handicap. He was fitted with the first of several prosthetic legs.

A 1928 article in *The Irish Times* reported that during Marshall's stay at London's St. Thomas Hospital, King George V visited the wounded soldiers. When asked to choose which of Marshall's legs was artificial, the King selected the wrong one.[32] Even so, artificial legs proved not only to

CHAPTER ONE

be challenging to maneuver, but painful—what Marshall would describe as "phantom pain," which, along with the ghosts of war, followed him for the rest of his life.

May 1, 1917 - *H.S. Jan Breydel* transported Marshall back to England; Aftermath: leg prosthetics; (May 28, 1918) Silver War Badge #393051 allotted to Marshall. The reward for disabled, disillusioned veterans

Herbert Marshall was among four actors in the London Scottish who would later find acclaim in Hollywood. Ronald Colman had enlisted two years prior to Marshall. Colman's army stint was short-lived after shrapnel ripped through his knee and ankle. He was discharged in May 1915, and left with a permanent limp which he disguised with a jaunty saunter. Claude Rains enlisted in February 1916. In November, his unit was bombarded by heavy artillery and poison gas. His right eye was impaired, and he was granted an officers commission based in London. Basil Rathbone enlisted in March 1916. He was awarded the Military Cross, "for conspicuous daring and resource on patrol."[33] Rathbone spied on the enemy during a daylight raid— disguised as a tree! That he survived was nothing short of a miracle. In 1957, commentator Edward R. Murrow asked Basil what was the toughest role he ever played. "Oh, a tree, Ed," answered Rathbone, "to a very unappreciative audience."[34]

British actor Brian Aherne, who was sixteen when the war ended, never forgot the accumulated horrors of a war-torn world, and its aftermath. He recalled in 1969, "Surrounded as we were by widows and orphans, by cripples on crutches and mutilated men in wheelchairs, and seeing as we did ex-officers of famous regiments standing in the gutter, trying to sell pencils or matches, we were all pacifists ... determined never, so help us God, would we fight again, for any cause whatsoever."[35] Aherne underscored the fact that war is never really over and done with.

American author Laurence Stallings lost a leg in battle. His autobiographical bestseller, *Plumes* (1924) (the basis for the 1925 block-buster film *The Big Parade*), detailed the grim realities faced by disabled, disillusioned veterans. Politics and corruption obstructed financial aid to these men—a situation mirrored in England. Both countries spent millions memorializing the dead with monuments, shrines and spectacle, but what about the living? Stallings exposed the hypocrisy and brutal realities faced by thousands of disabled surviving the carnage of battle. In 1918, Bart Marshall found himself very much like the protagonist in *Plumes*, unable to "romance about his wounds" and the glories of war. He had survived, alright. Damaged nerves were a reminder of that fact. As Stallings described, "I've got ten thousand flames of hell telling me that I'm alive."[36]

"Those first few months ... were the darkest," confirmed Marshall, "the most bitter of my life. I thought I was permanently handicapped in my profession. There are not many roles written for lame men ... ."[37] Although his spirits had been lifted by Uncle Bogey, Bart's obvious limp continued to play on his mind. On his own now, hopes at a standstill, Bart Marshall did what most English chaps would do under similar circumstances. He headed straight to the nearest pub.

CHAPTER 2
The Right Pub ... at the Right Time

It was a thick, foggy, London summer night. Bart Marshall, feeling like a ghost of his former self, headed toward a favorite pub. The war was still on, but by May 1918, the aerial threat to Britain was effectively over. Wireless communication enabled planes to be dispatched to the borders in time to counter attacks. Pubs were returning to their former relaxed and friendly atmosphere. Arriving at his destination, Bart milled through the crowd towards the bar. He had barely swallowed a mouthful when someone called out, "Herbert old boy! What about playing a part for me on a six weeks tour?"[38] He turned to see the cheerful, familiar face of actor-manager N. Carter Slaughter. Slaughter strolled over to him and shook hands. "I was still white and shaky," recalled Marshall, "and terribly, terribly scrawny. And miserably uncertain about myself and my ability to tackle life again." He elaborated further on this crucial encounter with Slaughter.

> I told him I wasn't sure I could act any more, that I wasn't fit for work yet. But the more I talked, the more he interrupted. He was sure I could play the part right now—and his faith restored mine. It was the beautiful casualness of the offer, the assumption that there was no reason why I shouldn't go out, no reason why I shouldn't pick up where I had left off that—well, that resurrected

me from the trenches, that healed my war wounds. God bless him for that. I want to give him very special honorable mention, for no story concerning me or my life could be authentic without him.³⁹

Come August 1918, Bart Marshall, resurrected from the trenches, returned to the stage as the wounded war veteran Dick Fellows, in the domestic comedy *Betty at Bay*. Ripe with sentiment and humor, the play told the story of a recently wed, working class English girl who must rely on her own inner strength upon learning (falsely, as it turns out) that her husband has been killed in the war. It had been sixteen months since Bart had last tread the boards, and he was saluted by critics for his courage. A Gloucestershire review nodded, "The part of Dick Fellows ... is well played by Mr. Herbert Marshall, whose limping movement across the stage is not put on, but the effect of wounds received in real battle."⁴⁰ Mention of Marshall's service on the Western Front was used in publicity for the play.

Betty at Bay was wrapping up tour, just as the Armistice was signed on November 11th. It marked a victory for the Allies and defeat for Germany. Six months of negotiations at the Paris Peace Conference concluded with the Treaty of Versailles. As pointed out, for many the battle was *never* over. The psychological distress of soldiers was hastily described as "shell shock," although many veterans not exposed to exploding shells had similar symptoms. Ignorance regarding what was eventually known as PTSD only amplified the problem. The most audacious statement regarding the disease came from a U.S. military medical officer, Major Frederick W. Parsons, in 1919. Parsons concluded, "War neurosis which persists is not a creditable disease to have, as it indicates in practically every case a lack of soldierly qualities ... no one should be permitted to glorify himself as a case of 'shell shock.'"⁴¹ Parsons' attitude still persists. The *American Legion* article, "Booted After Battle" (2016), details how many veterans with PTSD end up homeless, suicidal and on drugs, simply because commanders and government personnel have the opinion that "real men" don't get PTSD, and consider them "trouble-makers ...

not fit to deploy."[42]

Bart Marshall had the good fortune to find refuge from his war trauma. Instead of shutting down, he allowed other people to help. He was rescued by the kindness of his Uncle Bogey, who listened and bore witness to his young nephew. Then came the casual and confident offer from N. Carter Slaughter, who accepted Bart fully, as he was. And, subsequently, veteran actress Francis Wetherall. Wetherall introduced Marshall to actor-manger Nigel Playfair, who owned the Lyric Opera House, in Hammersmith, London. Immediately following *Betty at Bay*, Bart joined Playfair's stock company for two years.

Playfair was taking a big risk, as Hammersmith was considered a slum area. The theater itself was a shambles, referred to by locals as "The Blood and Flea Pit." It had once served as a mission, as well as a boxing ring. Bart was in the newly renovated Lyric's premier production, A.A. Milne's children's fantasy, *Make-Believe.* In this, no less than nine Hubbard children explore the power of make believe, creating scenes from fairy tales. Bart popped up as: The Red Prince, Baron Bluebeard, and Pirate Bill. Next up, was *The Younger Generation* which challenged puritanical attitudes and parental control—pushing the envelope for young people to let loose. In the aftermath of WWI, the 1920's were about to roar. The *New Statesman* cheered, "*The Younger Generation* is a good piece of realism ... neat and natural. Herbert Marshall is an actor on whom those interested in marking down new talent had better keep an eye."[43]

Bart then took a step back in time in John Drinkwater's hit, *Abraham Lincoln*. In this, Marshall essayed two roles: an emissary for the Confederate States, and as Lincoln's Secretary of War. The play was a hit and played at the Lyric for over a year. Critic Arnold Bennett offered his own modest assessment of the play, saying, "Nobody can dine out in London today and admit without a blush that he has not seen *Abraham Lincoln*."[44] Amidst all the brouhaha, one cast member was in the throes of constant pain. This was confirmed by actor Reginald Denham, who revealed exactly what Herbert Marshall was up against.

> We had rehearsed for three weeks and it was not until the dress rehearsal when we were taking off our clothes that we discovered that Bart had only one leg. Bart had one of the latest mechanical ones for which there was a growing demand. These postwar contraptions were extremely clumsy and would cause the wearer great pain. Several years later, Bart told me that he had played most of the run of *Lincoln* in agony.[45]

The dressing room was on the third floor. Marshall had three quick costume changes, which required he climb and descend stairs eight times a day. "Through all this crippling discomfort," said Denham, "I never heard Bart utter a world of complaint. Of course, we all tried to help him. His one reaction, apart from gratitude, was apologetic. He hated being, what he called, 'such a bloody nuisance.'" Denham never forgot Bart's reaction when one actor advised him to do clerical work at the front desk, instead of attempting a stage career. "Bart told this popinjay what to do with himself," said Denham, "in words that would have won the approval of Kenneth Tynan." A flamboyant British critic, Tynan was known for peppering his opinions with profanities. Denham, who would focus on becoming a director, placed Bart Marshall in a unique category, saying, "My own main memory of him is as a young eagle, a wounded eagle, with indomitable courage." Following a two-month run of St. John Ervine's powerful drama *John Ferguson* (February 1920), in which Marshall played the rebellious son of a rural Irish farmer, the "wounded eagle" made his final bow at the Lyric in Shakespeare's *As You Like It*.

For a single matinee performance at the Lyric, author and playwright John Galsworthy penned a one-act play, *Defeat: A Tiny Drama*. Most likely, Galsworthy wrote the lead with Marshall in mind. The story detailed a brief interlude in war torn London, between a soldier who is "a little lame," and a desolate prostitute (Cathleen Nesbitt). Prior to any intimacy, she inquires if he is glad to have killed Germans. His response? "I don't think so. We're all in the same boat, so far as that's concerned. We're not glad to kill each other—not most of us." His kindness enables her to reveal that *she* is German. "My dear girl," he replies, "who cares? We aren't fighting against women."

Galsworthy allows the prostitute to drive the point home that war is a sad solution to nothing. The soldier, however, draws back from her bleak outlook. He places money on the table and starts to leave. "You upset me," he explains. Outside the window, a newsboy declares another victory for the British. The woman picks up the money to give it back, but the soldier refuses, and bids adieu. The script then allows her to revert back in time, to her happy childhood in the fatherland. She rips up the English currency, and tearfully begins to sing "Die Wacht am Rhein." Outside, voices sing "Rule, Britannia!" Curtain. Galsworthy's point: patriotism dies hard.

The Lyric's ground-breaking version of *As You Like It*, with outré costuming and stage design, was met with controversy. One critic railed, "Treating Shakespeare as if he were some modern drawing-room playwright … is simply intolerable." Playfair realized he was creating something of a revolution. *The Times*, on the other hand, found it "brilliant and exciting." *The Observer* called it a "riot of pure color." As the melancholy traveler Jacques, Marshall provided the perfect contrast to Athene Seyler's exhilarating Rosalind, who fled from her uncle's court. *The Spectator* enthused, "Miss Seyler and Mr. Herbert Marshall made us conscious of the philosophy of life which runs under the play. Their acting was raised above that of the average … by their remarkable perception of this inner play." Marshall was afforded Shakespeare's famous monologue: "All the world's a stage, and all the men and women merely players … ." *The Saturday Review* nodded, "Herbert Marshall … the best Jacques we have ever seen." Years afterwards, Marshall admitted, "Jacques in *As You Like It* has given me more pleasure than any part I have played."[46] Before leaving the Lyric, Bart celebrated his thirtieth birthday. His parents, both retired, still lived on Sutton Court in Chiswick. They caught their son's performances at the Lyric and other West End theaters, such as The Duke of York's, where Marshall played Antonio in Shakespeare's *The Merchant of Venice*.

Brown Sugar (1920) Flapper Best confronts Marshall, as Lord Sloane

Now freelancing, Marshall had the good fortune to return to The Duke of York's for the comedy *Brown Sugar* (July-October, 1920), all about a chorus girl with a heart of gold, who marries into high society. *The London Illustrated News* referred to the leading lady as, "that stage-flapper *par excellence*, Miss Edna Best." It was the role that brought Best to stardom. Marshall played her husband, Lord Sloane. The Marshall-Best relationship was cordial, and in a few years would resonate off stage. In the meantime, cupid's arrow struck elsewhere. By December, the fair-haired, blue-eyed twenty-year-old Best, had the lead in a new play (*Peter Pan*), and a new husband, Seymour Beard, a star of musical comedy. Headlines blazed "Peter Pan Married!" "Peter Pan Secretly Wed!"

The Crossing – Caricatures of Marshall and Hubert Harben

Marshall contented himself with wife Mollie, and the life after death saga, *The Crossing*, in which he played a ghost. On stage, his psychic daughter beholds her beloved father's return from the great beyond. Family members are ecstatic at this turn of events, filled with, what drama critic Hugh Dryden called, "an abundance of words ... causing much exercise of grey matter." Dryden had praises for Marshall, nonetheless. "The acting is beyond praise. Herbert Marshall was superbly exalted as an idealist." *The London Mercury* thought Marshall, and the childlike charm of co-star Marjorie Gordon (the physic daughter) made the play worth seeing.

In January 1921, Bart joined the cast of *A Safety Match*. Critics agreed he was the one "bright spot." In *Count X*, he played an inventor who spars with a fraudulent spiritualist trying to steal his latest creation. *The Saturday Review* thought Marshall "stuck in a thankless role," and found *Count X* to be nothing short of "a cure for insomnia." Not to worry. Someone had her eye on Herbert Marshall. To his rescue came the highly respected actress Marie Lohr, who was the same age as Bart. Australian born, Lohr had been a leading West End star since 1908. In 1918, she and her husband took over the management of the Globe Theatre.

At the end of May, Lohr and Marshall co-starred in a Winter Garden performance of the one-act comedy *Mother of Pearl*. It was a charity event for the Royal National Orthopedic Hospital, and raised over a thousand pounds. In July, Marshall and wife Mollie, joined Lohr for another benefit performance of *Her Destiny*. It was at this point that Marie Lohr took Bart Marshall under her wing. Though only in her early thirties, she had grown rather matronly. Preparing for her first Canadian tour, Lohr realized that she needed the eloquent charm of a leading man like Marshall. She got her wish. On August 25, Bart, Mollie, Marie Lohr and her London Globe Company, boarded the *Empress of France* at Liverpool, and sailed to Quebec.

Upon arrival, the London Globe Company boarded a train and headed west to Ottawa, where they staged *Fedora*. They played to capacity houses at each stop across Canada. After playing Vancouver's Orpheum Theatre, the troupe returned east to Edmonton, where the Dramatic Society entertained Lohr and her handsome leading man to high tea. By December, the troupe opened in Winnipeg for an engagement in Robert Hichens' *The Voice from the Minaret*. In this, Lohr played an unhappy married English lady who is romanced by a dashing younger man (Marshall), a minister no less, who is tempted by the flesh. A vengeful husband (Edmund Gwenn)

complicates things, until he conveniently dies. The Canadian Press was thrilled that Lohr preferred to tour Canada *prior* to heading to the U.S. Other British companies went directly to New York. Ben Deacon, for the *Manitoba Free Press* predicted a new theatrical trend. "Miss Lohr and company have followed a different route," Deacon crowed. "They went first to the Dominion and after touring Canada, they condescended to come to New York."[47]

As important as the plays themselves, was the gracious, profoundly moving curtain speech that Marie Lohr gave following a performance of *The Voice from the Minaret*. She came to the defense of her leading man, after he unintentionally stepped upon the long train of her fabulous evening gown. The silky green fabric, embroidered with silver spangles, proclaimed to typify the latest in English couture. Marshall had tread upon this exquisite creation no less than three times during the play. Naturally, he was mortified, much to the audience's amusement. After the curtain came down (to tremendous applause), an indignant Lohr gave her audience a rapid once over, and began what amounted to a sermon. "If you had realized," she protested, "that Herbert Marshall had lost a leg in the war and was completely unaware that he was treading on my dress, I am sure, that not one of you, would have thought it amusing." The audience was staggered by her reprimand, having no idea about Marshall's traumatic war experience. The incident, mentioned in a 1960 issue of *Films and Filming*, concluded,

> They gave him an ovation that was so great and so spontaneous that throughout the length and breadth of Canada and the United States, he became front page news. After that, every city welcomed him as "the British soldier who fought adversity and returned to his career in the theatre." From then onwards he never looked back.[48]

The Voice from the Minaret (1921-22) Marshall avoiding Lohr's long train

The Vancouver Daily World review of *Fedora* (November 21, 1921) praised, "Herbert Marshall, one of the heroes of the war, who, despite the loss of one leg, strides through the play with astounding authority and deceptive ease." A few months later, Broadway's Burns Mantle echoed the sentiment, saying, "Herbert Marshall, who manipulates an artificial limb wonderfully, inspiring sobering thoughts of England's tragedy in giving of her best."[49] Marshall himself would often mention Marie Lohr as one of his champions. Although he was never prone to make a fuss over his war injury (in fact, he preferred not to talk about it at all), Lohr's concern for his well being was something he would treasure.

The last two months of the tour focused on the eastern seaboard of the U.S. *The Voice from the Minaret* opened at the Hudson Theatre in New York on January 30, 1922. *Theater Magazine* commented on Lohr's "theatrical gesture" and "old-style elocution," and that her leading man was "a bit young to lend verisimilitude to the romance between them." (Bart was actually two months older than Lohr.) Lohr's stage vehicles were far removed from the modern trend—"taken out of the urn of forgotten plays" as one wag put it. *Fedora* debuted in 1882. *The Voice from the Minaret* (1919) already carried the scent of lavender. Press releases described Lohr as "The Flower of the London Stage." To some, her bloom had begun to fade. Charles Darnton for *The Evening World* concurred with other reviews regarding the Lohr-Marshall love match. "In figure," wrote Darnton, "Miss Lohr did not realize the romantic type, especially when contrasted with the slender and boyish-looking lover."

In the romance novel *Pride's Court* (1980), Canadian author Joy Carroll, included a scene where the protagonist attends a 1921 Montreal performance of *Fedora*. One excerpt read: "as she watched Mr. *Herbert Marshall's* delicious limp (from a war wound, the newspapers had reported) and the somewhat overblown dramatics of *Marie Lohr* ... ."[50] Apparently, Bart's "delicious limp" was an object of, not only sympathy, but arousal. Bart's own assessment of his career at this juncture? "I was just another reluctant leading man in those days," he sighed.[51]

Upon returning to London, Marshall signed on for *Windows*, a drama by John Galsworthy, best known for his novel *The Forsyte Saga*. In *Windows*, a young girl smothers her illegitimate baby, serves time in prison, and then becomes a domestic servant for novelist Geoffrey March (Marshall). The play was intended to be a push to reform the prison code. *Windows*

left critics dissatisfied. *The Christian Science Monitor* praised the performers, but sadly concluded, "We expected to see more through Mr. Galsworthy's windows; but as things turned out, they were scarcely worth looking through." *Windows* lasted 39 performances at the Court Theatre.

Marshall spent the summer of '22 in the Globe's revival of the whimsical tale, *Belinda*. He played a globe-trotter who, after eighteen years, returns home to his wife Belinda. Critics raved about Irene Vanbrugh's genius as Belinda. "*Marshall* does his best ... ," stated one critic, but the role afforded him no real opportunities. Playwright Noel Coward came to Bart's rescue, along with producer Robert Courtneidge, who had jump-started Marshall's career after the war.

Young Idea (1922-23) Marshall pleads with Kate Cutler. Noel Coward and Ann Trevor look on.

The Young Idea, a comedy about the youthful members of society, had a tryout in Bristol. Notices were good. Courtneidge then opted for a six-week trial run in the provinces. Coward had written a role for himself, as Bart's son (!). Marshall, only nine years older than Coward, was apparently amused by the idea. Besides, the actress playing his wife, Kate Cutler, was twenty-five years his senior. Courtneidge had no problem with Cutler, but insisted that Noel was too old to play the son. Coward remained firm, and his decision came back to bite him. One critic snipped, "It was a pity that Mr. Noel Coward did not look younger."[52] The part of Marshall's daughter was written for Edna Best, who backed out due to contract obligations. Mollie Maitland was cast in a smaller role.

The Young Idea premiered at London's Savoy in February 1923. The convoluted plot centered on young siblings (Coward and Ann Trevor) trying to get their father (Marshall) to leave his boring second wife and return to their arty, raffish, mother (Cutler). One review praised, "Mr. Noël Coward calls his brilliant little farce a 'comedy of youth,' and so it is. And youth pervaded the Savoy last night, applauding everything." A drama critic for *The Spectator*, was quite taken with one performer in particular. "Mr. Herbert Marshall's acting ... is excellent. He has that most admirable possession for an actor, a face which it is a perpetual pleasure to watch ... every muscle is eloquent ... so realistic as to make [one] distinctly uncomfortable." Backstage, Coward found Bart Marshall to be "rather larky"—a mischievous prank player. Coward's secretary, Cole Lesley, later commented,

> He had lost a leg in the war, and the metal replacement, though he used it with apparent ease, often gave trouble technically. Noel was the appointed mechanic, a cause of hilarity between them, Marshall having to drop his trousers while Noel with a spanner tightened a loose screw, or loosened it if Noel had screwed the knee unbendably tight. Their humor centered exclusively below the waist.[53]

During one performance, Bart gazed "spellbound" at Noel's crotch, reducing him to a state of certainty that his fly was open. After Noel caught on, he intentionally came on stage with his fly buttons open, making them visible only to Marshall, who, in turn would wonder what Noel might next reveal to the audience. Coward, who was gay, never talked about his sexual orientation in public. This was understandable given that even private homosexual activity between adult men was not decriminalized until 1967, and there was a real risk of prison time or chemical castration for those men who dared to live their lives openly. Years later Coward did mention that, "There are still a few old ladies in Worthing that don't know."[54]

As a side note, Marshall's character in *The Young Idea* was named George Brent. In 1932, when Marshall's Hollywood star was on the rise, a young Irish actor named George Brent also proved to be a temptation for leading ladies to drool over. Only Garbo managed to nab both men to co-star with her in the same film, W. Somerset Maugham's *The Painted Veil* (1934)

※

Marshall's success in *The Young Idea*, coincided with the death of his mother, Ethel May. In November 1922, the Actors' Association notified the press of Mrs. Marshall's passing.[55] Ethel May was fifty-four-years-old. She never gained the kind of recognition that her husband or son achieved, but appeared content to be her husband's traveling companion and champion, and play whatever small roles were offered her. Following her death, Percy brought a close to his career of thirty-five years, and lived quietly in Chiswick. He would pass away five years later at St. Mary's Nursing Home, also in Chiswick. In his will, he left his son an impressive sum of £5,864.[56]

Soon after Ethel May's death, *The Journal of the Royal Army Medical Corps* published a report on war veterans with artificial limbs. Over 45,000 officers and men had suffered leg amputations—on a scale the world had never seen. In 1923, there was a push in Parliament to supply pensioners with a lighter metal limb, known as the New Desoutter duralumin leg, half the weight of previous versions. The report mentioned several success stories of the duralumin leg, including, "Mr. Herbert Marshall ... with an above the knee amputation, playing the lead in the theaters of London."[57] Defraying costs for the supply and maintenance of artificial limbs for veterans was steadily debated in Parliament. It would be years before the Ministry of Pensions, whose aim was to save taxpayers the expense of the war disabled, began to encourage pensioners to claim their rights. With his steady career (and hefty inheritance) Marshall was more fortunate than many.

Aren't We All? (1923) Marshall, Ellis Jeffreys, Charles Hickman, Patrick Gover

Fredrick Lonsdale's light comedy, *Aren't We All*, focused on aristocrats saying bright, witty things to one another. Marshall, as the rich and idle Willie Tatham, is beguiled into a kiss by a houseguest, just as his adored wife Margot (Marie Lohr) opens the door. Willie's worldly-wise father smoothes over his son's matrimonial tangle by contacting a young Australian with whom Margot had committed the same lip-locking indiscretion while she was on a holiday in Egypt. The Tathams finally reach a happy compromise. The actors carried the sprightly little play with the appropriate zest. A visiting critic for *The Montreal Gazette* thought Marshall, "one of the few really able actors of the younger generation." The play, lasting three months at the Globe, also opened on Broadway with Leslie Howard in the Marshall role.

Marshall moonlighted during the run of *Aren't We All*, in the political drama *The Machine-Wreckers*, by German playwright Ernst Toller. It focused on the workers' revolt after steam-engines caused unemployment and poverty among Nottingham weavers. The Luddites, as they were called, go on strike, with Jimmy Cobbett (Marshall) as their spokesman. He rallies people with the memorable line, "'Tis God who perishes when you destroy a brother's livelihood." *The London Illustrated News* remarked, "*Herbert Marshall, the hero*, the victim of the drama, excellent by such magnificence of diction that the character will be remembered when the play will rest in quietude with many other products of 'storm and stress.'" The critic for *The Nation and Athenæum*, concurred, "*Herbert Marshall* deserves special credit for endowing Jimmy with a dignity of his own, not the author's, creation."

In the director's seat for a June 1923 performance of *The Man Who Ate Popomack*, was Reginald Denham, a co-player of Marshall's during the run of *Abraham Lincoln*. *The Man Who Ate Popomack* told the dilemma of a man who ate the strange fruit known as popomack. He was left to face society exuding an overwhelming, nauseating odor. Marshall's own back-story charged his portrayal. Denham was haunted by what he saw. In 1958, he recalled, "Marshall gave an inspired performance that was deeply moving. He brought a note of high tragedy to the part of the man with the ghastly disability that was inherent though not evident in the writing."[58]

Alice-Sit-by-the-Fire Marshall, Elizabeth Irving, Graham Browne

Marshall would balance heavier turf with lighter fare such as a revival of J.M. Barrie's *Alice Sit-by-the-Fire*. Alfred Sutro's *Far Above Rubies*, which opened at London's Comedy Theatre (March 1924), had a stereotypically virtuous wife (Marie Lohr) using feminine wiles to get her husband (Marshall) a job promotion. Critics thought it old hat. *Variety*'s review was typical: "Halfway through Act I we know ... all that is in store." As for the actors, the review quipped, "Marie Lohr acts with her whole soul and very little brain. Herbert Marshall smiles famously and is, in consequence, beloved by the audience." Sutro's niece, Clare Sheridan, wrote to her uncle after witnessing the play and was frank with her opinions:

> Oh I wish you'd write a play about the man who tries to help his wife's career. I want you to do something so desperately modern. Don't you understand—we *don't* help our husbands any more. We've got our own work to

do. Listen: the *whole* problem of the world today is that women need wives. Just analyze that to yourself.[59]

It was obvious that the tide was turning against the author. The Roaring Twenties were doing just that—roaring, and playwrights who didn't get on board paid the price. The mighty roar was also fueled by what author F. Scott Fitzgerald called the "lost generation"—aimless, youthful Americans who were living the high life on their parents' bank accounts. Fitzgerald's wife Zelda and her childhood rival Tallulah Bankhead, both Southern girls, enjoyed shocking folks. By 1923, Tallulah, a reputed libertine, had moved to London. The following year, she found herself tempting Marshall on stage in Eliot Crawshay-Williams' *This Marriage*.

"In *This Marriage*," said Bankhead, "I was the seductress. Herbert Marshall was my prey. I was trying to steal him from Cathleen Nesbitt." [60] Nesbitt, as Marshall's wife, suggests a plan wherein both women could share him—a *ménage à trois* for the husband's good. *This Marriage* lasted two weeks, but was considered a respectable failure, at least for Bankhead—strengthening her fan base. A critic for *The Nation and Athenæum* explained, "Bankhead has an easier part because it is more satisfactorily realized by the author. Marshall had the worst task of all, because he was merely the symbol of a man in a mess."

The "modern woman" also helmed American playwright Jules Eckhert Goodman's *Morals*, in which a single pregnant woman (Edna Best) refuses not only money (from the parents of the reluctant expectant father), but the institution of marriage itself. She's not in love with their precious son. The parents are baffled. The family uncle (Marshall) is quite taken with the woman's strength and independence. He responds with his own proposal, but she prefers to go her own way. Helen Gahagan Douglas, who originated the role on Broadway (under the title *Chains*), thought the character to personify the modern woman. In London, the play was short-lived, but rekindled the relationship of Marshall and Best, who were ready for a change in matrimony themselves.

Pelican (1924) Marshall, Charles Cherry

Bart's role in *The Pelican* (October 1924-May 1925) was another step sideways. He played a man who divorces his wife, believing that their son wasn't really his. Years later, he bonds with the boy during the war, and decides to reinstate him as his heir. To do so, he must remarry the ex-wife, who is in love with someone else. Actress Josephine Victor, as the wife, stole the show. *Variety* announced "with one performance she has established herself in the front rank of actresses. Herbert Marshall makes use of his customary air of forceful restraint. He needs a change to get him out of the rut managers keep him in."

Instead of a change, Marshall was tossed into *Lavender Ladies*, about two proper, elderly women who are shocked into a more humane view of their fellow mortals. Marshall is a novelist-father, whose daughter (Elissa Landi) mirrors the unconventional life he writes about. Together, they determine that lavender ladies must change their tune. Although enthusiastically received, it did nothing to advance Marshall's career. Coincidentally, Landi, age twenty-three, had just completed her first novel, *Neilson*. *Spectrum* magazine marveled at author Landi's ability to convey contemporary youth as both responsible and undeceived, quoting the heroine's line, "Please don't think it clever to make me love you; it would be so easy if you tried."[61]

As Marshall's handsome, gentlemanly manner had an audience on both sides of the Atlantic, he negotiated for an American tour, boarded the *S.S. Mauritania* in Southampton on August 22, 1925, and sailed to New York. His career had long eclipsed that of his wife Mollie, and it was rumored that she preferred a "rather rougher type of man."[62] While abroad, Bart found true love in the arms of Mrs. Seymour Beard.

Publicity shot of Marshall. London's Reville Studios

Edna Best

(c.1923) Edna with her twins: James and John Beard (born December 16, 1921)

CHAPTER 3
Bart & Edna

Broadway producer Al Woods offered Marshall his first important role in the U.S. *These Charming People*, written by Michael Arlen, was a revision of Arlen's *Dear Father*, which Marshall had essayed for one performance back in November 1924. *These Charming People* was a huge success and would keep the actor busy for five months. For good luck, Bart's old mentor from *Grumpy*, Cyril Maude, had the starring role, touted to be his farewell performance. Producer Woods, who called everyone "Sweetheart," sweet-talked Marshall into repeating his more serious role in *The Pelican* at Times Square Theatre, prior to the opening of *These Charming People*. Woods was determined to get his money's worth out of Marshall.

At the premier of *These Charming People* (October 6, 1925), all eyes, including Bart's, were on leading lady Edna Best. The play was hailed by critic Percy Hammond, as an "adroit, worldly, and laughable bit of comedy acrobatics." Hammond felt that Edna Best, "beguiled the eye and satisfied the intelligence—a foxy post-war innocent." *The New York Times* praised Marshall's "rich voice and pleasant manner." This compliment had its roots in Percy Marshall himself, who was noted for his "rich voice" in an 1889 review from London's *Stage* magazine. It was obvious to many that Herbert Marshall had polished and deepened his art.

Arlen's thin plot depended on the irresistible pranks of Cyril Maude, a doddering Baronet coming to terms with his married daughter Julia (Alma Tell) falling for Geoffrey (Marshall), the son of a butler. *Their* butler. Best was on hand as Maude's younger daughter with modern ideas.

The cast of characters were a restless lot. *The New York Times* quipped, "Unlike the characters, the actors stood on their own feet." *The Sun* concurred, "The acting is performed by a band of English specialists in whimsicality ... clever talk and quick rejoinder." Alma Tell's line, "Geoffrey is adoring. He was born to be a co-respondent," turned out to be prophetic, off stage. However, the Marshall-Best relationship took its time. It would be another two years before Marshall had the honor of being named "co-respondent."

※

On Armistice Day, November 11, Bart and Edna attended a gala ball held at New York's Hotel Plaza. The event was sponsored by the British Great War Veterans. Guests that evening included English stars: Beatrice Lillie, Gertrude Lawrence and Jack Buchanan. Following the festivity, at the stroke of midnight, the occasion became one of solemn remembrance. Military leaders and guests stood for the Massing of the Colors. At the sound of the trumpeter's taps, the room darkened. Two minutes of silence was observed in memory of those who died in the World War—"our glorious dead" as they were referred to in Britain. It was a sobering moment. Eight years had passed since Bart's own traumatic injury. Proceeds from this event were distributed to disabled and destitute British veterans living in New York.

By New Year's 1926, *These Charming People* had left New York for a two-week run at Boston's Colonial Theatre. There were indicators that the Marshall-Best romance was in full-swing. A reporter for the *Boston Globe* waited in the lobby, wondering whether or not Edna Best was going to show up for an interview. She eventually appeared, chattering away as she led the gentleman to her dressing room. "You just want an ordinary interview?" she asked. "I've always been in comedies. I made two pictures in England, but I don't like them. It's such a job getting up and being ready with your make-up on at 9 o'clock in the morning."

CHAPTER THREE

Best, born March 3, 1900, in Sussex, made her London debut at the age of seventeen in *Charley's Aunt*. From there, her career was a mix of nonstop touring and London stage productions. Edna remarked to the reporter for the *Globe* that she enjoyed touring the small English towns, which was more profitable than playing London. She talked about her nice flat in the Adelphi section of Westminster. "Shaw and Barrie have flats right next to me. That isn't so bad, is it?" At this point, she abruptly got up, left the room and the interview, to confide something to an actor, who was outside waiting for her. A few moments later, she joyfully burst back to announce, "Well, that's all isn't it? You don't want any more do you? There's really nothing more to say, is there? Goodbye."[63] The interviewer, shaking his head, had no alternative. One is inclined to second guess who was out there waiting. There was no mention of her four-year-old twins, or husband Seymour, who, at that time, was having a successful run in the West End production of *No, No Nanette*.

At the end of the Boston run, the play went to Newark. Following a run at Cleveland's Ohio Theatre, Best sailed home for England. *These Charming People*, still turning a profit, went on to Washington D.C., before closing in Philadelphia. Marshall wasted no time in getting back to London, and within two days of his return, he was back at the Globe for the short-lived production *By-Ways*. Drama critic Hubert Griffith concurred with the *Morning Post* that the play was pure twaddle. "Among the queerest plays lately put on the London sage," he grumbled, before offering his one note of praise. "Herbert Marshall performed something like a miracle in the last act. When the audience could no longer control its derisive laughter, he compelled it to be silent and treat this tosh as if it were worth listening to."[64] The comedy *Engaged*, also at the Globe, was a slight improvement, but Marshall would have to wait until August before being rescued, once again, by his good friend Noel Coward. By September, Edna Best was also scoring a major hit with Coward as her co-star.

Engaged (1926) as Tom Harrington. Caricature by Irish cartoonist Edward S. Hynes

❧

Running for a profitable 136 performances, *The Queen Was in the Parlour* was filled with typical Noel Coward excesses. The fantasy plot concerned a displaced damsel in Paris, who becomes duty-bound to leave her true love behind, and become Queen of Krayia. Marshall shows up as Prince Keri of Zalgar, her royal suitor. Basil Dean was in the director's seat. Coward made note of Dean's insensitivity. "When I told him how bitterly he had offended so-and-so, or how unnecessarily cruel he had been when poor miss such-and-such had been unable to get the right intonation—I don't think it ever occurred to him that actors' feelings are notoriously nearer the surface than average peoples'. His actors, on a whole, were terrified of him."[65] Marshall remained unperturbed and worked with Dean in subsequent productions.

While Marshall romanced the Queen of Krayia, Best, with her trademark piquant charm, was enjoying what many consider the high point of her career, *The Constant Nymph*, also directed by Basil Dean. "Miss Edna Best," announced *The Spectator*, "by a performance of singular beauty, has come into her own at last." Her success came as no surprise to Noel Coward, who had commented on her "accurate timing and almost contemptuous restraint." In *The Constant Nymph* she portrayed an adolescent with the mind and heart of an adult, deeply in love with her cousin's husband, a composer (Noel Coward). Director Dean had persuaded Coward to portray the composer, a role which had been written for John Gielgud. Gielgud had no problem with losing the role, as he was completely smitten with Noel Coward.[66] Three weeks after the play opened, Coward had a nervous collapse, which afforded Gielgud the opportunity to take over. It proved to be a catalyst to his remarkable career.

In January 1927, Marshall took on the role that boosted his visibility in British theater, the bittersweet murder drama, *Interference*. The production marked the beginning of Bart's association with American impresario Gilbert Miller, who ran the St. James Theatre in London. After two weeks rehearsal, Gerald du Maurier, director and star of *Interference*, turned suddenly to Marshall and remarked, "Your part is much stronger as this play is written, and I never knew it before. We must play it that way." From that point on, Marshall took stage center, as the play's scoundrel, Philip Voaze.

Interference (1927) Marshall with Gerald du Maurier

Voaze, who had been reported dead in the War, reappears at the doorstep of his ex-wife, Faith, now married to an acclaimed physician, Sir John Marley (du Maurier). Faith reveals to Voaze that she is being blackmailed by an old flame of his. In the second act, Voaze, who suffers from a heart condition, attempts to redeem himself from an unscrupulous past. He arranges a reunion with his old flame, and takes along a vial of poison. The final act takes place at the Marley residence, where Voaze confesses to the murder. As a police inspector escorts him to the front door, Voaze, staggering from chest pain, offers the line, "For delivery to Bow Street. Marked Fragile." Bow Street was home to London's police force. A critic for *The Sketch* cheered, "Herbert Marshall reached the summit of his career by his vivid, appealing, powerful picture of the wasted life." For all the acclaim that Marshall received, he credited du Maurier. "Sir Gerald literally turned the play over to me, reversed the order of the thing, made my part bigger than his own, made it *the* part in the whole play. It was definitely he, who established me as an actor with capital letters."[67] *Interference* ran for 412 performances. In 1938, Marshall would repeat his role for *Lux Radio Theatre*, with Leslie Howard as Sir John Marley.

Interference Marshall as Voaze, poisons his old flame (Hilda Moore)

Although Edna had voiced her dislike for making films, Bart took the opportunity to sign with producer/director Herbert Wilcox at Twickenham Studios. During the successful run of *Interference*, Marshall made his film debut, playing Colonel Armytage in the war-themed *Mumsie*, starring Pauline Frederick in the title role. The story was written by Edward Knoblock, who had served in the British Army's Secret Service Bureau. Location scenes were filmed in the French village of Caudebec, on the bank of the River Seine. *Mumsie's* contrived plot unfolded thusly: a French woman, Mumsie, has a beloved son who turns traitor, divulging the secret location of a French munitions train. Colonel Armytage, a family in-law, shows up, and takes a fancy to Mumsie. Armytage offers the wayward son a choice: the firing squad, or carrying a dispatch which will save the munitions train. The boy dies a hero. Mumsie's bookworm husband succumbs amidst the bombings of worn-torn France. Armytage receives word that his wife died in an English asylum. Mumsie and the colonel live happily ever after.

Filming began in the Spring of 1927, and wasn't without mishap. An air-raid scene, filled with electrical-controlled explosions, left co-player Norman Keys in a state of collapse. Keys survived, but *Mumsie* was less fortunate. The film failed to reach the United States, which was the fate for many British films. *Mumsie* is now considered a lost film. Novelist Peter Batten, was on the *Mumsie* set as a bit player. He mentioned Marshall's superstitious habit. "Bart always carries in his right-hand pocket a brightly-polished penny ... the odd-copper in the first pay-envelope he ever received as a professional. He polishes it regularly, wouldn't be without it."[68] Marshall's other good luck charm was Pauline Frederick. He later recalled, "I shall never forget her kindliness and helpfulness to someone of whom she had almost certainly heard but whose bewilderment and fright must have been apparent. She eased me through my first day's work and I loved her for it."[69]

CHAPTER THREE

Mumsie (1927) Marshall said of Pauline Frederick: "She eased me through my first days' work and I loved her for it."

Upon completing *Mumsie*, Marshall faced issues surrounding his father's health. After his wife's death in 1922, Percy remained in Chiswick. At one point, it became necessary that he enter St. Mary's Nursing Home. As Percy was well-off financially, Marshall could attend to his career while checking intermittently on his father's needs. Edna Best was on hand whenever possible. This was confirmed in a letter written by John Gielgud, who was on tour with Best during the fall of 1927. On September 11, Gielgud wrote to his mother, following a Glasgow performance of *The Constant Nymph*,

> Edna asked us to sup with her and we went—politely but yawning—only to find sandwiches and lose at poker, and see her off by the beastly sleeper at 1:30 a.m. I was *very* cross. However—once bitten! Imagine her energy (and devotion to Mr. Marshall) going up to town for Sunday every weekend. These hearties![70]

By "up to town" Gielgud meant London, where Edna spent Sundays with Marshall. Gielgud himself was romantically attached to a young Irish actor (and future novelist), John Perry. They shared a flat in London's West

End.[71] As Gielgud indicated, Edna's "devoted" sojourns to London continued until the tour ended. Percy Marshall passed away on, December 28, 1927. By the time his estate was settled in March of 1928, Bart and Edna were in rehearsal for the play *Come With Me*. Basil Dean, their director, recalled that the twosome were "still in the heyday of their love affair."[72] The Marshall-Best romance had been an open secret for some time.[73] Naturally, fans were eager to see the illicit lovers in person.

Come With Me (1928) Marshall and Edna Best

CHAPTER THREE

Audience response to *Come With Me* kept the play going for a two-month run. The plot concerned a wealthy damsel named Cecil (Best), who marries Ronald (Marshall), a lower-middle-class auto enthusiast. When Cecil provokes the attentions of another gent, Ronald shoots him. The last act finds Ronald on trial for murder. *The Spectator* thought the courtroom dramatics "realistically acted— thrilling." The review was impressed by the "efforts of Miss Edna Best and Mr. Herbert Marshall who are great favorites ... at their best." Dame May Whitty and Ian Hunter were also in the cast. Prior to the opening of *Come With Me*, Bart and Edna made dramatic headlines off-stage.

In April 1928, Seymour Beard sued Edna for divorce, naming Herbert Marshall co-respondent.[74] Beard's divorce from Edna was secured in the London Divorce Court on April 30. Justice Hill also granted Beard custody of their twin boys. It was agreed that the twins would be taken care of by Edna's mother, as Beard was usually on tour.[75] In a cross-divorce suit, Hill simultaneously granted Mollie Maitland a divorce from Marshall on grounds of misconduct.[76] They had been married twelve years. A few months later, Bart and Edna took *The High Road* (the name of their new play) to the U.S.

Free at last, the divorced duo boarded separate liners at Southampton, arriving in New York three days apart. They opened at Broadway's Fulton Theatre on September 10. Posh Park Avenue residents attended in throngs. Frederick Lonsdale's *The High Road* had a successful four-month run—144 performances. *Variety* enthused, "Herbert Marshall is always the 100 percent lover and his scenes with Miss Best are the more interesting having been let into the secret of the romance between the two."

Lonsdale's comedy offered an abrupt assessment of the social classes. A young English lord falls for Elsie Hilary, an actress (Best). His father, Lord Trench (Frederick Kerr), intends to pay Elsie off with a hefty bribe. In retaliation, his son proposes marriage. As a compromise, the aristocrats invite the actress to stay a few months at the Trench country estate, replete with not-so-subtle insults. Perhaps she'll change her mind. She does. The Duke of Warrington (Marshall) is also a guest, and it isn't long before the two are desperate for one another. In a surprise twist at the finish, Elsie returns to the stage, and the Duke takes the "high road." New York critic Burns Mantel concluded, "Not much of a plot. Not much of a play. But peopled with charming actors and attractive personalities and therefore smart and satisfying entertainment." Long Island critic Harriet Menken thought Marshall to be the standout.

> He gives to the portrayal of the Duke of Warrington an understanding, an inflection, a power, a charm that has not been seen on these shores of late. It would be well for producers and playwrights if they could somehow ban Mr. Marshall's exodus from this side of the big pond.[77]

The High Road would translate less successfully on the big screen as *The Lady of Scandal* (1930) with Ruth Chatterton and Basil Rathbone in the leads.

❧

Friday nights were extra special for Bart and Edna, after he organized the West End Club. Its sole purpose was to provide a venue for British players, performing in New York, to fraternize. On board for these weekly festivities were: Gertrude Lawrence, Dennis King, C. Aubrey Smith, Beatrice Lillie, Noel Coward, Frederick Kerr and his son Geoffrey. Marshall and Best also campaigned for funds to provide a clubhouse for disabled men who had fought in the World War. Although they rarely gave interviews, the duo did agree to talk to Dixie Tighe, for the *Standard Union*. Tighe was taken aback by Marshall's reticence to talk about the war.

> Oh yes, I was in the service from the jump. And, in 1917 I received a very serious leg wound and it was in trying to overcome the set-back that this gave me—and it still tries to assert itself—that I determined to make a success of my work—gameleg or not.[78]

CHAPTER THREE

"And that is about all that Mr. Marshall believes that modesty will permit," concluded Tighe. Marshall's reticence wasn't unusual. Author Laurence Stallings' disabled veteran in *Plumes* recoiled from questions about his injury. "I fell out of an automobile on the way to a quartermaster's dance," was his snide answer to one inquisitive mind. Stallings revealed "the truth" in his writing. In his interview with Tighe, Marshall emphasized that he would "never forsake the speaking stage for the movies—no matter how great their development." He was, in fact, arising every morning at 7 a.m. to be at Paramount's Astoria studio, playing the lover of Jeanne Eagels in a film version of W. Somerset Maugham's *The Letter*.

In *her* interview with Tighe, Edna offered a clue to her success. "Of course you know that the way to prompt the audience to tears is to choke back in a very martyrly fashion your own grief. A flood of tears from an actress will never arouse much sympathy." Jeanne Eagels, on the other hand, never held back. Due to her erratic behavior, Eagels was suspended from the stage by Actors Equity. Paramount took a risk when they cast her in *The Letter*. Eagels, the same age as Marshall, offered a unique and raw performance. She didn't exactly arouse audience sympathy, but her "flood of tears" did garner her a posthumous nomination for Best Actress. Eagels, addicted to sedatives, alcohol, and heroin, died only months after the film's release.[79]

In *The Letter*, Eagels played Leslie Crosbie, the neglected wife of a plantation owner (Reginald Owen), in British Malaysia. She has a faithless lover, Geoff (Marshall), who has drifted into the arms of a Chinese woman Li-Ti (Lady Tsen Mei). The opening scene shows Marshall relaxing in the arms of Li-Ti. Their tête-à-tête is interrupted by the arrival of a threatening letter from Leslie, who begs Geoff to visit her posthaste. Perturbed, he complies, only to be confronted with one of her tantrums. Leslie, carrying the elitism and prejudice of her English upbringing, feels betrayed by Geoff's new relationship—a Chinese woman, no less. It is obvious that Geoff's lost interest. "I'm sick and tired of the whole thing," he tells her. "You're enough to drive anyone out of his senses." Marshall's facial expression and body language make it clear that he's heard it all before—an irritable woman, on a perpetual tirade. He confirms his disgust. "I'm sick of the sight of you. You wanted the truth. Now you have it." And yes, as he leaves, she riddles him with bullets from her husband's pistol.

The Letter (1929) Marshall and Jeanne Eagels (Paramount)

Maugham's 1927 play was based on a 1911court case involving a Mrs. Proudlock in Malaysia. Her lawyer provided Maugham the details, during the author's visit to Kuala Lumpur in 1921. The idea of "the letter" was Maugham's own invention—proof of Leslie Crosbie's love affair. Proudlock was sentenced to hang, but as there *was* no evidence, friends signed a petition which resulted in a pardon from the sultan. In the aftermath of Maugham's play, the English colony in Malaysia resented his intrusion for, as one member of the Malayan Civil Service put it, "ferreting out the family skeletons of his hosts."[80] A Malaysian newspaper railed, "Mr. Maugham has explained the worst and least representative aspects of European life in Malaysia—murder, cowardice, drink, seduction, adultery. No wonder that white men and women who are living normal lives in Malaysia wish that Mr. Maugham would look for local colour elsewhere." This didn't stop Maugham. Such depictions of "small lives of unremarkable individuals" in the colonies was his life's blood.[81]

French director Jean de Limur had his challenges with the fledgling "talking film" technique. On the set one evening, Eagels, smoking gun in hand, crouched over Marshall's "dead" body. There was a loud crash. A guitar had fallen from the hands of one of the musicians. The sound take was ruined. Eagels stood there, nervously. Marshall rolled over and laughed. The scene had to be reshot pronto, as Marshall had to leave for the theater (*The High Road*) in ten minutes. Reporter Rosa Reilly was a witness to this mishap, and described Eagels as a "high-strung, nervous racehorse ... waiting for the webbing to go up." Marshall's nonchalance as he leaned against a tall light fixture, was betrayed by his edgy fingers trying to light a cigarette. Once again, a red light flashed, and two cameras rolled for a successful take. Marshall left immediately for the Fulton Theatre, by subway. Electricians and carpenters headed for the streetcar. The Long Island studio felt deserted. Reporter Reilly approached director de Limur, who groaned, "These new talking pictures they are like that animal that you call the Ass ... stupid, stubborn ... we don't know what to do with him."[82]

Marshall's two scenes in *The Letter* were effective. The remainder of the film centered on Eagels, on trial for murder, lying to the jury that Hammond tried to rape her. Eagels' restless, agitated interpretation was considered an "acting triumph" by *Variety*. The *New York Telegram* voiced the critical consensus: Eagels held audiences with "compelling intensity." On the other side of the big pond, *The London Illustrated News* diagnosed that Eagels' "emotional outburst ... spared neither herself or her audience." The review found "distinct relief" in the "admirable" support of Marshall and Reginald Owen. A 2011 assessment by film critic Michael Barrett, referred to Marshall's "exquisitely weary and caddish" portrayal.[83] Marshall's own opinion of the film? "I felt I was no good for the screen."[84] In 1940, he would essay the trusting husband in a Bette Davis remake of *The Letter*—a tribute to Marshall's range as an actor.

Prior to filming *The Letter*, Marshall, Reginald Owen and other Broadway stars, on behalf of the Actors' Fund and Authors' League, donated their services to play "bit" roles in director Robert Florey's 3-reeler comedy short, *Pusher-in-the-Face* (1929). A stage melodrama within the film (which is apparently lost), shows Marshall about to be stabbed by a Chinese gentleman. *Motion Picture News* thought it "all very amusing."

Pusher-in-the-Face (1929) Star Lester Allen is about to push-in-the-face of an annoying woman. Marshall (listed on the back of this still as "Bart Marshall") lies on the stage floor below a Chinese man wielding a knife. (Robert Florey estate)

CHAPTER THREE

December 27, 1928: Bart and Edna marry in Jersey City

When filming on *The Letter* wrapped, Bart and Edna tied the marital knot. The cast of *The High Road* presented the couple with an English wedding scroll, and a good luck dinner. The following morning, November 26, 1928, Judge Leo Sullivan, in his chambers at Jersey City's First Criminal

Court, presided. The crime, matrimony. "Stage Love Becomes Reality" cried one headline. Lord Cowley (who had worked on stage with the bride and groom) was best man. Mrs. H. Gordon Turner was maid of honor. Dudley Malone filled in as majordomo. English actress Fay Compton was also present. Lord Cowley was a grandnephew of the First Duke of Wellington. He and his London actress wife were currently embroiled in tempestuous divorce proceedings that wouldn't find resolve until 1933. Who could have asked for a better best man? Dudley Malone, an attorney, was an early champion for women's suffrage, an anti-war activist, co-counsel for Clarence Darrow in the John T. Scopes "Monkey Trial," and character actor. Obviously, Marshall included a stimulating mix of acquaintances to help celebrate his second marriage.

On December 5, the new Mr. and Mrs. Marshall had luncheon at the Algonquin, surrounded by the wit and humor of Noel Coward, Gertrude Lawrence, Fay Compton, Harpo and Chico Marx. A few weeks later, Coward, Lawrence, Compton, Beatrice Lillie and other British stars gave a tea for the newlyweds at the Embassy Club. *The High Road* closed on Broadway on January 13, then set out for a lucrative tour: Philadelphia, Boston, Washington D.C., and lastly, Chicago's Blackstone. As Marshall explained to a reporter for the *Boston Herald*,

> Because of equities ruling, you know, foreign actors are only able to act on the stage in America a certain length of time. Since that is so, I should like to be able to spend the Spring and Summer in England and the Fall and Winter in America. And I should like to act in Frederick Lonsdale's plays all the while.[85]

The reporter enjoyed Marshall's sly sense of humor. "In England," mused Bart, "the newspapers don't devote half the space to the theaters as they do here, and it certainly is a very laudable thing to do, for surely a country's drama should be as important as its murders."

On March 14, Bart and Edna boarded the *RMS Olympic* for England.

CHAPTER THREE

Over the next several years Marshall listed his London address as: 180 Sloan St., London, SW. It was the residence of Edna's mother, Mrs. Clara Best. Once settled in, Bart and Edna found themselves bound for Paris, figuratively speaking. They contracted for a London production of Philip Barry's American success *Paris Bound*, about a married couple who remain spiritually committed while philandering with others. Edna's line summed it up best: "Married people need a holiday from each other once and awhile."

When *Paris Bound* opened at the Lyric, drama critics were enthused with (some) performances, but not the play. "Thin," "painfully weak," "rather unsatisfying," were the usual complaints. Even though audiences were enthusiastic, it was considered a flop, lasting only four weeks. A young Laurence Olivier was cast as a composer who carries a torch for Best—pleading that their affair must be consummated in order to complete his latest composition. Critics took Olivier to task, with one review grumbling that his portrayal was "beyond our endurance." Marshall concurred with this assessment. He was perturbed by the twenty-two-year-old. "It was an inoffensive little play," Marshall said afterward, "but it could have been better had Larry taken more interest. As it was, he moped about, forgot lines, and was totally undisciplined. There was no chance of ensemble playing with him in it."[86]

The film version of *Paris Bound* (1929) opened three months later. In the hands of Ann Harding and Fredric March, critics were ecstatic. Advertisements promised, "You'll gasp at every spoken word!" *Time* magazine raved, "An immediate and brilliant success." The Marshalls had no choice but to let go of *Paris Bound*, and laugh it off at the Theatrical Garden Party held in Chelsea. Aside from forty sideshows and a casino, entertainments included Gerald du Maurier's popular "frivolity in six spasms" at the Grand Giggle Theatre. Noel Coward had the feminine lead. Bart and Edna also joined the onstage antics.

Marshall-Best attempted a revival of a 1921 play, *A Bill of Divorcement*—playing the father-daughter roles that John Barrymore and Katharine Hepburn would essay in director George Cukor's 1932 screen success. A visiting critic for the *San Francisco Chronicle* thought Best "colorless," but Marshall faired "better" as the gentle father, Hilary, who escapes a psychiatric asylum, believing he's cured. The play was penned by Clemence Dane, a prolific British playwright, and part of Noel Coward's inner circle of friends. *A Bill of Divorcement* asked uncomfortable questions: Was Hilary really a victim of shell-shock? If not, was his mental illness hereditary? The play underscored the issue of returning soldiers being a disturbing presence in the family circle. *A Bill of Divorcement* is dated, but it managed to put in a time-capsule questions that were being asked in post-war England.

"OLD FRIEND, WE'VE BEEN PARTED TOO LONG," Mr. Herbert Marshall as the cynical drunkard of Heat Wave

Heat Wave (1929) Marshall displayed his "wonderful organ" for an extended run. Here with Ann Todd

CHAPTER THREE

In the fall of 1929, Marshall took a sabbatical from co-starring with his wife. He tackled the role of a cad and ladies' man in Roland Pertwee's *Heat Wave*. The play focused on the insularity of Colonial compounds, specifically India, where ladies and gentlemen drank whiskey and soda, while being fanned by natives—or, as *Variety* put it, "Englishmen going to pieces morally, in the tropics." The review admired the melodrama's "brilliant" wit and "intelligent" direction, adding, "The piece is splendidly acted by Herbert Marshall ... the venture has every indication of substantial success." London critic Ursula Greville zeroed in on Marshall, to say that she had changed her tune about the actor.

> I have usually been a little fussed about Herbert Marshall's voice, for he has so often seemed to use it as though he was conscious of it as a wonderful organ, and so I have noticed voice instead of play. But in *Heat Wave* he was artist from beginning to end.[87]

A favorite line was uttered by Marshall as he gazed fondly at a bottle of scotch whiskey. "The only angel that came out of Scotland," he sighs. "Old friend, we've been parted too long." The charged atmosphere in *Heat Wave* settled down to an extended run at the St. James.

To start off 1930, the Marshalls teamed again for what proved to be one of their biggest successes, A.A. Milne's *Michael and Mary*. The consequences of mixing bigamy and marriage proved to be a provocative topic. The title characters meet accidently in the British Museum—Mary, deserted and left penniless by her selfish husband, and Michael, a promising author who takes an instant liking to her. They marry and have a child. Twenty years pass. The husband returns with only one thing in mind, blackmail. *The Spectator* described *Michael and Mary* as a "wallow in bigamous bliss." The play scored a five-month run at the St. James. The following year,

Victor Saville directed the film version starring the Marshalls. An article for *Photoplay*, thought the film captured "something of the rare sweetness which belongs to this couple in real life."

Real life would place the careers of Bart and Edna in what was touted as the "world's record for long-distance commuting," London-to New York-to Hollywood and back. A 1932 news item calculated that Marshall's return to England was his tenth crossing on the Atlantic Ocean. It was actually his twelfth. At that point, he and Edna, often mentioned in the same breath as Lunt and Fontanne, had made seven voyages in tandem. Their careers, on both sides of the Atlantic, were flourishing to critical raves, raking in box-office gold.

Michael and Mary (1931) Mr. and Mrs. A.A. Milne visit the film set. Director Victor Saville stands behind Edna.
(below) Michael and Mary mixed bigamy with marriage (Gainsborough)

Marshall, ready for Hollywood

CHAPTER 4
Back & Forth Across the Big Pond

In early 1933, Marshall reflected on his marriage to Edna,

> We've spent most of our on-stage hours together as well as our off-stage ones. In London, the public will have none of one of us unless the other is present, too. In fact, we dare not appear in roles which require us to quarrel with each other. I suppose that is because a happy marriage is the ideal deep within everyone's heart.[88]

The Swan, by Ferenc Molnar, fit the formula that Marshall described. It was Bart and Edna's ninth play together, and opened at the St. James immediately after *Michael and Mary* closed. In Molnar's adult fairytale, Edna played Princess Alexandra, betrothed to her cousin Prince Albert (Marshall). Colin Clive, tutor to Alexandra's brother, proves to be a tempting distraction for her, throwing a royal monkey wrench into the proposed merger. *The Swan's* philosophical insights on love and the social classes lasted three months. *The Spectator* quipped that Best was neither swan nor goose, but rather "a dear little docile dove." The audience only cared that she "finally settled on Mr. Herbert Marshall."

In October, Colin Clive left the cast, and sojourned to Hollywood for his iconic performance in *Frankenstein*, crying the immortal lines, "It's Alive! It's Alive!" Clive, hating to leave Bart and Edna in the lurch, asked

Maurice Evans to take over his role in *The Swan*. "I sensibly buried my pride and said *yes*," recalled Evans. "For me it turned out to be one of the most stimulating months I have ever spent in the theatre: a good tragicomedy, a pair of eminent actors to work with, and a beguiling drama to boot." During the run of *The Swan*, *Variety* columnist, Frank Scully, made bold quips about Marshall in an article titled, "All Over the Place on One Leg." It read,

> The hit of the show is the performance of Herbert Marshall's duraluminum leg. Marshall plays Prince Albert, and he plays it perfectly, thanks to a load of great courage and a perfectly made artificial leg. He had, you know (and he's no longer secretive about it, now he's a star) his left gam bobbed nine inches from the hip in the war. He walks with a grace that defies the keenest eyes. No peg-legged, stiff-kneed stuff. It was an invention (shrapnel) that blew his leg, but other mechanical gadgets seem to have put him on his feet again. Such contradictions in life are known as "progress."[89]

The poignant finish to Scully's commentary is understandable. During the war, Scully was also the recipient of shrapnel in his leg. He suffered a decade, before amputation. Perhaps he felt *entitled* to divulge information about Marshall, who was less inclined to mention it at all. In fact, Marshall included a clause in all his stage contracts, *not* to mention his infirmity in press releases.[90] Scully, on the other hand, had spent so much time convalescing in hospitals, trying to save his leg, that he was compelled to write a book, aptly titled, *Fun in Bed*. It was a best seller.

CHAPTER FOUR

The Swan (1930) In Molnar's play, Bart and Edna maintain the "love ideal" fans expect

After *The Swan* closed, Bart opted to leave England to escape typecasting. *Variety* reported that he planned to negotiate with Charles Dillingham for the lead in *Cynara* on Broadway. He and Edna boarded the *S.S. Majestic*, arriving in New York on December 9, 1930. They checked into the city's Midtown beaux arts Hotel Carlton. Upon their arrival, Marshall's second talkie was released in the U.S., helmed by Britain's "Master of Suspense," Alfred Hitchcock.

Murder! & HITCHCOCK

In *Murder!*, Alfred Hitchcock's trademark ingredients were coalescing into the smooth machine for which he became famous. One senses the genius behind the camera. The director was in the process of adapting new sound techniques. We hear Marshall's inner dialogue as he shaves before the mirror, listening to a radio broadcast of *Tristan and Isolde*. Hitchcock recalled,

> What people most remember about *Murder!* was Herbert Marshall's soliloquy in front of the shaving mirror. This was 1930, and we didn't know much about sound mixing. The only way to do it then was to record Marshall beforehand, and then play his voice back while we shot the scene, with a thirty-piece orchestra in the background.[91]

Marshall played a celebrated actor-manager, Sir John Menier (patterned after Sir Gerald du Maurier). He is summoned to be juror in a murder trial. Menier is convinced that the young actress accused of the crime is innocent. While she awaits the executioner, Menier sets out to find the real culprit. In true Hitchcock fashion, the plot introduces a mix of curious characters.

"I intended it as a satire on the theater," explained Hitchcock. "In those days the actor-manager was king. Du Maurier used to have an office over His Majesty's Theatre. That's why I dressed Herbert Marshall … like a cabinet minister. They never went to the provinces. So, when my actor-manager does … he feels the suffering and indignity of a lower order of actor." Inevitably, Sir John finds himself in a rooming house in the provinces. He's lying in bed with a cat, surrounded by children, while landlady Una O'Connor, blathering on and on, reveals a clue. It's unlikely that Marshall was privy to Hitchcock's attitude about du Maurier, definitely one of Marshall's champions.

On screen, Sir John narrows the suspects down to one: Harold Fane

(Esme Percy), an actor and trapeze artist who specializes in cross-dressing. Fane is also a half-caste—determined to conceal his racial heritage and protect his career. The murder victim was about to divulge Fane's dark secret. Hitchcock did not conjure animosity for the murderer. In the climactic circus scene, Fane realizes the odds are against him. While on the high wire, he offers a memorable finish for the crowds below. They watch in horror as the elaborately gowned transvestite creates a noose out of trapeze rope—enabling *him* to be his own executioner. In Hitchcock's view, the villain was no *real* villain at all. "He was a half-caste homosexual," said Hitchcock in 1972. "In those days being half-caste was very serious ... you weren't accepted. But the element is surely dated now."[92]

Hitchcock's *Murder* (1930) Marshall and Esme Percy (British International)

In interviews with French director Francois Truffaut, Hitchcock noted, "It was Herbert Marshall's first (sic) talking part and the role was perfect for him; he turned out to be excellent in the sound medium."[93] Marshall's performance was solid. His conviction for the task at hand, his compassion for the innocent victim, rang true. *Variety* praised, "Herbert

Marshall beats the cast to it as the knighted actor who turns amateur detective. [*Murder!*] contains all ... the pet Hitchcock technique from quick cutting to skillful dialogue blending. *Murder* is by miles the best so far." Britain's *Film Weekly* honored Marshall with fifth place in the top ten film performances of the year.

While filming the German-language version of *Murder!*, Hitchcock locked horns Alfred Abel, a German actor who played Marshall's role. Abel made numerous demands, and insisted on having a comfortable lounge chair like the one that had been provided for Marshall. Hitchcock complied, without explaining to Abel that Marshall had been a war casualty, hence the accommodation. When Abel attempted to sit in his own lounge chair, which was far more elaborate-looking than Marshall's, "the whole contraption collapsed to the ground."[94] Hitchcock looked on with a "puckish grin." As TCM host Robert Osborne explained when telling the story, "Don't mess with Alfred Hitchcock!"[95]

In January 1931, Edna headed to Hollywood to play opposite film idol John Gilbert. It was considered her "big chance" at screen stardom. Marshall stayed behind in New York. Instead of *Cynara*, he decided to star in Philip Barry's new play, *Tomorrow and Tomorrow*. The domestic drama, directed by Gilbert Miller, involved a noted psychology professor Dr. Hay (Marshall), and Eve (Zita Johann), the wife of a friend and colleague. Eve is childless and depressed. Hay's sympathetic nature does wonders for her. Ten years pass. Eve now has a young son, who is traumatized after falling off a horse. She beckons Dr. Hay for help. Hay complies, only to learn that the boy is his. It was Hay who had provided Eve the necessary biological component for motherhood. The husband (Harvey Stephens) has remained clueless.

CHAPTER FOUR

Tomorrow and Tomorrow (1931) Osgood Perkins and Marshall

Critic Burns Mantel thought the play superior to Eugene O'Neill's *Strange Interlude*, which carried similar themes. "Miller has directed this exquisite drama with an art that conceals art. Herbert Marshall plays the doctor with distinction and winning charm." Arthur Pollock, for the *Brooklyn Daily Eagle*, concurred, "Mr. Barry never showed himself before so deft a dramatist. Herbert Marshall plays with the simplest, frankest intelligence." The play ran for 206 performances. The film version of *Tomorrow and Tomorrow* (1932), starring Ruth Chatterton and a somber Paul Lukas, opened to mixed reviews. *The New York Times* cautioned, "Paul Lukas weakens the narrative for those who saw Herbert Marshall in the same role on stage."

Marshall had his fans, but wife Edna headed the list. She shocked everyone when she fled Hollywood and the arms of John Gilbert, to be back with Bart in New York. This "scandal" left the MGM production *The Phantom of Paris*, in the lurch. Best had completed four British releases in 1930. *Variety* noted that she was London's "best talker bet." It was assumed that she was ready for Hollywood. But, after a few weeks at MGM, being groomed for stardom, and only one day of shooting scenes, Edna got the jitters. On the morning of February 17, John Gilbert paced the floor, as director John Robertson kept an eye on his watch, waiting for Edna to show up. "Maybe she wasn't feeling well," suggested Gilbert. Robertson kept quiet until a telegram arrived. "Well, I'll be damned!" he blurted, handing the message to Gilbert. It read:

> Please forgive me. I am on my way back to London and my husband. I am awfully homesick and besides I am just afraid I wouldn't be any good in the picture.[96]

Marshall was actually visiting friends on Long Island when he received a long-distance call from Edna explaining her decision. He did not protest, but offered apologies once Edna arrived on the east coast. "I'm afraid I'll have to admit I was the sole reason my wife left the films. You see, we've been married three years and never separated longer than three weeks. It was a clear case of lonesomeness." Later on, Marshall remarked that the part simply wasn't to Best's liking. Ten days prior to her fleeing the film capital, Best asked for a release from her contract. Metro's attorney J. Robert Rubin encouraged her to remain. It was finally announced that her contract would be suspended "until she and her husband can reside in Hollywood together."[97] Gossip columnist Louella Parsons added her own spin, saying that Best had developed an "inferiority complex." "She looked at Norma Shearer, Greta Garbo ... and a galaxy of MGM favorites, and said, 'I just know I wouldn't be any good.'" Parsons saw daggers whenever anyone had the audacity to snub the holy shrine of Hollywood.

Edna channeled all her pent up angst into a new play, titled, *Melo*. In this, she played a suicidal wife who almost poisons her husband in order to run off with his best friend (Basil Rathbone), a concert violinist. She opts to throw herself in the Seine, instead. New York critic Gilbert Gabriel, enthused, "Until now we had seen Miss Best over here only in comedy and fluff. We were unaware of what bonfires lay under the snow." The bonfires lasted 67 performances, so that Edna could join Bart on his return to England. They were under contract to co-star in films for London-based Gainsborough Pictures.

Secrets of a Secretary (1931) Marshall and Claudette Colbert (Paramount)

During the run of *Tomorrow and Tomorrow*, Bart, at the behest of Paramount and Claudette Colbert, completed his third "talkie," *Secrets of a Secretary* (1931). His Broadway triumph had prompted more than one film offer. "I believe *deluge* is the word," quipped Marshall. "I had three and when an actor gets three offers in America, his public statements should read, 'deluged.'"[98] After the deluge, Marshall made the decision to go with Colbert at Paramount's Astoria studio on Long Island. For *Secrets of a Secretary*, Marshall was able to display his on-screen charm. Unlike most leading men, he didn't rely on "attitude"—he was different from the rest. *Photoplay* raved, "It is Herbert Marshall, English-actor husband of Edna Best, who makes this picture more than ordinary interest. When you see him you will know why Edna ran away from Hollywood to be with him." The magazine rated Marshall and Colbert among the "Best Performances of the Month."

Secrets of a Secretary has enough dash and brilliance to grab attention. A blonde and beguiling Colbert, offers her trademark sparkle as a rich man's daughter. On a whim, she marries a scheming gigolo (George Metaxa). When her father dies, leaving her penniless, the gigolo deserts her. Colbert is hired as social secretary for Mrs. Merritt (Mary Boland), whose daughter (Betty Lawford) is betrothed to the titled Lord Danforth (Marshall). Thirty minutes into the film, Marshall shows up to make a distinct impression on Colbert, and vice-versa. They are both intelligent enough to see through the charade of upstairs-downstairs, rank and position. They also have instant cinematic rapport. After Marshall is stood up several times by his fiancé (who prefers the deadbeat gigolo), he makes a pitch for Colbert. "I am dying from lack of food and pleasant company," he tells her. It's an offer she's unable to resist.

Towards the finish, racketeers raise their evil heads, along with blackmail, murder and melodrama. Colbert is interrogated by the police. The film, according to the *Boston Herald*, "loses its identity, becomes a hybrid" filled with "dramatic futilities." Despite such complaints, Colbert and Marshall entice the viewer, making every second count—the lighter moments, as well as the dramatic. In this respect, *Secrets of a Secretary* was a career boost for them both. "You're going to rave about Mr. Marshall," cheered Columnist Jimmy Starr. "Herbert has everything Ronald Colman has," cooed Louella Parsons, "and he is much better looking." Charles Brackett, who penned the story *Secrets of a Secretary*, told Colbert biographer Lawrence J. Quirk, that Marshall "found Colbert a tasty dish indeed, but … she was having no part of any romancing away from the camera."[99] Bart was looking a bit wistful on the final day of shooting, but he and Claudette would co-star twice more on screen.

Once safely across the big pond, Marshall and Best completed films for Gainsborough British-Lion, and prepared for their next London stage "smash hit." Their first film release, *The Calendar* (screened in the U.S. as *Bachelor's Folly*), was an improbable yarn about a wealthy racehorse owner Garry Anson (Marshall), who agrees to intentionally throw a race at Ascot. He admits his blunder to Lady Panniford, who determines to have Anson disqualified from the Jockey Club. Best was cast as Lady Panniford's younger sister, who worships Anson from afar. *Variety* concluded, "First-class performance by Herbert Marshall," but "Edna Best has nothing to do." The trade paper *Hollywood Filmograph* warned American audiences, "Like most British pictures the action was a trifle slow." Ironically, it was directed by an American, T. Hayes Hunter, known mostly for his work in silent films.

There's Always Juliet Apollo Theatre, London

In October 1931, London's Apollo Theatre welcomed the Marshall-Best duo in John Van Druten's fragile romantic comedy, *There's Always Juliet*. *Stage* magazine observed that the Marshalls "entranced the first night audience." After a month's run at 50% profit, producer Gilbert Miller arranged to take the play and cast to New York. Broadway's Empire Theatre welcomed the production on February 15, 1932. Critic Burns Mantel reported, "The Marshalls are back, and that means much to this theater." Mantel offered a rundown of the plot. A London socialite (Best) meets an American architect (Marshall) at a cocktail party. They abandon their respective dinner dates and motor to Sussex Downs for a glorious two-day rendezvous. Upon receiving an urgent cable to return home, the architect faces the reality of being a divorced man with a six-year-old son. Dame May Whitty played Best's chaperone, and Cyril Raymond was her London love interest. "Lightly, brightly written," noted Mantel, who qualified, "It conceivably could be quite trying if uninteresting people were to play it. All four performances are beautifully finished."[100]

CHAPTER FOUR

Bart and Edna's stay in the U.S. was eight months long, mostly due to his being so much in demand. It is interesting to note that on the ship manifest for the *S.S. Berengaria* (dated February 9, 1932) under the column "Marks of Identification"—the forty-one-year-old Marshall was designated: "Amputation - Left Leg - Above Knee." Aside from Marshall and Ronald Colman, two other romantic leads in their forties were wounded in the Great War. Maurice Chevalier received shrapnel in his back. Germans held him prisoner for two years. Clive Brook sustained shell-shock during the Battle of Messines in 1918. Marshall's intermittent operations for his leg, however, were a constant reminder of things past.

In mid-May 1932, Paramount was in a furor to acquire Marshall's services. Director Josef von Sternberg had seen the long lines of women buying tickets to see Herbert Marshall in *There's Always Juliet*. At von Sternberg's insistence, Paramount paid off the cast, the theatre, projected profits, and other expenses (five weeks worth, totaling $36,000) for *There's Always Juliet* to close its doors.[101] Von Sternberg wanted Marshall camera ready for his fifth production starring Marlene Dietrich, *Blonde Venus*, post-haste.

Marshall, now under contract with Paramount, had a difficult time coming to grips with von Sternberg. "The role in *Blonde Venus* opposite Marlene Dietrich appealed to me," said Marshall, "so I came to Hollywood." Following the film's release, Marshall opened up during an interview with writer Laura Benham.

> I was very unhappy while working on *Blonde Venus*. Mr. von Sternberg and I did not get along. I could not understand his method of working and evidently he could not understand mine. It was only by keeping a firm grip on my self-control—by reiterating to myself that it really wasn't so important whether or not I liked working with von Sternberg—that I was able to go on. No matter how unpleasant conditions were, they could not last forever.[102]

May 1932. On the set of *Blonde Venus* (Paramount)

Benham was left speechless. "Mr. Marshall was talking as no Hollywood actor has ever dared to speak of a director. And it never occurred to him to doubt his right to freedom of speech ... it was refreshing." Marshall wasn't alone in his opinion. Clive Brook told Marshall that while filming *Shanghai Express* (1932), he told von Sternberg to go hang himself. Screenwriter Jules Furthman recalled Gary Cooper, on the set of *Morocco* (1930), grabbing von Sternberg by the neck, calling him "a god-damned kraut."[103] Sylvia Sidney, who starred in *An American Tragedy* (1931) waited until 1994 to lash out her feelings. "Von Sternberg was a dreadful person," she complained. "Oh God, I hated him. He didn't give a damn about actors at all."[104]

Under the helm of the "dreadful" von Sternberg, Marshall's portrayal of the emotionally torn Edward Faraday, a scientist suffering from radium poisoning, comes across as genuine. *Blonde Venus* does a fine job of establishing the dramatic conflict in the first half of the film. When Faraday travels to Dresden for a six month cure, his wife Helen (Dietrich) returns to her nightclub career to help finance the procedure. Helen catches the eye of the suave political boss Nick Townsend (Cary Grant) who provides her money in exchange for sexual favors. Faraday returns home cured, but is faced with his wife's indiscretion. Of the two men, Marshall's character is the more vulnerable. He's deeply hurt, crushed, and offers no reconciliation. He demands custody of their son Johnny (winningly portrayed by six-year-old Dickie Moore).

Blonde Venus (1932) Dietrich and Marshall (Paramount)

Helen flees, taking Johnny with her. She entertains at clubs and solicits sex for cash, before hitting rock bottom—a prolonged, muddled process. The *Boston Herald* observed, "Miss Dietrich plods dispiritedly along her way; Mr. Marshall struggles vainly to create something out of a vacuum. Dietrich needs the guidance of a new director." Dietrich, von Sternberg's protégé femme fatale, offered a vacant stare into the camera during scenes that required much more, especially when she and Marshall finally reunite (a studio imposed ending). As film critic/author Mick LaSalle points out, "Dietrich always stays on the outside of her performances. Her distance prevents her from touching the emotions. One watches Dietrich to bask in her beauty and to enjoy her good-natured cynicism."[105]

Marshall, mostly on his own, registered the necessary dramatic intensity. *The New York Times* acknowledged "Marshall's valiant work in a thankless role." *Blonde Venus* proved to be a box-office disappointment.

The erotically charged *Blonde Venus* has the advantage of smart editing, enticing background music, and excellent cinematography (Bert Glennon). The film is remembered for Dietrich's outré musical numbers. In a European nightclub she performs in her signature coat and tails, flashing a salacious grin at a chorus girl. An earlier sequence, "Hot Voodoo," has Dietrich being pulled on stage dressed as a gorilla. She emerges out of costume in ostrich feathers, and dons a wild blonde wig. It was during this outlandish (eight minutes long) number that Cary Grant shows up—devouring Dietrich's every move.

Marshall's main recollection of working with Dietrich, involved her being the recipient of kidnapping threats. The kidnap and murder of aviation hero Charles Lindbergh's baby was still making headlines when filming of *Blonde Venus* got underway. Marshall said of Dietrich,

> She had a very worrying time ... for it was then that the kidnapping scare was at its height ... mysterious telephone calls, anonymous letters. She received several threats. We were more than two months working on *Blonde Venus* and all the time there was a terrible fear at the back of her mind that some danger might overtake her little daughter, Maria. Kidnapping is a nightmare in Hollywood and I certainly would think twice before al-

lowing a child of mine the freedom to which our kiddies at home are accustomed.[106]

Several months after *Blonde Venus* was released, Edna gave birth to a daughter, Sarah Lynn. True to his word, Marshall's little girl spent the bulk of her early childhood in England, away from the "nightmare in Hollywood."

Trouble in Paradise & LUBITSCH

Ironically, Sarah Lynn Marshall was conceived in Hollywood, while her father filmed one of the great classics of the Pre-Code era: *Trouble in Paradise*. Marshall was in a good mood during production, and had nothing but praise for director Ernst Lubitsch. He explained to Laura Benham,

> When a player is cast in a Lubitsch picture his worries are over. He can be completely assured … that Lubitsch will bring out in him a better performance than he ever suspected himself capable of giving. There is not one thing— not one detail—about acting, that Lubitsch does not know. He never wastes words, but in his soft rather guttural voice explains quietly just what he wants you to do. And he is always right. It's a pleasure and an education to work with Lubitsch.

When asked, director Lubitsch took no credit for Marshall's flawless performance. "He is one actor who doesn't need direction," acknowledged Lubitsch.[107] *Variety* rated *Trouble in Paradise* as the film that "clinched a prominent spot for [Marshall] in Hollywood-made-films."[108]

Many consider *Trouble in Paradise* Lubitsch's best film. The "trouble" in *Trouble in Paradise* was Marshall choosing between the luminous Kay Francis, or the loyal, if high-strung, Miriam Hopkins, his partner in crime. Lubitsch's satirical treatment of jewel thievery begins with Mariette

Colet (Francis) losing her enormously expensive handbag at the opera. She offers a substantial reward for its "Honest Finder" (the film's original title). Much to her delight, Gaston Monescu (Marshall) shows up with the bag (and a new name, Monsieur La Valle). He murmurs his way into Mariette's employ and boudoir. With flirtatious charm, he critiques her love letters, offers her advice on the correct shades of lipstick, and chastises her for not having more than 100,000 francs in her safe. "If I were your father, which fortunately I am not," he advises, "and you made any attempt to handle your own business affairs, I would give you a good spanking. In a business way, of course." Mariette asks, "What would you do if you were my secretary?" "The same thing," he assures her. She leans back in her chair, smiling and *very* interested. "You're hired!" she declares.

Mariette is the owner of Colet and Company, a French *perfumerie.* Their motto is: "Remember, it doesn't matter what you say, it doesn't matter how you look, it's how you smell." As the affair between Mariette and Gaston ripens, the famous "Lubitsch Touch" fills the screen. An Art Deco clock defines the length of a romantic interlude; a telephone rings, unanswered; parting glances contain revelations of unspoken dialogue. The erotic triangle is established when Gaston hires an assistant, Lily (Hopkins). The two plan to run off with 100,000 francs that the compliant Mariette has now stowed away in her safe. In Lubitsch's world, people like Madame Colet are begging to be robbed.

One of the film's most tantalizing moments has Mariette postponing her departure for a dinner engagement. We see an adoring Gaston, encouraging her to leave. He tells her that he's concerned about her reputation. "I wouldn't hesitate one instant to ruin *your* reputation," she smiles. "*Shut up ... kiss me!*" When Mariette finally learns the truth about Gaston, she's saddened, but philosophical. He returns to his "sweet little pickpocket," Lily. It's an intoxicating world that Lubitsch offers. One that embraces, wholeheartedly, the romantic, sexual being.

CHAPTER FOUR

Trouble in Paradise (1932) In real life, Bart and Kay remained lifelong friends (Courtesy of Larry Smith)

Film reviews for *Trouble in Paradise* were glowing. Llewellyn Miller, for the *Los Angeles Record*, approved, "*Trouble in Paradise* is as fragile as an orchid and just about as rare. It is pictures like this which make people like me decide that life spent in theaters is worthwhile after all." The *Los Angeles Times* enthused, "Mr. Marshall realizes for the first time on the screen precisely the opportunities that have made him extraordinarily successful on the stage." "You haven't seen the real Herbert Marshall until this picture," echoed *Photoplay*, who placed Marshall and his lovely co-stars in their "Best Performances of the Month" category. British novelist Leslie Storm, concluded, "The scenes between Herbert Marshall and Kay Francis are unequalled in my mind … consummate artistry … wits and skill lightly, piquantly played."[109] *The New York Times* offered a toast to, "Ernst Lubitsch's shimmering, engaging piece of work."

The scourge of the Production Code (July 1934) kept *Trouble in Paradise* out of circulation for decades. It was only shown at private film festivals. Lubitsch was in attendance at a 1947 screening presented by the

Great Films Society at Rexford School in Beverly Hills. Buoyed by an appreciative audience, Lubitsch knew *Trouble in Paradise* would always be a consensus classic. He died a few months later.

4 pm—Teatime, per Bart Marshall's insistence. With Kay Francis and Ernst Lubistch

For co-star Kay Francis, who had forfeited a European honeymoon in order to work with Lubitsch, Marshall had this to say. "Kay is generous to a fault. Her generosity even led to several mock fights between us, during the making of *Trouble in Paradise*. It was sometimes necessary for one of us to have a shoulder to the camera and there was always a tussle as to which of us it should be! Kay invariably wanted me to have the honor of facing the camera and more than once I had to use main force to turn her round!"[110] Only Marshall's back is visible when he runs up a flight of stairs. The back, of course, was that of his double.

Lubitsch biographer, Scott Eyman, wrote in *Ernst Lubitsch: Laughter in Paradise* (1993), that Marshall had affairs with both Francis and Hopkins. In her personal diaries (available at Wesleyan University), Kay was candid about her sexual affairs, and usually named names. There is no indication of an affair with Marshall. Besides, Bart and Edna were busy trying to make a baby. Bart insisted they stay in a posh Hollywood hotel during their stay. "So that my wife wouldn't have any housekeeping worries," he explained. During "production" they attended Carole Lombard's surprise 40th birthday party for husband William Powell. Also joining the festivities were Kay Francis and husband Kenneth MacKenna, director Howard Hawks, Chester Morris, and Ronald Colman.

Evenings for Sale was yet another exquisite soufflé—perfect turf for Marshall to display his undeniable charm, dashing masculinity, and that hint of melancholy which made his characters so human. In this, he plays Count von Dopenthal, whose ancestral castle and fortune have ended up in the hands of creditors. Marshall sweeps you into the tale's dream-like quality, as the Count abandons his plan for suicide, opting instead to be a gigolo at a popular cabaret. He falls for a young woman named Lela (Sari Maritza), who is equally smitten, until she learns about his new profession. Mary Boland shows up as a wealthy American with a Merry Widow complex. She has come to Vienna to live out her fantasy in the arms of a dashing count. The touching simpatico between Marshall and Boland is what makes the film a standout. They give humor and heart to the proceedings. Co-star Maritza was brought to Paramount as a threat to the troublesome Marlene Dietrich, who wanted to work exclusively with von Stroheim. Maritza barely caused a ripple in *Evenings for Sale*, and would soon vanish from the screen. The *Boston Herald* thought her, "Attractive but chilly." *The New York Times* rated her "satisfactory," but placed the picture's success into hands of "Herbert Marshall's clever, restrained acting."

Evenings for Sale—Gigolo Marshall obliges Mary Boland (Paramount) (Courtesy of Larry Smith)

❧

Upon completing his films at Paramount, Bart decided it was Edna's turn. She wanted him to appear with her in a London production of *Another Language*. They arrived at Southampton in October, and went directly into rehearsals. Prior to opening, Marshall, along with a majority in the British Actors' Equity Association, voted in favor of a closed shop for London theaters. Union membership would be required beginning January 1, 1933.

Another Language opened at the Lyric on December 1. The play detailed a family of four brothers who, along with their wives, gather round their tyrant mother each Sunday evening for tea. Breaking from the mold are one daughter-in-law (Best) and a nephew (Louis Hayward), who become smitten with one another. The critic for *The Era* found it "well worth seeing," and had to admit, "I fairly reveled in the spectacle of Herbert Marshall and Edna Best having a domestic scrap." Marshall played the husband of the rebel daughter-in-law. His understudy, Rex Harrison, took over the role of the nephew when Louis Hayward left the cast. (Another bit player was a youthful Errol Flynn.) When Bart and Edna's old chum Noel Coward set eyes on Louis Hayward, he found him "irresistible," and immediately took him under his wing, casting him in a revival of *Hay Fever*, and a new comedy *Conversation Piece*. Coward also rewarded Hayward with a romantic Mediterranean cruise.[111]

On January 9, 1933, Bart and Edna took, what turned out to be, their final theatrical bow together. Best announced that she was expecting, and Celia Johnson took her place until *Another Language* closed a few weeks later. Bart sailed for New York, and Edna stayed with her mother (180 Sloane Street, London) until baby Sarah Lynn was born on May 25, 1933. In early 1932, Marshall had emphasized, "There is a satisfaction in stage work which I am not willing to relinquish." He mentioned the rewards of audience contact, the bursts of applause and laughter. "Or, better still," he quipped, "that dear, almost forgotten sound—a sniffle followed by a hearty blowing of the noise!" After 15 years on stage, Marshall couldn't see himself putting it out of his life. "Not, that is," he added, "with any happiness."[112] After the close of *Another Language*, it would be another seven years before Marshall set foot on stage. As he predicted, this decision didn't necessarily bring happiness. On a personal level, he was left vacillating, conflicted.

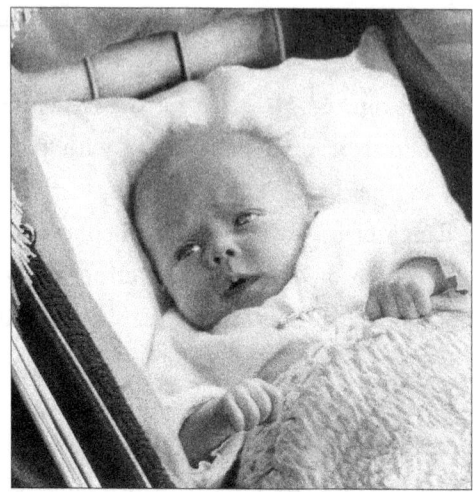

Sarah Lynn Marshall - July 1933

Almost unnoticed in the wake of Marshall's Paramount films, was his and Edna's final film for Gainsborough, *The Faithful Heart* (1932). It was touted to be "a love story as tender as their own." The film begins at a Southampton pub, where a cocky sailor named Waverly (Marshall), and a barmaid he christens "Blackie" (Best), have a romantic interlude. Twenty years pass before Waverly, now a Lieutenant-Colonel in the British Army, is confronted with the reality of having a daughter (also played by Best), the fruit of his forgotten affair. Will he forgo the opportunity of marrying an attractive, upper-class sophisticate, or take the orphaned, illegitimate daughter under his wing?

In 2016, London-based writer Graceann Macleod witnessed what she described, "an exquisite, silvery black and white print" of *The Faithful Heart*, digitized by the British Film Institute. She found the low-key lighting of pioneer cinematographer Mutz Greenbaum (aka Max Greene), "beautifully composed," but felt the story itself, "creaky, stodgy and stagy"—Marshall's "loathsome character," at the film's outset, "not believable." "While he gives it his best," noted Macleod, "the character fits him poorly." However, when Marshall reappears as a veteran of the Great War, Macleod embraced his performance wholeheartedly. "*This* is the Herbert

Marshall that makes sense," she observed, "a mature, sensible and kind gentleman who is now literally getting to act his age." Macleod suggested that perhaps it was the film's intention to show how the war and intervening years had softened him.

> *The Faithful Heart* is very good at ... hinting at the challenges faced by returning servicemen at the end of the Great War. At one point, one of them says "this demobilizing is most demoralizing." I'm sure Marshall brought his own memories to bear on these segments of the story.[113]

The Faithful Heart with Edna Best

One London critic was outraged by the idea of Marshall's woman-hungry cad seducing a barmaid, then being awarded the Victorian Cross. "I say that is a tremendous issue, which cannot be glossed over ... something to be drowned in a pot of beer."[114] A year would go by before *The Faithful Heart* was briefly screened in New York. The U.S. distributor

(Helber Pictures) had the temerity to redub all the actors with American voices. Marshall threatened to sue if the film wasn't withdrawn.[115] Understandably, he was too well known to have his voice dubbed. A critic for the *New York Evening Post* rated the dubbed film, "a fairly satisfactory specimen of British films at their worst." Mordaunt Hall, for *The New York Times*, was unimpressed with Victor Saville's direction, and felt that Marshall and Best were unable "to distinguish themselves." "They are victims of the direction," emphasized Hall.

The Faithful Heart—Bart and Edna, "victims" of director Saville, in their final film together (Gainsborough)

Years later, director Saville made it clear that he favored the talent of Best, and remarked, "Edna was technically the best actress I ever worked with; it was she who taught her husband Herbert Marshall, Bart as he was known, all he knew about acting and succeeded so well that she lost him to Hollywood and Gloria Swanson."[116]

Marshall and Swanson kept gossip columnists busy during 1934-36

CHAPTER 5
Marshall & Swanson

One fan magazine credited Herbert Marshall for introducing a new love code to "us crude Americans."[117] Marshall registered a smoldering subtlety that placed him face-to-face with the queens of cinema, all waiting in line: Shearer, Garbo, Hepburn, Stanwyck, and eventually, Bette Davis. Almost on the list was Jeanette MacDonald. In February 1933, she and Marshall were in London doing publicity for a Lubitsch film to be shot in England, *The Queen's Affair*.[118] Sadly, Lubitsch wasn't feeling well and dropped out, as did Marshall and MacDonald. Compensation to Marshall, MacDonald, and working staff resulted in a $200,000 payout.[119]

Prior to his daughter's birth, Marshall sailed to New York to negotiate with Paramount officials. He stayed at the upscale Hotel Lombardy for two weeks. Along with Kay Francis, and her almost ex-husband Kenneth MacKenna, Bart attended the premier of the Katharine Cornell hit, *Alien Corn*.[120] *The Hollywood Reporter* noted, "Poor Herbert Marshall. He was mobbed." Marshall promptly returned to London where he scheduled a tea and a chat with British novelist, Elinor Glyn. Her novel *It* (1927), championed the idea that if you had the magnetism of "It," you would be able to attract both sexes. When Glyn asked Marshall why his relationship with Edna had lasted, he confided, "It is because we follow inclination, not convention."[121] This pleased Glyn, who raved about Bart's "whimsical sophistication." He was genuine, unselfconscious, and capable of catching "the finest shades of meaning." When Glyn approached the subject of the stork, Marshall remained silent. "I saw at once that this subject is sacred," wrote Glyn, "and means deep things to this attractive man ... and I determined to pry no more."

Marshall was busy filming the taut WWI drama, *I Was a Spy*, directed by Victor Saville. The true story was based on the life of Marthe Cnockaert (played by Madeleine Carroll), a young Belgian nurse involved with British espionage. Conrad Veidt offered his signature, chilling portrayal as a German commander who woos Carroll, before sentencing her to be executed. Marshall, a hospital orderly involved with the secret service, is Carroll's true love. He sacrifices himself at the finish, on her behalf. The film didn't champion the British or the Germans. The characters in *I Was a Spy* are caught in an uncompromising machine. Director Saville himself stated, "With the powerful memories of 1914-1918 ... no film about war could be other than antiwar. I felt no need for heroics."[122]

I Was a Spy with Madeleine Carroll (1933) (Gaumont-British)

CHAPTER FIVE

A powerful scene occurs after Carroll is compromised into making love with the German commander. Carroll's facial expression tells Marshall everything he doesn't want to know. In turn, he reaches his hand out, letting *her* know that his love remains intact. Writer Laura Wagner wrote in 2010, "There is no dialogue, simply looks and gestures. It is a beautifully played moment."[123] *The New York Times* admired the plausibility and dramatic impact of the film, adding, "Miss Carroll is both beautiful and convincing. Herbert Marshall is splendid." In 2013, author Anthony Slide rated *I Was a Spy* as one of Saville's finest British films, "noted for its high production values, … and its quiet, controlled acting by Madeleine Carroll, Herbert Marshall, and Conrad Veidt."[124] During WWII, Carroll would put her own life on the line working with the severely wounded for the Red Cross in Italy.[125]

While on the set of *I Was a Spy*, Marshall mentioned plans to return to Hollywood. "We had hoped to do Noel Coward's *Design for Living*, but unfortunately it is thought that it may not be suitable for film purposes." It wasn't long before Coward's ode to *ménage a trois* went before the camera, without Marshall. Director Ernst Lubitsch opted for a loose adaptation of Coward's play, with Fredric March and Gary Cooper as the male leads. On screen, Coward's clever (censorable) lines, were, as *The New York Times* put it, "tossed to the four winds." Marshall was set to co-star in Paramount's *White Woman* with Dorothea Wieck (known for her role in the 1931 German film *Mädchen in Uniform*). When Wieck backed out, so did he. Upon arriving in Hollywood in July, Marshall went directly into *The Solitaire Man*, an MGM "quickie." During the shoot, Ronald Colman hosted Bart and Edna at his home on Mound Street in Hollywood Hills. Sarah Lynn had stayed behind in London with Edna's mother.

Edna and Sarah arrive in Hollywood February 1934

When questioned as to whether or not fatherhood had affected his sex-appeal, Marshall was amused. "I do feel changed, rather. I got a great thrill from the birth of my daughter. I can't predict what it will do to my screen personality—but I assure you that it wouldn't have stopped me from becoming a father." Marshall admitted that he didn't want "to go on too much" about Sarah Lynn, and then did just the opposite. He told writer Elisabeth Goldbeck (sister of screenwriter Willis Goldbeck), "[Sarah Lynn] has a definite personality already. She's a gay little thing. Bright and jolly. And she always was attractive. Never went through that mottled stage. I spend just as much time with her as the nurse will allow. She's always shooing me out of the room." Bart then mentioned his eleven-year-old twin stepsons, James and John. "They're glorious," he enthused, "and they're with us a great deal. When our baby was born they wired, 'So glad to hear of the arrival of Sarah Lynn. Does that make us triplets?'" Bart registered relief in having a girl. Knowing the man, his reasons were understandable.

> We thought we'd rather have a girl in case of the next war. We'd much rather have her rolling bandages for the Red Cross than fighting in the trenches. For anyone who was really in the last war, and for anyone who can realize what the next one will be like, its unbearable to think of having a son involved in it.[126]

As for sex appeal, the lean, six-foot, hazel-eyed, Marshall scoffed that he lacked the necessary "rich smile" of he-men like Gable. He felt that talent and modesty, not looks, had propelled him forward, especially in the romance department. His only comment about his face was, "My cheeks feel like floating sweetbreads." He told Goldbeck, "I would choose to be known and liked for a certain forthright quality, an honesty and directness. And humor. I made a point of writing the vice-president of Paramount a special request that I be allowed to spit in somebody's eye in my next picture. I'm so tired of kissing hands and being a gentleman." Marshall qualified, "I'd want to treat women on the screen as they like to be treated in life, and still have the men like me." His role in *The Solitaire Man* fit the bill.

The Solitaire Man — Lionel Atwill, May Robson, Ralph Forbes, Marshall, Elizabeth Allan, Mary Boland (MGM)

In *The Solitaire Man*, Marshall, in the title role, leads a group of con-artists. Just as they are ready to retire from a life of crime, he is implicated in a murder. They find themselves flying across the English Channel to escape the law. "It didn't cost Metro a lot of jack," observed *Variety*, "but the quality throughout is deluxe and the direction is shrewd. Herbert Marshall is especially able as the mastermind." *Picture Play* raved that Marshall's "restrained and ingratiating art has never been seen to better advantage." Mary Boland, a cheeky, wealthy American, shows up as a fellow passenger aboard the plane. Her outpouring of off-the-wall remarks makes up for the lack of mobility in cramped quarters. A Salt Lake critic concluded, "the big Boland woman practically steals the picture."

By the time *The Solitaire Man* was released, Bart and "the big Boland woman" had sojourned to the Big Island of Hawaii for Cecil B. DeMille's *Four Frightened People*. Reporters found co-star Claudette Colbert "vivacious and sparkling" when she joined Marshall aboard the *S.S. Lurline*

CHAPTER FIVE

(September 9) in San Francisco. She had just undergone an appendectomy. Paramount attempted to replace her with Gloria Swanson. Due to Swanson's salary demands, the studio waited for Colbert to recover. Colbert recalled in 1978, that she arrived on the set with a nurse from the Good Samaritan Hospital. DeMille confirmed his reputation as a tyrant by insisting that she step into a swamp for her first scene. "Two days later," said Colbert, "I was bedridden with a 104-degree temperature, and I really thought I was going to die. DeMille was very apologetic. 'It's just an act,' he told me. 'People expect that of me. I'm not really like that underneath.' By that point, I didn't care what he was really like underneath. But I liked the old boy."[127] Colbert was being generous. DeMille's celluloid misfire was a mistake for everyone involved.

Marshall and Colbert on location in De Mille's *Four Frightened People* (Paramount)

In *Four Frightened People*, Hawaii served as a Malaysian jungle for a quartet of passengers who escape a Dutch steamer riddled with bubonic plague. Before long, they come face-to-face with their true selves. "They Shed Civilization as They Shed Their Clothes!" cried the ads. Colbert, a schoolteacher, is liberated from her mousy demeanor. Marshall, a chemist, abandons his defeatist attitude. William Gargan, a blowhard newsman, feels a temporary loss of self-importance. Socialite Mary Boland, a champion of birth control, provided comic relief. Soul-searching is frequently interrupted by hostile natives, or wild beasts.

After two weeks of filming, word arrived in Hawaii that Edna had, once again, abandoned Hollywood. She tested for a Paramount contract, then hopped an ocean liner bound for Hawaii, and Bart. When she arrived at the Hilo Hotel, cast and crew were making daily sojourns to the slopes of Mauna Loa. The volcano last erupted in 1926, destroying a small village. Mary Boland bemoaned the 4 a.m. breakfasts, and daily fifty mile trek into the jungle. A subsequent journey took them to the Kona side of the island where crews blasted a path across ancient lava beds, no doubt angering Pele, Hawaii's volcano goddess. While Pele behaved herself, Boland was impressed with Bart Marshall's noncommittal, "ex-trawdn'ry!"—for every impossible tangle in which he found himself.[128] When the cast shed their clothing, costume designers had a heck of time disguising Bart's artificial leg, draping heavy furs around his waist, which made him, according to co-player William Gargan, "sweaty as hell." Colbert had much admiration for her leading man.

> He has a miraculous quality of sincerity and great sympathy ... at no time did I have the feeling we were merely *acting*. It all seemed to be ... part of our own very personal existence. Absolutely no artificial note. He kept everyone in a good frame of mind on that hazardous trip we made for *Four Frightened People*. His remarkably good disposition under the most trying circumstances—his even, unruffled temper, stood up infallibly under the test. I think women sense this as soon as they see him.[129]

CHAPTER FIVE

Four Frightened People — William Gargan and Marshall on the Hilo side of the Big Island (Paramount)

Pele also sensed Bart's "good disposition," and took mercy on the doomed production. Mauna Loa waited until *after* DeMille and Co. were safely back home before erupting a ring of fiery lava. News reports on December 4, described columns of smoke a mile high. For forty-eight hours the island of Hawaii "resembled a land of seething fire." One news blurb wagged, "Was DeMille to Blame?"[130]

DeMille strips down in the jungle heat to confer with Marshall and Colbert.

Four Frightened People baffled the critics. Despite good performances, and a novel approach to self-transformation, the script lacked the necessary ingredients to stay afloat. Critic Walter Ramsey aptly scribed, "This little opus goes wandering around until it gets almost as 'lost' as the four people." *The New York Times* thought Marshall offered an "ingratiating portrayal." He even managed to pull off the impossible line, "Shut up! You're beautiful. I'm sorry." DeMille counted *Four Frightened People* as one of his "notable failures."

CHAPTER FIVE

In November, Edna returned home to England. Marshall stayed behind, still planning on what he called a double career on stage and in films. "I am grateful to say that the salaries in Hollywood are an inducement to concentrate on talking pictures," he pointed out, "and I would gladly do so except for the debt that I owe the English stage. Perhaps my efforts are being directed over too much territory, but as long as I continue acting I hope to work on both sides of the Atlantic."[131] He mentioned that Edna had the same plan. "I'd rather play with Edna than any other actress in the world," he enthused. "There's no trace of professional jealousy between us. I don't like to talk about our happiness, Edna's and mine. You don't talk about the things which are closest to your heart. And I always have the fear that, by the mere speaking of the words, I'll break the spell."[132] His words proved prophetic.

Marshall contracted with MGM to co-star with Norma Shearer, who had had her eye on him ever since seeing *Secrets of a Secretary*. "The first time I ever saw Mr. Marshall on screen," said Shearer, "was in a picture with Claudette Colbert. I thought I had never seen a lady so thoroughly and convincingly loved. He has a charm that is always part of him. He has that great faculty of making you feel he never takes himself too seriously."[133]

Marshall and Shearer lock eyes, while Clark Gable grins.
Academy Awards March 16, 1934

By mid-December things were going smoothly on *Riptide*, produced by Shearer's husband, Irving Thalberg. Shearer played Mary, a vivacious American party girl who marries Lord Rexford (Marshall), an Englishman. Five years into marriage, Rexford leaves on business. Mary ventures to Cannes where she meets up with American playboy, Tommy Trent (Robert Montgomery). Their innocent flirtation makes headlines; Rexford accuses his wife of infidelity. Director Edmund Goulding, who concocted this flirtation with conventional morality, underscored one aspect of Marshall's screen success. "It's in his voice," said Goulding. "He has the most seductive voice on the screen."[134] And ... off the screen, for that matter.

In early January, Marshall attended a dinner party filled with celebrities. Goulding took the opportunity to introduce him to Gloria Swanson, the former silent screen star whose career was on the decline. She was being considered, along with Marshall, to film the Elinor Glyn romance *Three Weeks*. Swanson biographer, Stephen Michael Shearer (who accessed Swanson's personal papers) wrote that Marshall's "charm and courtliness impressed and tantalized her ... he asked at the end of the evening if he might call her ... . Gloria effusively and unashamedly wrote that within a week, she and Marshall were deeply in love."[135] Swanson, who had recently separated from her fourth husband, was smitten by Bart's "gentle face ... soft brown eyes ... and one of the most perfect musical voices I had ever heard."[136] On January 14, Bart and Gloria made an appearance together at crooner Russ Columbo's birthday bash at the Beverly Wilshire. Before long, the duo became fodder for gossip columnists.

The Marshall-Swanson affair was *the* red-hot topic when Edna arrived from London in early February 1934. She brought along eight-month-old Sarah Lynn, planning to make Hollywood their future home. Bart had imported his Italian car, a Hispano, to America. He mused, "We own an Italian car with English money, for driving around in America. Edna, Sarah Lynn and I." Edna signed on with Warner Bros., to replace Kay Francis in *The Key*, a romantic triangle set during the Irish Revolution. On their first night together, Bart opened up about his relationship with

Swanson— that he found her "utterly fascinating." "It seemed to me that the world had stopped," Edna confessed shortly afterward. "He told me that he did not want a divorce. He asked me to stand by, and be patient for a little while. I am going to do just that. I'm going home to England as soon as my picture is finished. I don't blame any man for being attracted to Gloria Swanson. The tragedy is ... the admiration of the world goes to the woman who is fascinating enough to interest a man—no matter what his ties are."[137]

It wasn't long before Edna met her rival face-to-face. She was determined to set the matter straight. Author Shearer, states: "At their meeting, Best ... asked if Gloria was in love with her husband. Gloria said yes. Edna asked if she knew about his drinking. Gloria said yes. Edna asked if Gloria understood there was a child involved, a young daughter. Gloria said yes."[138] After a decade of knowing the man, Edna was well aware of the demons her husband faced, and of the impending emotional conflicts he would suffer if Swanson involved herself any further. Swanson would hear none of it.

LA BELLE SWANSON

Born in Chicago in 1899, Swanson made her film debut in the summer of 1914. She began as an extra for Essanay Studios in Chicago. The first day on the set Gloria noticed a burly actor in drag, playing a Swedish maid in a slapstick comedy—actor Wallace Beery. Biographer Shearer, noted that sex "held a deep and insatiable fascination" for Gloria, and that Beery "was exactly what the impressionable Gloria Swanson was looking for."[139] After a morals charge, Beery hightailed it to California. It wasn't long before Gloria joined him in matrimony (March 1916). Swanson appeared in Mack Sennett comedies, before Cecil B. DeMille turned her into a romantic lead, skyrocketing her to stardom. Following her box-office success in W. Somerset Maugham's *Sadie Thompson* (1928), Swanson's career took a nosedive, and stayed there. Between 1916 and 1934, Gloria found herself perpetually married, with four husbands to her credit. She truly needed a break from matrimony, and Bart Marshall fit the requisite romantic interlude she had in mind.

Marshall's turmoil regarding his new romance, his commitment to Edna, and his fatherly responsibility to Sarah, began to take its toll. His British fan base, so devoted to the Marshall-Best combination, was yet another concern. Bart's heavy drinking and guilt created problems on the set of *Riptide*. The film itself centered on the problems of infidelity. Life was reflecting art, and for Marshall there was no escape. To top things off, he was adjusting to an artificial leg replacement, experiencing tremendous "phantom pain." He had holes cut in the pockets of his trousers in order to loosen the strap during painful episodes. One day, he crossed over to Norma Shearer for an intimate scene. To everyone's dismay he fell directly in front of her. The leg ricocheted and tore through his pants. Robert Montgomery recalled that Shearer's husband, who had serious health issues, rushed down to the set to calm everyone down. "It wasn't good for his heart," said Montgomery. "[Thalberg] liked Bart and knew he'd wind up giving a fine performance, as he always did. I remember him commenting that if he had had to hobble around for all those years with an artificial leg, *he* might have wound up an all-out alkie."[140]

Riptide was a comeback for Shearer, who had been nursing Thalberg back to health following a heart attack. She had insisted they take a long voyage to Europe, before resuming her career. Thalberg stated that his wife "literally kept me alive."[141] During *Riptide*, the Thalbergs and director Goulding empathized with Bart's situation. Shearer and Goulding tactfully persuaded him to stop drinking, for the time being. Marshall turned in a stellar performance as the disgruntled husband. Even so, Shearer confessed to co-player Lilyan Tashman, that she was terrified that Marshall's limb might break and injure her. Tashman herself was dying of cancer, and would succumb a few weeks after *Riptide* was completed. Goulding was caring for his invalid wife, suffering from tuberculosis. No, Marshall wasn't the only one facing physical challenge and transition on the aptly titled *Riptide*—a potentially strong current, hazardous to individuals caught in its path.

Riptide — Director Edmund Goulding and Shearer bolster Marshall during a difficult time (MGM)

Following a preview of *Riptide*, scenes were cut and retakes were ordered. Released just prior to enforcement of Hollywood's Production Code Administration (PCA), *Riptide* was condemned by Catholic Father Daniel Lord, author of the Code. Father Lord, determined to immerse the Ten Commandments into film-making, attacked *Riptide*, and Thalberg, for casting "his charming wife in the role of a loose and immoral woman." Lord took things one step further. "We advise strong guard over all pictures which feature Norma Shearer. They are doing more than almost any other type of picture to undermine the moral code."[142]

Marshall and Shearer play scenes for *Louella Parsons* radio show, March 14, 1934 (CBS)

A more rational critic for *The New Outlook* summed up, "Into the capable hands of Miss Shearer, Mr. Marshall and Mr. Montgomery has been placed a luscious, sloppy glob of whimsical elfishness, and they have done their honest best with it." Critic Walter Ramsey nodded, "Herbert Marshall almost steals the picture in the role of the jealous husband." *Photoplay* agreed, "Marshall ... gives a flawless performance." His performance may have been flawless, but it would have been better had Goulding kept this frolic in the same key as Noel Coward's *Private Lives*—allowing Marshall's Lord Fenwick a sense of humor in the marital mix-up. *The New York Times* deduced: "As for Mr. Goulding, it is another instance of his being a better director than an author."

Marshall's only comment on *Riptide* would wait until 1963, when he casually remarked, "In the old days, we'd get on a Norma Shearer picture and shoot on and on for 15-16 weeks, with two hour lunches and no hurry about anything."[143] Production delays on *Riptide* had, in fact, prevented Bart from returning to England to co-star with Edna in the premier of John van Druten's *Most of the Game*. Ironically, "no hurry about anything" allowed the Marshall-Swanson affair to go full-steam ahead.

Marshall was now renting Goulding's beach house, where he and

Gloria could rendezvous unnoticed. While William Powell and Colin Clive vied for Edna's affections in *The Key*, she dealt with her husband's obsession with Swanson. On March 16, Bart and Edna attended the Academy Awards dinner at the Ambassador Hotel. Irving Thalberg made a point of dancing three times with Edna, which helped ease "the situation."[144] Following the premier of *Riptide*, Bart and Edna made an entrance at the cast supper party. Edna was "unsmiling and mask-like" as they made rounds to various tables. Moments later, she left—alone. Their public appearances together had become "very conspicuous," observed columnist Mollie Merrick, "all due to the gossip about La Belle Swanson."

Prior to her departure for England, Best stated, "There's nothing a wife can do but stand by waiting, when her husband's name is linked with that of another woman. I wouldn't lift one finger to keep Herbert's love if he wants to give it to another." Reporters noted that when Bart saw Edna off at the Pasadena train station she was in tears. Fans and columnists were having difficulty reconciling Herbert Marshall with the man who was involved in an extra-marital affair. *Modern Screen* theorized, "Hollywood is very much against the Best-Marshall split because they know the inside story about the famous and much-married femme star who has caused the whole thing ... she took advantage of her position to break the marriage up for good."[145] It was these kinds of reports that threw Swanson into a panic about the success of her "big comeback."

In April, Swanson arrived in New York to perform on the vaudeville circuit and promote her anticipated film for MGM. She checked into the Waldorf-Astoria, and received a long passionate letter from Marshall. One ardent line read, "Oh darling heart and wife of my eternal being."[146] Upon his arrival in New York, Marshall gave a party for Swanson at the El Morocco. A photographer sneaked into the nightspot and began taking photos. According to writer Regina Cannon, Marshall went into a "spectacular rage," demanding to know why his privacy was encroached upon. Cannon scoffed that the El Morocco was about as private as Grand Central Station. There were other instances of Marshall raging at photographers, most likely at Swanson's prompting. She had been cautioned by MGM not to flaunt their affair. These episodes subsided when Swanson announced her plans for divorce (April 23).

In spite of everything, Marshall was as much in demand as ever. In an interview with Laura Benham, he candidly theorized, "A man can be sincerely devoted to one woman, want her always in his life, without losing his desire to be with others at times. The regard he has for his wife is a permanent and solid thing, unaffected by his casual friendships with other women. Much heartbreak would be avoided if wives would only realize that a husband's harmless contacts with other women in no way jeopardize their marriage ... if she grants him enough freedom."[147] Benham drew her own conclusions from Marshall's ramblings. "No wife of spirit can remain idly on the side lines waiting for him to grow tired of his new playthings. The friendship of Gloria Swanson and Herbert Marshall will end as painlessly as it began, with neither party harboring regrets or disillusionment."

Benham was correct on both accounts. Bart later revealed his fantasy of playing the role of *Jurgen*, in which the protagonist has numerous erotic encounters with legendary women, before returning to the arms of his spouse.[148] Bart would perplex reporters by announcing, "Divorce is the farthest thing on my mind now. If I should be indiscreet later, well, that's a different story." The implication being that Swanson was a temporary indiscretion.

Instead of co-starring with Swanson in *Three Weeks*, which kept being delayed, Marshall was teamed with Constance Bennett in *Outcast Lady*, a ponderous version of Michael Arlen's scandalous play *The Green Hat*. Swanson was galled that Bennett had requested Marshall as her leading man, which only amused him.[149] Bennett was married to Swanson's third ex-husband, Henri La Falaise, a French nobleman.

To appease the PCA, most of the scandal in *The Green Hat* was tossed overboard. The original plot had newlywed Iris March discover that her groom had contracted syphilis. After he jumps to his death out of a hotel window, Iris drifts from man to man. She is finally reunited with her one true love, Napier, a diplomat, but he marries a respectable woman instead. After Iris bears Napier's illegitimate child, she opts to drive her sports car, at top speed, into a tree.

Outcast Lady (1934) Marshall remained "cool as a cucumber" during numerous retakes. Here with Hugh Williams and Constance Bennett (MGM)

Bennett was cast as Iris March, and Marshall, Napier. Instead of syphilis, the suicidal husband (Ralph Forbes) served time in prison for a "horrifying, shocking" (and as far as the script was concerned, unmentionable) crime. Iris' illegitimate baby is never conceived. Her deliberate smash-up into a tree, had less dramatic impact. *Variety* assessed, "*Outcast Lady* is the chassis of *The Green Hat* with the motor taken out." Dramatics are sluggish until the final scene, when Napier rails at his father (Henry Stephenson), who had obstructed his marriage to Iris. Marshall offers a rousing climactic moment, one of the best of his career. Bennett biographer, Brian Kellow, observed that after heavy rewrites and costly retakes, *Outcast Lady* "wasn't about much of anything."[150] Despite the flaws, Louella Parsons insisted that Marshall's voice made it "worth the price of admission just to hear him speak his lines."[151]

Veteran writer J. Eugene Chrisman visited the set of *Outcast Lady*. Marshall was doing a scene with Hugh Williams, who played Bennett's alcoholic brother. Things weren't going smoothly. "Williams lacks the calm placidity of Marshall," wrote Chrisman. Retakes caused Williams to become more flustered, while Marshall remained "cool as a cucumber on Christmas." Bennett remained haughty, and Marshall remained polite. He simply avoided the usual chit-chat between scenes with his glamorous co-star. "The greatest event of his day," concluded Chrisman, "is the whiskey and soda which is fixed for him the moment the day's work is over."[152]

MGM was more than pleased with Marshall, and announced in trade journals that *Marie Antoinette* had been purchased as a vehicle for Norma Shearer and Charles Laughton, and would provide Herbert Marshall "an opportunity for his most appealing charms."[153] Irving Thalberg would produce. Thalberg's death in 1936, put this block-buster on hold until 1938. Robert Morley and Tyrone Power were allotted the roles intended for Laughton and Marshall.

Nothing seemed to fall into place for Swanson, except her extra-marital affair. She had become a social exile. Norma Shearer rescued the illicit lovers with an invitation to an evening soirée at the Thalberg residence. "The message was very clear," wrote Swanson. "It was time to declare us socially acceptable again."[154] At the end of July, after being deemed "acceptable," Swanson was loaned out to Fox for the Jerome Kern-Oscar Hammerstein musical, *Music in the Air*. Despite good reviews, the film was a commercial failure. Swanson would have to wait another sixteen years, before her stunning, Oscar-nominated comeback as Norma Desmond in *Sunset Boulevard* (1950). As filming wrapped on *Music in the Air*, Marshall volunteered, "I would never try to make a 'comeback,' as they call it. If I knew my time was up, I'd run like blazes and try and find a little corner on the stage."[155] Swanson resisted his advice, and kept playing the publicity game. "Yes, I plan to make more pictures," she frequently announced. "I will never make another picture until I make a great one." It was as if she was writing lines for Norma Desmond, herself.

In November 1934, Swanson was granted a divorce. She gained custody of her two-year-old daughter, Gloria. Though gossips slated Marshall to be the "Fifth Mr. Swanson," he denied any intention of divorcing Edna. *Variety*'s review of *The Key*, deduced that Edna reflected "enough beauty, poise and charm to make her a worthy contender in Hollywood." Even so, Edna was content to stay home in England, where she was busy filming Alfred Hitchcock's classic, *The Man Who Knew Too Much*.

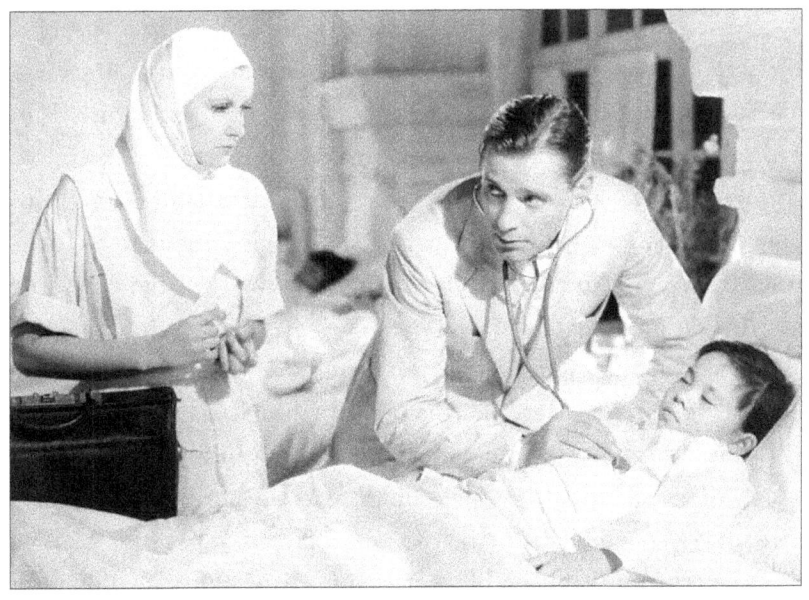

Garbo reunites with Marshall to save humanity in W. Somerset Maugham's *The Painted Veil* (MGM)

As Bart finished *Outcast Lady*, filming for Garbo's *The Painted Veil* had already begun. "I ended a very intensive scene with Miss Bennett at one o'clock," he explained, "and at 2:30 I was rehearsing a major scene with Miss Garbo." Marshall understood Garbo's solitude and seclusion. "I enjoy similar seclusion on the sound stage, to ponder over the lines and problems of the scene that is to follow. I believe that Miss Garbo and I have managed to play our scenes together instinctively."[156] Marshall emphasized, "One reason I like my present role with Garbo, is that though the character is a nice gentle fellow, he can and does, become beautifully angry."[157]

W. Somerset Maugham's *The Painted Veil* had exotica, erotic undertones, and a million dollar budget. During 1919-1920, Maugham's wanderlust had taken him to the Far East. Focusing on his fascination with the expatriate milieu, he took copious notes from his encounters and the stories he heard. *The Painted Veil* was partly inspired by a notorious scandal involving an Englishwoman in Hong Kong. Maugham, when writing his version, took the precaution of changing his leading lady's nationality.

On screen, Garbo played Katrin, a restless Austrian on the verge of spinsterhood. When her father's associate Walter Fane (Marshall) proposes marriage, Katrin sees an opportunity for escape and adventure. Fane's medical research will take them to China. Once there, Fane keeps busy battling a cholera epidemic, while Katrin is escorted around by British diplomat, Jack Townsend (George Brent). The plot begins to boil when Fane arrives home to discover his wife's bedroom locked and Townsend's hat lying on the table outside the door.

Maugham's story provided perfect turf for Marshall, once again, playing the wronged husband. Maugham biographer Selina Hastings, noted, "There is a great deal of the author himself in Walter Fane."[158] (In the future, Marshall would be called upon twice to portray Maugham on screen.) *Variety* nodded, "Acting honors really go to Herbert Marshall. He is especially fine in the big scene, immediately after he's found out about Garbo and Brent." The film's finish (altered from the novel) was particularly powerful. Katrin is left with no choice but to accompany her husband inland where the epidemic is rampant. Once there, the tempo slows down as she absorbs death and dying closing in on her. Katrin learns to appreciate the full spectrum of Fane's work and his dedication to help the suffering. Her affair with Townsend looks small in comparison. She isn't so much redeemed as she is enlightened.

CHAPTER FIVE

Andre Sennwald, for *The New York Times*, praised the "superb presence of Miss Garbo," and nodded that Brent made "an agreeable and intelligent chap of the lover." "As the husband," said Sennwald, "Mr. Marshall provides one of his best screen performances." "Marshall's artistry as an actor appears to be infallible," wrote Los Angeles critic Elizabeth Yeaman. When Maugham was invited to watch Garbo in the film, he recoiled, "I cannot bear seeing my works when they are made into pictures."[159] Interesting to note that in 1930, Bart and Edna were being considered for the play version of *The Painted Veil*.[160]

In the 1990's, former *Our Gang* child star Jean Darling recalled visiting the set of *The Painted Veil*. She heard the rumors, and was determined to know if Marshall really had an artificial leg.

> I saw Mr. Marshall sitting in a director's chair reading the script. I came over and leaned on the arm of his chair and sort of idly ... put my hand on his knee and tapped it. Then I went over on the other side and did the same thing, and he said, "It's the right (sic) one! Why didn't you *ask* which one?"[161]

Darling, who was twelve at the time, explained that she didn't want to be rude. Over sixty years had passed since the incident, and so had Darling's recollection of the correct leg.

George Brent became a major distraction for Garbo. He went so far as to build a gigantic concrete wall around his home at Toluca Lake to keep prying eyes from spying on his reclusive and frequent visitor. Brent didn't talk about Garbo, and Garbo didn't talk at all. "It's a great combination," quipped one columnist.

While Marshall didn't have to build a gigantic wall for Swanson, he was protective. Besides run-ins with photographers, he made front page news following a scrap with the screenwriter, John Monk Saunders, husband of Fay Wray. "Marshall Takes it on the Chin in Hollywood Party Brawl," headlined the United Press. On September 24, 1934, Bart and Gloria attended a party at the home of Ernst Lubitsch. The gala event was in honor of producer Max Reinhardt, who had fled Germany, and was staging *A Midsummer Night's Dream* at the Hollywood Bowl. The two couples left the party, to play a few rounds of ping-pong at Swanson's home. When they returned to the Lubitsch soiree, both men were literally in their cups. It wasn't long before Marshall was lying on the floor, unconscious.[162]

According to Saunders, Marshall got upset, called him "a name," but failed to smile. Saunders felt that Marshall shouldn't have used "that word" without smiling. "I felt it necessary to let Mr. Marshall have one on the chin," he boasted. Witnesses, including Reinhardt, were aghast. Marshall was seated at a table when the blow occurred. He told the press, "I can only say that Mr. Monk Saunders' statement is the best proof that he is a writer of melodramatic fiction. The only active part I played in this melodrama was to resent his insulting behavior to a lady at my table."[163] The lady, of course, was Swanson. The following day, the two lovebirds were seen lunching together on the Fox lot. Bart, showed no visible signs of the previous night's tussle.

CHAPTER FIVE

He Didn't Smile

HERBERT MARSHALL

Screen Writer Claims Knockout Over Gloria Swanson's Escort

John Monk Saunders Trounces Herbert Marshall At Film Party

Scenarist Declares Actor Forgot To Smile On Making Certain Remark Concerning Woman's Beauty.

Writer Floors Movie Star in Fight at Party

Herbert Marshall Accuses Saunders of Striking Him While Sitting

Marshall Takes It on Chin In Hollywood Party Brawl

Resents Insulting Behavior of Author in Gloria Swanson's Presence at Affair Honoring German Producer

Hollywood—(UP)—A new champion was crowned today in another of Hollywood's many one-punch "battles of the century."

He was John Monk Saunders, writer, who was unofficially acclaimed after he reported a knockout over Herbert Marshall, English actor, at a party attended by many film personages.

The one-punch encounter occurred at the home of Ernst Lubitsch, the director, during a party honoring Max Reinhardt.

September 17, 1934. Prior to being surrounded by sensational headlines, Gloria Swanson signs autographs, while Marshall looks on.

Years later, Fay Wray wrote in her autobiography that Swanson made it impossible for any kind of reconciliation during the incident. "She flew about in all directions in a furious display of hysterics," said Wray. The problem began when Saunders seated himself next to Swanson, eyeing her décolletage. Wray elaborated, "[Bart] called him a bestial bastard, it was surely not with vitriol but, rather, kindly, a statement of fact." In the wee hours of the morning, Wray received a phone call. It was Gloria, declaring that Bart had a gun, and was on his way to their house. Wray listened as Swanson went on and on about the "enormous differences" between "the drinking style of Europeans and Americans." Wray didn't believe a word of what Swanson told her about Marshall. "A man who could say what he said about John," deduced Wray, "would not be out with a gun. He probably didn't have one."[164] Over the next few years, Saunders accumulated insurmountable problems with drugs and alcohol. He hung himself shortly after divorcing Fay Wray.[165]

Since he began making films in the U.S., Marshall had no complaints except for his run-in with Josef von Sternberg. In the fall of 1934, he signed on for the innocuously titled *The Good Fairy*, directed by William Wyler and starring Margaret Sullavan. It provided Marshall yet another opportunity to let off some steam about his director *and* co-star. "They were both too intense," complained Marshall, "too pig-headed, too hell-bent on having their own way."[166]

CHAPTER FIVE

Bart brought his sad-eyed English Setter to Hollywood

Marshall and Margaret Sullavan in Wyler's *The Good Fairy* (Universal)

The Good Fairy — Frank Morgan, Margaret Sullavan, Reginald Owen, Marshall (Universal)

CHAPTER 6
"I'm sick and tired of being a gentleman"

"I'm sick and tired of being a gentleman," complained Marshall. "To me the term implies artificiality—a studied pose, and I'm damned if I'm artificial!"[167] To fans, Bart epitomized the perfect English gentleman. A Dallas critic wagered, "Mr. Marshall, at this writing, is perhaps the most attendance-compelling leading man on the screen, deferring only to such acknowledged stars as Cagney, Gable, Cooper and Mickey Mouse."[168] Due to demand, Paramount had loaned Marshall out for over a year. The studio reaped a profit well in advance of the monies they had agreed to pay him. It took a new contract to ensure that he would make three pictures on his home lot in 1935-36.[169]

Bart's affair with Gloria Swanson hadn't curbed his popularity, at least in the U.S. Back in London, friends of Edna Best revealed that she expected Marshall to accede to her wish that he return to her and Sarah Lynn. She had purchased a home outside the city, and planted Bart's favorite Japanese cherry trees around the property.[170] It was a curious move, as Bart preferred the big city, and disliked what he referred to as "material problems." "I am not domestic," he admitted. "I like sophisticated men and women, intelligent talk about good books, plays, the enterprises of others. I should like enormously to write."[171]

The Good Fairy & WYLER

Bart had the good fortune to be cast in director William Wyler's *The Good Fairy* (1935), based on a play by Ferenc Molnar, who had penned Marshall's stage hit, *The Swan*. Screenwriter Preston Sturges had his work cut out for him thanks to the PCA. Sexual innuendo had to be eliminated, and the camera could not linger on "provocative" items such as: "a divan, sofa, settee ... ," per Joseph Breen, chief of the PCA. As cameras rolled, Sturges kept working on the script, a short jump ahead of the microphone. It was as if the whole production was being filmed off-the-cuff. Also in the cast was Bart's dear friend, Eric Blore, whose Hollywood career took flight after he played a headwaiter in the Astaire/Rogers film, *Flying Down to Rio* (1933). In *The Good Fairy*, Blore offered some hilarity as Dr. Metz, a perpetually tipsy Budapest dignitary.

As the story unfolds, young, naive Luisa Ginglebuscher (Margaret Sullavan), leaves a Budapest orphanage to be an usherette. Ignorant of the facts of life, she discovers her own way of dealing with the male gender: as if she were living in a fairy tale. Luisa tells a stage door Johnny (Cesar Romero) that she's married to a waiter, Mr. Detlaff (Reginald Owen). She then fends off Konrad (Frank Morgan), a middle-aged tycoon, who tells her they should make babies, who will call him "papa." She also tells him that she's married. "To whom?" Konrad asks. "What does he do?" Sturges' clever, convoluted dialogue has them *both* deciding that her husband must be an attorney, a poverty-stricken one (selected out of a telephone book). His name is Dr. Max Sporum (Marshall), a rather cynical man, whose cherished goal is to acquire a hand-cranked pencil-sharpener. Luisa, always intent on doing her daily good deed, decides that Konrad should hire Sporum and shower him with gifts. Konrad obliges. Unwittingly, Luisa delivers Sporum his new pencil-sharpener, only to be struck by cupid's arrow.

Luisa's suitors eventually learn the truth about her "husbands" and her "good fairy deeds." Konrad takes pity, and keeps Sporum under his employ, so that Luisa can become Mrs. Max Sporum. At the finish, Frank Morgan offers the hilarious, "If there's any good fairy around here, it's *me*!"

CHAPTER SIX

Marshall's comic turn proved refreshing, different from anything he had done on screen. He joined in the antics providing contrast to the frantic styles of Morgan and Reginald Owen. Whether fussing with his beard, or waxing ecstatic over his beloved pencil sharpener ("Glorious! Like a needle! Did you ever see such a point!?!"), Marshall is equally amusing. His character's underlying warmth is especially effective when he discovers the ruse behind his new employment. He scoffs while repeating his personal motto, "Honesty is the shortcut to success. Integrity brings its reward." The ensemble spirit behind a cast of quirky characters buoyed the film into something special. Sturges' script took a poke at upper class pretention, in the new genre of screwball comedy.

Variety predicted, "The box-office reaction should be robust." It was. The *San Francisco Chronicle* thought Sullavan "engaging," and Marshall "highly satisfactory as the bewildered benefactor." Andre Sennwald, for *The New York Times*, found Marshall "entirely effective," and went on to cheer the "scatter-brained skill of Frank Morgan and Reginald Owen" in what he called, "an engaging and often uproariously funny work." In 2015, New York critic David Noh nodded to Sullavan's performance. "Nobody did wide-eyed, irresistibly maddening innocence better," he wrote. "You just want to eat her up." Marshall, it could be said, found her less than appetizing to work with. Ditto for director Wyler.

Years later, Marshall recalled the combustible atmosphere on the set. Margaret Sullavan was prone to tantrums, and clashed repeatedly with her director. "She was forever testing the exasperated Wyler to see how much she could get away with," said Marshall. "And he was equally tough."[172] Marshall's calm, even temper was a more practical choice. "When I have anything to argue about," he mused, "I say it quietly to the person concerned."[173] One day, Wyler bawled Sullavan out in front of the entire cast, then took her out to dinner. Several weeks later they married, but continued to lock horns. Six months after that, they were living apart.[174] The final straw was Sullavan's decision to get an abortion without telling Wyler.[175] She quipped that she was ultimately left with two choices, "Jump in the lake, or get a divorce."

Sylvia Sidney pegged Wyler in a 1990 interview. Wyler directed her in *Dead End* (1937) soon after he and Sullavan divorced. "Wyler was … a sadistic son-of-a-bitch," said Sidney, known for her salty interviews. "He had a habit of treating you badly and then trying to make love to you. At least that was my experience with him."[176] Following *Dead End*, Wyler tried his technique on leading lady Bette Davis. While filming *Jezebel*, she was most compliant. "I adored Willie," cooed Davis. "He was the only male strong enough to control me. The sexual sparks were there from the beginning."[177]

In November, as Bart completed scenes for *The Good Fairy*, he was being considered to join Kay Francis at Warner Bros. for the Frank Borzage film *Living on Velvet* (a role that went to Warren William). Unfortunately, he was needed for retakes on *The Painted Veil*.[178] Although "sick and tired of being a gentleman," Bart rose to the occasion and penned a nice "thank you" to Wyler on November 8.

> My Dear Willy,
>
> Re-takes at Metro prohibit me from coming out to Universal and telling you personally what a pleasant time I had with you — and I'm leaping off to the Desert to-morrow. I enjoyed myself enormously and I shall use my next drink into toasting you and wishing you and the company and Preston a successful picture, artistically and box-officially.
>
> You might please tell Margaret, with my regard, that in spite of any view she may have to the contrary, her gum-chewing is nowhere near as good as her acting, and God knows her chewing is superb and adroit.
>
> Yours sincerely,
>
> Bart[179]

CHAPTER SIX

The Flame Within — Henry Stephenson, Ann Harding, Marshall (MGM)

Hollywood Hotel (CBS) broadcast scenes from *The Flame Within*. Marshall, Ann Harding, Edmund Goulding, Louis "Sugar" Hayward

Five years later, Marshall would team once again with Willy Wyler for two Bette Davis successes: *The Letter* (1940) and *The Little Foxes* (1941).

After retakes at Metro, Bart and Gloria flew from Hollywood to Yuma, Arizona, for a wedding. Fortunately, it wasn't theirs. They stood in as witnesses for British stars Evelyn Laye and Frank Lawton. (Yuma had also accommodated Wyler and Sullavan when they tied the marital knot.) *The Good Fairy* premiered in Hollywood on February 12, 1935. Bart and Gloria were in attendance, before joining in an evening of revelry at the Trocadero.

Instead of returning to Paramount, Bart, along with Ann Harding, teamed at MGM for *The Flame Within*. Both stars were delighted at the prospect of working with director Edmund Goulding, who had written the scenario. Goulding kept cameras rolling for longer takes than usual—which were beautifully sustained by the actors. Harding played a psychiatrist, Dr. Mary White, who develops a romantic attachment for one of her patients, a young alcoholic named Jack (Louis Hayward). Initially, she was dealing with Jack's suicidal sweetheart Linda (Maureen O'Sullivan), but decided that the real problem was Jack. Her skill pays off. The young couple wed. After the honeymoon, Jack confesses his love for the woman who cured him. Resisting her own romantic feelings, Dr. White encourages Jack to "do the right thing" for his young bride. Marshall was on hand as Harding's devoted suitor, someone she could bank on. As written, his support eventually serves as a death knell to her professional career.

Some balked at the film's final moment. Psychiatrist Harding loses confidence in herself, and gives up. "I'm not going on with the work," she tells Marshall. "What are you going to do?" he asks. "*You* tell me," she replies. In his critically acclaimed *Complicated Women* (2000), author Mick LaSalle, wrote, "Everything about the moment is designed to indicate a happy ending ... except for Harding's performance. Harding plays the moment like she has just had a lobotomy. She plays it as a moment of abject defeat and soul death. ... The best she can do is slip out a message, like a captive in a totalitarian land. That message is for us."[180]

LaSalle was referring to the PCA's edict that a woman's place was *not* in the professional world. *The New York Times* pointed to the weak ending. The *Los Angeles Times* concurred, "Least convincing are the closing moments. The story, one feels, does not end here, except perfunctorily." Marshall suffered patiently in the background, until Harding relents to his proposal of marriage. As pointed out by *Variety*, "Marshall's role is a trifle stiff since he is called upon to impersonate a passive pillar of moral strength upon whose shoulder the confused lady doctor may at last rest." Director Goulding's camera had a tendency to dote on Louis Hayward who was making his Hollywood screen debut, after critics singled him out during the Broadway run of Noel Coward's *Point Valaine*. Biographer Matthew Kennedy noted that "Hayward ... was given generous screen time by Eddie," and "rewarded with positive reviews."[181] Hayward subsequently broke up with Coward, who referred to his young protégé as "Sugar." Their affair would end "bitterly."[182]

Later that year, Marshall teamed again with Harding for *The Lady Consents* (released in 1936) with better results. It was his first film for RKO, where he signed a five-year contract with yearly options. This time, it was Harding's character that suffers, while husband Marshall, a physician, leaves her to marry one of *his* patients—a manipulative, young social climber (Margaret Lindsay). A pivotal scene has Marshall returning home from the hospital at 5 a.m. He is in dire need to share his despair after failing to save the life of a close friend. His new wife does not want to be bothered. Realizing his mistake, Marshall shows up at his understanding ex-wife's apartment. *The Lady Consents* was an intelligent twist on a familiar theme. Only, this time around, Marshall is not inclined to give up his profession. When Lindsay refuses him a divorce, Harding suggests, "Let her keep the title ... but *I'll* be your wife." (Surprisingly, this line, implying that she could be his mistress, got by the censors.) "I'm not worth that," he replies. With a loving smirk, she responds, "I know that." No doubt many fans were reminded of Edna Best, back in London, patiently waiting for her husband to lose interest in Gloria Swanson. Such a prospect was in the back Marshall's mind, too. But, he kept putting it off.

The Lady Consents — with Ann Harding (RKO)

Harding's gallant lady image (which had boosted her career), was wearing a bit thin by this time. *Hollywood Citizen News* complained that the "routine expertness" of her suffering had become "tiresome." On a personal note, Harding's ex-husband, actor Harry Bannister, made headlines during a custody battle in which he claimed she was an "unfit mother" for their six-year-old daughter Jane. He sent wires and letters demanding up to $100,000—blackmail, for not releasing "certain revelations" that could lead to public scandal.[183]

With such strikes against Harding, *The Lady Consents* still made profit for RKO. *The New York Times* felt she etched a believable portrait of "articulate despair." A San Diego critic praised, "Herbert Marshall, by force of his personality and dramatic technique, scores with one of his best performances."[184] Harding's contract with RKO was ending, and she was looking forward to an extended stay in England. She had quizzed Marshall on the set of *The Lady Consents* about attractive places to stay while abroad. He had to admit that he was somewhat out of the loop as he hadn't been home for three years. That would soon change.

Typecasting had soured the marquee value of other stars—from Dietrich's exotic creatures to Garbo's sad ones. In a June 1935 column,

CHAPTER SIX

Mollie Merrick designated Herbert Marshall as "the savior of all slipping stars." Merrick announced that Bart would step in to save the career of Dietrich. "If the appearance of Gary Cooper in her present picture [*Desire*] and the help of Bart Marshall in the next ... can't do the work ... Marlene just hasn't got it in her."[185] Fortunately, the film with Dietrich, *I Loved a Soldier*, went into production without Marshall. Filming was brought to a halt due to script problems and altercations between Dietrich and director Henry Hathaway. As far as being typecast, Marshall himself had to be on guard against roles that pigeonholed him as the long-suffering husband or lover. "I want roles I can get my teeth into," he insisted, "characters instead of carbon copies."

Sketches by Scottish artist Alan Ritchie from 1935

After a brief respite with Swanson near Palm Springs, Marshall had the good fortune to return to comedy, and the Paramount lot. He was to co-star with Sylvia Sidney, considered to be the quintessential Depression heroine. Sidney's films usually placed her in city slums. In *Accent on Youth*, she found employment as secretary to playwright Marshall. Along with director Wesley Ruggles, they created one of the box-office champions for 1935.[186] While Marshall's middle-aged playwright tackles the subject of May-December romances, he unexpectedly finds himself in a similar situation with his young secretary. Life imitates art. The engaging chemistry between Marshall and Sidney, combined for diverting screen fare. Marshall is particularly delightful when manipulating egos of the actors cast in his play. *Variety* praised, "Marshall's restraint makes a difficult acting assignment thoroughly convincing." A Brooklyn critic found the performances "refreshing," but Ruggles' direction "unenterprising." The latter half of *Accent on Youth* lacked a brisk tempo for complete success. Years later, Sidney minced no words in relating her feelings about Ruggles.

> Wesley Ruggles ... was another son-of-a-bitch! Marshall had lost a leg in World War I, but he used to cover this handicap. On stage, you never noticed it. When he was in films, you didn't notice it. It was only apparent in *Accent on Youth*, because Ruggles' set was too difficult for Marshall to walk around on. Other directors had accommodated Marshall.[187]

Accent on Youth — with Sylvia Sidney (Paramount)

CHAPTER SIX

During production, Bart was called away from the set to offer encouragement to a Paramount electrician, who survived the disastrous Sky Chief crash of May 6, 1935. (Myrna Loy had the good fortune to cancel her flight reservation at the last minute.) The transcontinental flight took the lives of both pilots, and New Mexico Senator Bronson Cutting. Cutting was outraged when Congress passed the Economy Act of 1933, reducing benefits for disabled veterans. He was headed to Washington D.C. to reverse the decision, and accelerate payment of veteran's bonuses. Also on board was a Paramount film unit bound for Annapolis for location shooting on *Annapolis Farewell* (1935). Upon impact, the studio's chief electrician C.G. "Pat" Drew, of Santa Monica, was left with a badly mangled leg.

After Drew was transferred to Los Angeles, his leg was amputated. He remained in critical condition.[188] Physicians feared that hysteria would cost him his life. One doctor, familiar with Marshall's amputation, telephoned the actor. Thirty minutes later, Bart walked into Drew's hospital room. He looked at the patient and smiled, "You know, I got a bit shot up during the war. But I feel better now than I ever did." Drew reached a new calm, and his temperature subsided. Doctors claimed that Marshall, not themselves, had saved Drew's life.[189] However, the studio felt that Drew was unemployable. It took someone like Carole Lombard to come again to his rescue. She had a clause put in her contract that Pat Drew be assigned to all her pictures.[190] Tragically, Lombard herself would die in an air crash during a War Bond tour in 1942.

※

In June 1935, Marshall advanced to the prestigious studio of producer Samuel Goldwyn, joining Merle Oberon and Fredric March in a remake of the 1925 silent hit, *The Dark Angel*. Marshall was cast as a WWI veteran, caught in a love triangle. Set in the English countryside, *The Dark Angel* begins with a dispensable flashback to establish the devotion of three childhood friends. Ten minutes later, ten years have passed. At the outbreak of the Great War, we see two enlistees, Alan (March) and Gerald (Marshall), in love with the same girl, Kitty (Oberon). When they arrive home on leave, Kitty reveals that it's Alan she wants to marry. Gerald takes it on the chin, until the men are called back to the front. As his commanding officer, Gerald denies Alan leave to see Kitty. In the aftermath, Alan is presumed dead.

Toward the finish, Kitty and Gerald reunite with Alan, who was blinded during battle. Not wanting to be a burden, Alan attempts to fool them into thinking that he can see. Marshall's poignant recognition of Alan's ruse, and what is *really* going on, brings the film to a heartfelt and memorable closure. *Film Daily* enthused, "Stellar honors are divided evenly" between the three stars. Without a doubt it was Oberon who gave this tear-jerker the necessary heart. She got an Oscar nod for Best Actress. Lillian Hellman and British playwright Mordaunt Shairp shared credit for *The Dark Angel*. Hellman later referred to the film as "an old silly directed by Sidney Franklin."[191]

The Dark Angel — Fredric March, Merle Oberon, Marshall (UA)

In some respects *The Dark Angel* felt dated. Novelist Graham Greene's review in London's *The Spectator* summed up, "The silly sentimental war story of *The Dark Angel* ... a very manorial, very feudal film ... is one you should go a very long way to avoid."[192] In the U.S., however, critics waxed poetic about the film. *Photoplay* ranked the trio of stars and the film in their "Best of the Month" category. "Miss Oberon is a revelation," lauded *Variety*. "Marshall and March are superb." Philadelphia critic Mildred Martin pointed directly to "the fine-grained artistry of Miss Oberon and Mr. Marshall." Martin was less enthused about "Mr. March's somewhat clumsy attempts at pathos and unconvincing work as a blind man with a pride complex." March had inherited his role from Leslie Howard. Prior to filming, Oberon and Howard were engaged in an off-screen love affair. She had requested he play her love interest in *The Dark Angel*. The romance cooled. Howard lost interest in doing the film, and returned to his wife.[193]

The film's gala premier at Grauman's Chinese Theater, had a big turnout of celebrities, minus Bart Marshall, "owing to his aversion to crowds," explained the *Los Angeles Examiner*. Gloria Swanson, who frequently showed up on the set of *The Dark Angel*, was escorted to the premier by MGM baritone Nelson Eddy, who was about to leave for Lake Tahoe and location shooting on *Rose Marie*. Metro was still fumbling around trying to find a role for Swanson, and, as her biographer Shearer put it, "mercifully she still received her MGM weekly paycheck."[194] Swanson's 1935 wages at Metro (for doing nothing) totaled $53,000.[195]

In October, Marshall and Swanson showed up at the Shrine Auditorium for the performance of Evelyn Laye in Noel Coward's *Bitter Sweet*. Reportedly, Swanson dazzled the crowds with her flame-red velvet gown. Walter Winchell promptly blabbed, "The Gloria Swanson-Herbert Marshall romance is far from cooling. In fact, it's hotter than ever."

If Only You Could Cook — with Jean Arthur (Columbia)

In her tome *5001 Nights at the Movies*, critic Pauline Kael rated the romantic comedy *If Only You Could Cook* (1935), "eminently watchable ... remarkably good-natured and fresh. Jean Arthur brings out the best in Marshall." Filmed at Columbia, the plot finds unemployed Jean Arthur sitting next to Marshall on a park bench. She's reading the want ads, and assumes he needs a job, too. She suggests they team-up as a married cook-and-butler. Marshall, a wealthy auto magnate, takes her up on the offer. He wants escape from a fiancée who only loves his money. It isn't long before their new employer, an ex-bootlegger mobster (Leo Carrillo), smells not only garlic the kitchen, but the aroma of an imposter ... Marshall. Marshall's droll delivery is perfect, especially when Carrillo's mob kidnaps him from his own wedding. Marshall quips, "In one way boys, I don't mind this at all."

In the director's chair was William Seiter, who raved about Marshall. "What an actor! He'll work until he drops dead. Nothing is too much trouble for him. He never complains—I'm nuts about him!"[196] Some critics felt that the film would have fared even better under the helm of

CHAPTER SIX

Frank Capra, who had scored five Oscar wins for *It Happened One Night* (1934). When *If Only You Could Cook* was released in England, Columbia Pictures president Harry Cohn, wanting to cash in on Capra's popularity, made sure it was advertised as "A Frank Capra Production." Capra was furious, and confronted Cohn, who argued, "Does it kill ya, for crissake, to see Columbia make a few more bucks in England? Maybe we can cut you *in* for a slice … ."[197] Capra sued. The incident was resolved a year later, after Cohn bought film rights for the play *You Can't Take it With You*, allowing Capra to direct.

Marshall enjoyed comedy, telling Sheilah Graham, "The fan mail I received following *If Only You Could Cook* cheered me no end. They all wrote, 'Thank goodness, you played—for once—a lighter part.' I am tired of making people weep." He wanted to work with Capra, calling him "the best in the business." Jean Arthur was fortunate. Her next film was the Capra classic, *Mr. Deeds Goes to Town*, which propelled her to international stardom. Marshall went back to making people weep. He starred in two back-to-back dramas at Paramount. His leading lady in both films was Gertrude Michael, best known for her role as the jealous chanteuse in *Murder at the Vanities* (1934), in which she sang the cult classic, "Sweet Marijuana."

Till We Meet Again, a WWI saga, was originally proposed for Marshall and Sylvia Sidney in 1933, under the title *Reunion*. Filming finally got under way in January 1936, under the helm of Robert Florey, whose direction added momentum to an otherwise routine romantic spy-drama. Marshall, a British matinee idol, and his fiancée, a Viennese stage beauty (Gertrude Michael), are separated at the outbreak of war. "I love you more than my country," declares Marshall, but the two are soon pitted against one another as counterspies. Marshall strikes an authentic chord when impersonating a shell-shocked prisoner of war. Memories of his comrades in London hospitals (1917-18) allowed him to register grim realities on screen. In 2015, Australian author/critic John Howard Reid observed, "When called upon to act the shell-shocked veteran, Marshall's mighty convincing."[198]

Till We Meet Again — Director Florey and his trio of stars: Marshall, Gertrude Michael and Rod La Rocque (Paramount) (Courtesy of the estate of Robert Florey)

Rehearsing with Gertrude Michael for *Till We Meet Again*. Director Florey, at far right. (Paramount) (Courtesy of the estate of Robert Florey)

CHAPTER SIX

Till We Meet Again allows the lovers to renounce war, and flee to neutral territory, Holland. As Dallas critic John Rosenfeld wagged, "As has been the custom of spy pictures lately, lovers will look after themselves and let their respective fatherlands go hang." Rosenfeld considered Marshall's performance the standout, "Mr. Marshall seems never to be acting, yet never fails to point up every dramatic element ... with plausibility and punch." Making a comeback attempt, was Bart's friend Rod La Rocque, who played an English spy left with no choice other than honorable suicide. The real surprise in *Till We Meet Again* was hearing Marshall sing a chorus of Strauss's "Tales of the Vienna Woods." This occurs in a café during the film's first ten minutes. His pleasant baritone blends alongside the voice of Gertrude Michael, with charm and simpatico.

Robert Florey, Marshall, and La Rocque were well-acquainted. Florey biographer Brian Taves contacted this author in 2017, saying, "I'm not sure how Bob and Bart first met, but it seems they were old friends. There were snapshots of trips across the border to Mexico—Bob, Bart, Rod, and Fredric March, ca. 1936. I think *Till We Meet Again* encapsulated both Florey's feelings about WWI, and his own wish to do more romantic stories."[199] According to Taves, the cast eased tension on the set with a few "gag" photos—shots of Bart and other actors in evening clothes "relieving themselves" on a wall below a sign proclaiming, "Commit No Nuisance!'" La Rocque, it must be noted, was a former lover of Gloria Swanson. Their 1924 romance was filled with lovers' quarrels and a proposal of marriage. "He was physically beautiful and had a brilliant mind," wrote Swanson in her memoirs, "I wanted to be with him every minute."[200]

Marshall and Jim Gerald being "disobedient" on the set of *Till We Meet Again* (Courtesy of the estate of Robert Florey)

In mid-production, King George V passed away. *Variety* reported that out of respect for the King, several British stars joined together for a quiet dinner at the Beverly Wilshire. They included: Marshall, the Basil Rathbones, the Edmund Gouldings, Merle Oberon and C. Aubrey Smith. Years later, it was revealed that His Majesty's final words, "God damn you!" were addressed to a nurse administering him a sedative.[201] Marshall came close to cursing when screenwriter Sada Cowan asked, "How does it feel to be a gentleman in the midst of a lot of actors?" He replied softly, but definitely, "I am *not* a gentleman."

> To understand me, you have to know what the word 'gentleman' means to a Britisher. It means 'well born.' And I am decidedly not what a Briton means by well

born. I come from a substantial middle-class family. So you see, on the face of things I am not a gentleman. I don't like the word anyway. There is a famous line in one of your old American plays—*The Virginian*, if I'm not mistaken—in which one man insults another and the insulted one, with a gun in his hand, answers, 'When you call me *that*, Stranger, *smile*.' In England we feel a bit that way about the word 'gentleman.'[202]

Marshall's reference to *The Virginian* was an obvious dig at John Monk Saunders, who quoted the same, after socking Bart in the jaw. Cowan had no choice, but to concede, "Herbert Marshall is not a gentleman!"

Forgotten Faces with Gertrude Michael (Paramount) (Courtesy of Jenny Paxson)

Critics were less enthusiastic when Marshall and Gertrude Michael re-teamed for the grim melodrama *Forgotten Faces* (1936). "Herbert Marshall deserves a far better fate than his present one," said Ohio critic

William Blair. "*Forgotten Faces* has all the marks of being turned out quickly." In this third remake of William Walburn Child's 1919 story, "A Whiff of Heliotrope," Marshall played a gambler, who relies on the scent of heliotrope to bring him good luck. Instead of luck, he catches his wife (Michael) in the arms of another man, whom he kills. Before spending a life behind bars, he arranges for his baby daughter to be adopted by a wealthy couple. On parole, seventeen years later, Marshall discovers his wife is attempting to blackmail the couple. At the finish, Marshall and Michael both end up in the morgue. As critic Blair summed up, "it never quite gets away from the sordidness." *The Dallas Morning News* offered kudos to Marshall. "It loads onto the rather gallant shoulders of Herbert Marshall the most insufferably burdensome script of his career. The best to be offered is a toast to his noble effort." *Forgotten Faces* is considered a lost film.

"Queen of the Hollywood Extras" Bess Flowers faces Marshall in *Forgotten Faces* (Paramount) (Courtesy of Larry Smith)

Gloria Swanson dropped in on the set of *Forgotten Faces* to watch Bart at work. He escorted her away from the turgid dramatics, and onto the circus set of *Poppy* where W.C. Fields displayed the art of ad-libbing. While there, Gloria introduced Bart to director Eddie Sutherland and gag writer Bobby Vernon. Both had co-starred in her silent film *The Danger Girl* (1916). Marshall and Fields stood by as the old co-stars talked and talked. Fields finally broke it up, blurting out, "Funny, how I always get thirsty." He left to take care of the problem.²⁰³

On the set of *Poppy* with W.C. Fields

The completion of *Forgotten Faces* coincided with Warner Bros. wrapping up *The White Angel*, starring Kay Francis. She had the tough assignment of playing Florence Nightingale, Britain's celebrated founder of modern nursing. Kay's diary indicated that she relaxed at Marshall's home drinking absinthe (which was illegal at the time).²⁰⁴ It made sense that Kay would seek out Bart's counsel and indulge in a glass of Bohemian contraband. *The White Angel* was a difficult shoot. "Experts" from England were brought in to make sure that Kay's performance revered Nightingale. The script was compromised by the Lord Chamberlain himself. The film's failure at the box-office, meant the beginning of the end of Kay's reign at Warner Bros.

Although Bart still retained British citizenship, he wagered that his career from here on out would be on U.S. soil. He insisted on being offered a raise with each new contract, but his salary ($40,000 per film) was substantially lower than those of his British counterparts Ronald Colman ($150,000) and Leslie Howard ($75,000).[205] Regardless, Bart remained optimistic. "When the day dawns that I shall have to get along with a slashed budget I'll find a way. I've done it before."[206] As summer 1936 approached, Bart announced plans for a short visit in England. He envisioned boarding the zeppelin Hindenburg for Germany. From there, he would take a plane to London. His getaway would have to wait. He had three more films to complete.

※

Bart made a smart move (initially), to 20th-Century Fox for a film adaptation of Ladislas Fodor's play *Matura*. Re-titled, *Girl's Dormitory*, Marshall played Dr. Stephen Dominik, headmaster of an all-girls school in the Swiss Alps. Ruth Chatterton was his leading lady. She lent authenticity to her role as Anna, a school instructor. Third billed, was French actress Simone Simon, who played Marie, a student who develops a crush on Dr. Dominik. Simon had a reputation of being temperamental. She had been axed from a role opposite Ronald Colman in *Under Two Flags*. Upon completion, *Girl's Dormitory* was a well-written, dramatically sound film. Unfortunately, producer Darryl Zanuck decided to tamper with it. In doing so, he lost both the backbone and fragility of the original play. Zanuck turned the ending on its head for publicity purposes—he was determined to make a star of the youthful, kittenish Simon.

Simon's name dominated advertising for *Girl's Dormitory* with the tagline: "Introducing the new discovery star of 1936!" Marshall and Chatterton were delegated to the smaller print. Lying on the cutting room floor was the original, adult Marshall-Chatterton love story. In its place, headmaster Marshall and pubescent Simon share the fadeout kiss. This change made critics cringe. "The culmination of this definitely absurd romance," said Los Angeles critic Elizabeth Yeaman, "is a jarring note at the conclusion of an otherwise appealing little human interest tale. Marshall … must have squirmed inwardly when he fulfilled the final requirements of his role."[207] Pittsburgh author Florence Fisher Parry spelled out exactly what happened.

> Originally the story ended thus: Simone Simon, convinced that Ruth Chatterton and Herbert Marshall are really in love and meant for each other … leaves him. Marshall turns to Ruth, and takes solace in a renewal of their romantic friendship. But after the picture was released, a new ending was manufactured, false and patched and showing concessions in every line.[208]

Parry added, "I don't know how old the girl is … but she doesn't look over fourteen. That is the only weak spot in *Girl's Dormitory*. The girl is too much of a child." Another critic barbed that the film was a "great piece of cradle-snatching." When Marshall and Simon were called back to reshoot the ending, a number of extreme close-ups of Simon were inserted to exploit her impish appeal. *International Photographer* pointed to the "outbursts of mediocre cutting" and "distortion" resulting from "its forced change from a vehicle for Chatterton and Marshall to a builder-upper for Simon." In the aftermath, Simon became known as "one of Hollywood's most spectacular failures."[209] The real surprise was Tyrone Power Jr., who appeared in three small scenes. Fox signed Power to a seven-year contract and gave him a massive build-up.

Girl's Dormitory — Director Irving Cummings with Simone Simon, Marshall and Ruth Chatterton (20th Century-Fox)

Marshall was considerate of Simon. She expressed her gratitude, in her best English, thusly, "I cannot say how kind he was to me, that man. When I am mixed, he tells me softly the word, so nobody shall hear. When I was so worrying, he would give me a helping look."[210] Marshall appreciated the fact that it was Simon's first American film. "You couldn't take direction if you couldn't understand it," he rationalized. "That, I believe, was Simon's trouble."[211] The next question was, could Marshall maintain his equilibrium while playing opposite the outspoken, headstrong, and talented Katharine Hepburn?

A Woman Rebels — Hepburn benefited from Marshall's "admirable reserve" (RKO)

Zaza Claudette Colbert puckers up for illicit kisses (Paramount) (Courtesy of Larry Smith)

CHAPTER 7
A to Z

A WOMAN REBELS (1936) - ZAZA (1939)

Prior to leaving for England, Marshall came close to buying a $40,000 citrus ranch. "It will be a good hideaway for rest between pictures," he wagered. After much press coverage, he backed out, opting instead to lease a cottage from actor Charles Farrell. Marshall had other financial concerns. For several months he continued to pay the salary of his chauffeur, who was hospitalized.[212] Marshall reached into his pockets again, donating money to lettuce strikers in Salinas, whose wages were reduced from fifty cents to thirty cents an hour. Donations from celebrities totaled over $5,000. The biggest donors were: Marshall, Gary Cooper, Brian Aherne, Gloria Stuart, and Ginger Rogers.[213] PCA officials and producers set off alarms saying that sympathy to lettuce strikers would endanger the whole studio system. *The Dallas Morning News* labeled them "Red Actors."[214] The two-day standoff ended poorly for the strikers, who were exempt from legal protection.

In October, after signing a five-year contract with Columbia Pictures, Bart boarded the *S.S. Aquitania* (instead of the Hindenburg). His anticipated fifteen-day trip to London was extended to a month-long stay. Edna, who was in rehearsal for *As You Like It* at the Old Vic, made it clear that she had no plans to meet with him, although she anticipated they would talk things over. "What form a discussion would take," she told the press, "I cannot forecast, as I don't know what is on his mind."[215]

Upon Bart's arrival on October 21, reporters made further inquiries. "I shall be disappointed and deeply unhappy if I do not see Mrs. Marshall," he replied nervously. "All kinds of things have been said, I know, but we have not said them. This is the first time that studio arrangements have permitted me to come to England."

November 1936 - Bart and Edna join Rod La Rocque hitting London night spots

The time Bart spent with Edna was buoyed by the support of friends like Rod La Rocque, who was also visiting London. The trio were seen out together at various nightspots. Bart and Edna seemed to be enjoying each other's company while dancing at Sherry's Dance Hall in Brighton. Bart was also delighted to visit the all-male, London-based Garrick Club (for actors and men of refinement), in which he had retained his membership. It was reported that the Marshalls stayed together in an apartment of a friend.[216] In fact, Edna withdrew from the cast of *As You Like It*. London's *Stage* magazine mentioned that her doctor recommended rest.[217] Her absentee husband was in town.

CHAPTER SEVEN

Upon his return to the U.S. on November 23, Bart appeared to be significantly happier. When asked about his wife, he replied, "We are the greatest pals." At the mention of reconciliation, he just shook his head.[218] In Hollywood, writer Gladys Hall invited herself over for tea at Charlie Farrell's charming English cottage. Bart drew out his pipe, and relaxed. His dog crouched down by his feet in the sitting room. A cozy fire blazed as tea was laid out. "I like this room," he said.

> It fits my moods—and I have them, I'm afraid. Red, black, blue. We have great talks here, David Niven and I, Ronnie [Colman] and I, groups of us. Whenever I have problems to work out they seem to work out here, by the fire. Yet I shall be leaving it soon—when my little daughter comes to stay with me. I fell in love with my little girl. I knew that I would feel as I do, of course, but I didn't know in quite what a deep way. I knew it from pictures, from the letters her mother sent me. Perhaps the discovery strikes so deep with me because I am not such a very *young* father. And as we grow older lovely things are not taken lightly, are they?
>
> I didn't know, for one thing, the way in which she would laugh or what it would do to me when I heard it. It is the sunniest, jolliest, most bubbling little laughter. It is like being constantly by a singing brook.

He paused briefly, then continued. "She is so happy," he said wistfully, "That she felt like sun in my heart." Hall felt her throat tighten. The moment was poignant, due to the significance he gave it. Marshall looked up and smiled, "I didn't at all realize what a jolly thing it would be to have a little pair of arms clamped around my neck. Nor did I have any idea, nor much hope that she would take to me as she did." Marshall chuckled to himself. "It was love at first sight with both of us. She made it so delightfully clear that I was pretty much alright with her." Marshall took great pleasure in accompanying Sarah to her dancing lessons, watching boys and girls bowing and curtseying. "I cried like a fool," he admitted. Marshall reflected back to his own youth—an only child raised by maiden aunts. "I never really had a child to play with before. It was all so new to me, so blessed." When it came time to return to Hollywood, he found it difficult. "I have said many goodbyes in my lifetime—but none more difficult than that one."[219]

Whatever transpired between Bart and Edna during his London visit, enabled them to remain friends, "pals" as he put it, and let bygones be bygones. As a result, Marshall allowed himself a new sense of mental and emotional freedom.

Marshall's last two films for 1936 (his busiest year on screen) came out in November. *A Woman Rebels*, based on an English novel by Netta Syrett, was set during the Victorian Era, and championed a woman's right to work. Katharine Hepburn offered a gentle, restrained portrait as Pamela Thistlewaite, the crusading editor of a feminist publication *The New Woman*. Determined to remain independent, she raises her fatherless child—the result of an affair with a married man (Van Heflin in his film debut). Reluctantly, Pamela represses her feelings for a diplomat (Marshall), who admires her ambition as the "new woman." Years later, her daughter (whom she is raising as her niece), falls for a young man who is really her half-brother. In order to protect the daughter, and keep "her past" a secret, Pamela ends up as co-respondent in a divorce court case. Marshall's character, after learning the truth from Pamela herself, diplomatically resolves her dilemma.

One critic marveled, "Miss Hepburn seems more assured in her present picture than in several recent roles, and strikes no false notes. Herbert Marshall's admirable reserve contributes a great deal to the film and may even have curbed Miss Hepburn in her moments of more flighty tendencies."[220] Cleveland critic, W. Ward Marsh, concurred that Hepburn "turned in one of her finer, less bizarre characterizations ... and never stoops to the familiar Hepburn tricks. Herbert Marshall, as usual, gives a careful and charming account of his faithful lover role." *Variety*, however, found the overall effect of the film to be "rambling and without cumulative sock."

Hepburn biographer Anne Edwards determined that *A Woman Rebels* "lacked vitality." Edwards felt that director Mark Sandrich was "out of his element" (Sandrich was known for Astaire-Rogers musicals). The film lost $222,000, Hepburn's third box-office flop in a row.[221] The problem with *A Woman Rebels* is in the telling. Instead of focusing on the challenges of a feminist publisher, tackling issues with bite and promise, we are left with a handsomely filmed soap-opera, highlighted by Miss Hepburn's exquisite Victorian gowns by designer Walter Plunkett. In lieu of dramatic tension, we are faced with a meandering series of vignettes.

Freelance writer Katharine Hartley, who frequented the RKO lot, relished the sound of Hepburn shouting at someone. She was a spitfire, and made good copy. Back in 1931, Leslie Howard complained of Hepburn's "insufferable bossiness"—he couldn't work with "that beanpole."[222] Howard applied pressure to have her removed from the Broadway cast of *The Animal Kingdom*.[223] What was Bart's opinion of the temperamental Hepburn, who would accumulate a total of twelve Oscar nominations for Best Actress? He graciously admitted, "Oh, I burst out at times. I fight for my rights. Don't think that I don't."[224] Marshall himself had asked for revisions on the script for *A Woman Rebels*.[225]

As far as Hepburn's demand that visitors be barred from the set, Marshall was also on the defensive. "I can't say that I blame her. I can make love to a girl with an electrician two feet away holding a spotlight ... because he belongs there. No one can be expected to do good work with strangers watching. Outside of the studio I know nothing of Miss Hepburn." When push came to shove, Marshall qualified, "Temperament takes too much time and energy and is so foolish. No one with brains goes in for it."[226] In lieu of temperament, Marshall reached into his pockets to buy crew members at RKO gifts upon the completion of *A Woman Rebels*. This time, he gave away lapel strap watches that he had purchased at a Hollywood jewelry store.[227]

Following his cautious remarks about Hepburn, Marshall backed out of co-starring with her in *Quality Street*, which was in production when he had left for England. Franchot Tone took his place.[228] Without Marshall there to curb Hepburn's "flighty tendencies," critics, once more, were giving her a hard time. *The New York Times*, warned, "Such flutterings and jitterings and twitchings, such hand-wringings and mouth-quiverings, such runnings-about and eyebrow-raisings have not been on the screen in many a moon."[229]

Make Way for a Lady (originally titled *Daddy and I*) focused on Anne Shirley, publisher Marshall's adolescent daughter. Shirley feels obligated to find daddy the perfect wife. She decides on a novelist (Margot Graham), a woman he detests. Besides, he already has his eye on Shirley's teacher (Gertrude Michael). One New York critic aptly summed up, "a forced, artificial little thing that overtaxed credulity." *Variety* agreed, saying that Marshall "mostly stooges" for Anne Shirley. One expects Marshall to give her a good dressing down by the finish. He doesn't. Nonetheless, Marshall's reaction to his meddlesome daughter was the film's highlight. His scenes with Gertrude Michael have a warmth and charm that helps keep the film afloat. Bart expressed his admiration of Michael, and told Sheilah Graham, "I'm extremely fond of her. But not in the coy Hollywood manner. She is a woman of real acting ability."

The only person who got something out of *Make Way for a Lady* was Burgess Meredith, who was on the RKO lot filming his Broadway success *Winterset*. Meredith marveled at Marshall's astute sense of focus, as he repeated identical actions up to a dozen times, for various camera moves. "He never varied one small movement," said Meredith. "It takes an enormous amount of ability to put a thing like that across."[230] Meredith liked the "indifferent ease" with which Marshall was able to provide "action" in the film's most static moments.

CHAPTER SEVEN

Make Way for a Lady (1936) Marshall stooges for Anne Shirley (RKO)

Anne Shirley had a line in *Make Way for a Lady* that Marshall took to heart: "Daddy, you must begin to think about your waistline. You'll soon be forty!" (He was forty-six.) Bart's typical lunch at the studio consisted of water with lemon juice, avocado (no dressing), and a slice of cream cheese. For obvious reasons, Bart's idea of a good workout was a steam bath and vigorous rubdown. But he took it a bit further in 1936, purchasing a mechanical horse designed to burn calories. In mid-August, he gauged the horse at full-speed and was hurled over the horse's head and onto his own. Dr. Irwin Cooper had to stitch up the actor's scalp. "My horse threw me," he explained to those inquiring about the heavy bandages.[231] On the mend, Bart attended to his hobby of sketching and painting, and drawing risqué cartoons (according to one columnist).[232] British poker pals, David Niven, Ronald Colman, Eric Blore and Alan Mowbray helped keep Bart in good humor.

The major reason for Marshall's new lease on life upon his return from London, was his decision to let go of Gloria Swanson. In early

1936, *Screenland* magazine reported that the Marshall-Swanson romance was "dying a natural death." In July, upon their arrival at the premier of Ronald Colman's *Anthony Adverse*, an orchestra struck up the tune "Why Do I Love You?" Marshall was asking himself the same question. He was tired of being front page news. At one point during their relationship, Bart was compelled to dish out $227.05 in hush money to "prevent the publication of an unfavorable story." Was he trying to protect Swanson? He mistakenly attempted to use it as a tax reduction, until the Internal Revenue Service caught wind of it.[233] Biographer Shearer, indicated that Gloria had already begun a clandestine affair with the twenty-six-year-old Hungarian piano prodigy Ervin Nyiregyhazi. "Neary," as she referred to him, was a clinically confirmed sex addict.[234] Swanson jockeyed this affair with a brief relationship with New York broker Jerry Gordon. Shearer surmised that Gloria's "legions of paramours more or less served their purposes for whatever amount of time she allotted them. She never found in a man the love she felt for herself."[235]

Fall of 1936. The Swanson-Marshall romance "dying a natural death" at the races with Eddie Goulding, Rod La Rocque (Gloria's ex-lover), and his wife Vilma Banky

In her 1980 autobiography, Swanson concocted a dramatic telephone scene for her and Bart. The call took place soon after his October 1936 arrival in London. Gloria answered the phone and listened as Bart apologetically explained his "reconciliation" with Edna, who Gloria considered "the ghost" that stood between them. Swanson struggled to control herself. "Why Bart? So that I can go through the pain of being that other woman who broke up a happy home all over again? Oh, Bart!" She hung up, and began to sob. "I might go on loving him," wrote Swanson, "but I would never respect him again."[236] All this from a woman who had two other lovers on the side ... just in case. As mentioned previously, Marshall never announced a reconciliation with Edna, he simply said they were "the best of pals." Marshall may have relied on the counsel of Rod La Roque, a previous Swanson conquest of 1924, who had had difficulty reconciling her "exhaustive romantic past."[237]

Swanson, knew that she was no prize herself. Following her third divorce she admitted to "the difficulties in being married to me."[238] In most respects, Swanson was an unhealthy influence. Biographer Shearer points to her tendency to seduce and dominate. "Her self-absorption, which doomed her marriages," wrote Shearer, "equally distanced her from her children ... ."[239] By 1938, her film career going nowhere, Swanson quit Hollywood and left for New York. She moved into an apartment gifted to her by her lover Gustave Schirmer, heir to the Schirmer music publishing firm. Nonetheless, in 1951, writer Adela Rogers St. Johns still had to admit, "To see Bart and Gloria Swanson together was to believe in all the romances in history."[240]

※

Swanson theorized that Marshall "had serious weaknesses, the greatest of which was his overly docile disposition. He couldn't bear to hurt anyone, or disappoint anyone, or shock anyone. He would always turn to alcohol rather than face a painful scene."[241] She did clarify, "He was essentially a social drinker, but a heavy one," but failed to mention that alcohol provided the only relief from his struggle with phantom pain.[242] The "painful scene" that Marshall faced on a daily basis was physical. The humbling ordeal of war was a contributing factor to his "docile disposition," or more kindly put, his self-control, his thoughtfulness. When Bart reasoned in a 1938 interview, "Kicking up a row takes too much energy," it was based on life experience, not some psychological weakness.²⁴³ By 1980, Gloria couldn't recall the correct leg that her lover had lost—claiming that "his right leg had to be amputated."²⁴⁴

Other than a distinctive upright, deliberate gait, and his need for a double in certain scenes, Marshall's injury rarely compromised his performances. Even so, he suffered from intermittent "phantom pain" for the remainder of his life. His discomfort came from damaged nerves, and pressure from various prostheses. Phantom pain, particularly stump pain—a stabbing sensation, is not uncommon among amputees. Depending on the intensity of the pain, the vestigial limb can jerk in reaction. This may explain the aforementioned incident on the set of *Riptide* when Marshall's stump ricocheted and tore through his pants.

Bart's preferred pain remedy was alcohol—not an unusual choice for the times. A 1941 report in *Time* magazine, detailed a study at Cornell University, which concluded that whiskey was "one of the cheapest and best known pain killers to man." A 2011 study found that as many as 28% of those living with chronic pain use alcohol as a strategy for relief. In theory, alcohol (and other analgesic drugs) have the ability to affect the brain and central nervous system, resulting in a mild amount of temporary pain reduction. Over time, it may take a higher dose to produce the desired effect.²⁴⁵ In the aftermath, depression and melancholy induce yet another phantom to deal with. Options for relief were few and far between during Marshall's lifetime.

At the close of 1936, Bart appeared in a much acclaimed radio broadcast (*Lux Theatre*) of Noel Coward's *Cavalcade*. He and co-star Madeleine Carroll portrayed an upper class British couple, Robert and Jane Marryot, facing the major historical events of the early twentieth century. Ohio critic Robert Stephan, praised that the entire production "approached the dignity of legitimate theater. Carroll and Herbert Marshall deserve special applause for their work." It was at this time that Marshall began enjoying the company of Lee Russell, a young model who had relocated to Hollywood from New York. The duo were listed among the new twosomes frequenting the Brown Derby.²⁴⁶ They were also seen night after night, at the popular café La Maze. The orchestra leader would strike up Bart's favorite tune, Cole Porter's "Easy to Love," as soon as they walked in. The music of Porter was a logical choice for Marshall. It mirrored the wistful, romantic style he portrayed on screen. Louella Parsons made a point of saying how "all very amusing it was" that Russell had an estranged husband living on the East coast.

Angel (1937) Marshall, Dietrich, Melvyn Douglas and their director fail to create ... "The Lubitsch Touch" (Paramount)

In March 1937, Marshall finally had the opportunity to "rescue Marlene Dietrich" (as columnist Mollie Merrick once suggested). Marlene was still in need of a box-office hit, and her upcoming film *Angel* sounded promising. Director Ernst Lubitsch announced, "The story is half drama, half comedy and has the terrific lightness of touch with which I am associated."²⁴⁷ By September, *Angel* had been riddled with intrusions from censors, rewrites, and retakes. After six previews, the "Lubitsch Touch" upon *Angel*, felt heavy-handed.

Dietrich herself summed up *Angel* with the line, "I thought we were going to have an amusing evening, and now it's become serious." The tale of an English diplomat (Marshall) and his neglected wife (Dietrich), begins with her flirtation with a handsome gentleman (Melvyn Douglas) in Paris. Marshall is away conferring with The League of Nations. Douglas, it turns out, is an old war buddy of Marshall's. In fact, they had shared the amorous attentions of the same call girl. However, they are not inclined to share the extravagantly gowned Dietrich. She must choose between them. Douglas' somber manner, and Dietrich's brooding allure, keep things at a distance. *Variety* summed up, "Marshall is excellent as the duped husband ... Dietrich is wearing eyelashes you could hang your hat on ... Douglas is not a particularly sympathetic character. Nor is Dietrich for that matter." New York critic Howard Barnes underscored, "Miss Dietrich is ... more aware of camera angles than the vitalizing of an intriguing character."

Camera angles and Dietrich *Angel* (1937) (Paramount)

Off-screen dramatics between Dietrich and Lubitsch were part of the problem. Melvyn Douglas later told author Charles Higham, "There was some conflict between them as he reminded her constantly, 'This is a *lady* you're playing, not a demimondaine [prostitute].'"[248] Biographer Scott Eyman, noted that the director and his glamorous star "crossed swords more than they ever had before." By the end of production they were not speaking. Eyman concluded, "Despite a fine cast, a provocative central situation, and his painstaking directorial attention, Lubitsch's rhythm was alarmingly off. By any standard, *Angel* is a failure ... ."[249]

Dietrich demanded close-ups and insisted on facing the camera in every scene. Hollywood reporter Paul Harrison barbed, "Lubitsch feared audiences might forget what Miss Dietrich's leading man looked like." Once Marlene left for Europe, Lubitsch did retakes pointing the camera toward Marshall, and over the back of Dietrich's stand-in.[250] *Angel*, at a pricey sum of $1.4 million, failed to "fly" at the box-office. Dietrich was released from her Paramount contract, and labeled "box-office poison." As far as the long delay during production (March 22-June 14), Marshall had no complaints. He received $10,000 a week. Besides, he had a new good luck charm. When a slew of reporters showed up on the Lubitsch set, Bart pulled out a tiny gold electric fan, showing it off with a grin. Marshall explained that he received it from an admirer, "because he was so hot."[251]

For Marshall's first teaming with Barbara Stanwyck, comedy took precedence over plot. In *Breakfast for Two*, wealthy Texas socialite Stanwyck falls for New York playboy Marshall, and sets out to reform him. She buys Marshall's faltering steamship company, and wants to seal the deal with matrimony. When Stanwyck cuts off his income, he sneers, "You're the type of woman who likes to wear the pants! Alright Mister, wear them!" He proposes to someone else. The stars, with the added help of Eric Blore, as Marshall's manservant, manage to invigorate the routine direction of Alfred Santell. "*Breakfast for Two* won't disappoint those who come for laughs," cheered *Variety*. "Barbara Stanwyck and Herbert Marshall turning in slick performances."

Stanwyck went to New York after filming wrapped. She talked about *Breakfast for Two* with Irene Thirer of the *New York Post*. "It's gay and slapstick—you know, the trend they're now going through. I do very little in *Breakfast for Two*. It's practically Herbert Marshall's picture." The "gay and slapstick" trend, critics called "screwball." Doing "screwball," according to Stanwyck, was "awfully easy ... like a vacation." Her comment about Marshall was generous. Some critics thought him miscast. On screen, Marshall displayed an absent-minded charm, and appeared to be enjoying himself, even during a Stanwyck-Marshall boxing match. In Thirer's review of *Breakfast for Two*, she argued, "Herbert Marshall does not steal the picture. Eric Blore's buttling does." The two play nicely off each other, especially when Blore implores Marshall about his spending. "Stop nagging," Marshall snaps. "You're being feminine and I don't like it."

July 16, 1937 — Bart and Eric Blore help Stanwyck celebrate her birthday on the set of *Breakfast for Two* (RKO)

Blore had been a steady influence on Bart for twenty-seven years. He was even prone to write birthday prose to Bart. One whimsical composition began, "If words were birds and flew away and left me dumb this very day ... ." The verse was inscribed in the flyleaf of a dictionary Blore gave him—underscoring deep friendship and good things to come.[252] When asked about his adjustment to living in Hollywood, Blore enthused, "Just think. I can telephone Bart Marshall any time I want to. He's right here. In the town with me. Before this I'd maybe see Bart fifteen minutes every four years between jumps at Chicago." Blore felt that he had "been hitting a new high" ever since he met Bart Marshall in 1910.[253]

❧

As 1937 came to a close, four-year-old Sarah Lynn never made it across the Atlantic to visit her father. They would have to wait another two years for their reunion, and a rather dramatic one at that. The rise of Nazism and Hitler's vast machine of war was hovering over Europe. By the summer of 1939, when Edna brought Sarah Lynn to the U.S., traveling the Atlantic was considered risky.

Following a month's vacation in New York, Marshall went to Universal for his first musical comedy, *Mad About Music* (1938). He managed to get through it without singing a note—that was left to teen soprano Deanna Durbin. Durbin was thrilled at the prospect of working with Marshall, and a tad nervous. Prior to their first scene, she burst out, "Please, Mr. Marshall, may I just look at you for a long time?" Marshall was inclined to pay his young co-star compliments. "Deanna is delightful ... and don't you believe those rumors that she's really a grown woman. She used to bite her fingernails and try and hide them from me; that's a sure sign of being 15."[254] As far as playing Durbin's father, Marshall said, "It's rather a relief. I'd rather be a father with 16 screen children than 'good old Marshall,' the wandering wife's last resort!"[255]

On screen, Marshall didn't exactly play Durbin's father, but her *imaginary* father. Her mother (Gail Patrick), a famous movie star desperate to hold on to her youth, had placed teenage Deanna in an all-girls school in Switzerland—and out of the public eye. Marshall, a gentle-mannered composer visiting the Swiss village, sympathizes with Durbin's situation after it is revealed she has convinced her school chums that he is her father, a big-game hunter in Africa, no less. Author Clive Hirschhorn assessed in 1983, that it was Marshall's "polished presence" in *Mad About Music* that "elevated the nonsense to credibility." Marshall brought the requisite tenderness, humor and emotional punch to the proceedings. Coupled with Durbin's winning personality and vocal talent, producer Joe Pasternak had an irresistible hit on his hands. The film was nominated for four Academy Awards. Durbin herself received a special Oscar.

Mad About Music Box-office hit with Deanna Durbin (Universal)

"Marshall's performance is a gem to behold," enthused *Movie Mirror*. "Anyone else in the role would be unthinkable," echoed the review in *Picture Play*. *Photoplay* editor Ruth Waterbury joined the chorus, "Look at Herbert Marshall in *Mad About Music*. You will respond all over again to his really ingratiating personality ... after that long line of gloomy, betrayed husbands he has suffered with." Waterbury may have spoken too soon. Marshall's next three releases were all tearjerkers.

In January 1938, Marshall headed to San Francisco's Civic Auditorium to participate in President Roosevelt's annual Birthday Ball. This event was followed by two months of relaxation in Palm Springs, where Bart's romance with Lee Russell flourished amid rounds of socializing and cocktail parties. Bart then headed to the MGM lot for the taut romantic drama *Woman Against Woman* (1938). The film holds up very well, thanks to the three principals: Marshall, Virginia Bruce, and Mary Astor. As the title suggests, Bruce and Astor have a head-on collision when Marshall brings his new bride (Bruce) back to his hometown. Astor, as the self-martyred ex-wife, turns the townspeople against Bruce, who gets the cold shoulder wherever she goes. The film builds to a climactic moment when Bruce confronts Astor at a country club function. Marshall finally mans up to do the right thing, and is especially good delivering Astor an ultimatum. He and Bruce now have the upper hand, and Astor, we are left to believe, becomes a human being.

Woman Against Woman (1938) with Mary Astor and Virginia Bruce (MGM)

The Los Angeles Times praised Marshall and Bruce for giving "sincere and smooth performances." *Hollywood Citizen News* complimented the deft direction of Robert Sinclair, and thought Astor "could not have been more convincing." Astor relished her role as the "heavy." "Someone who messes up the plot," she told one reporter, "is always more interesting than someone who just lets the story do things to him or her."[256] It was this type of role that paved the way to an Oscar win for Astor in 1941's *The Great Lie*. Marshall and Virginia Bruce were a good match on screen, and would reteam three years later.

While filming *Woman Against Woman*, Marshall made news headlines that directly pitted him "man against man." In April 1938, United Press reported that Lee Russell's ex-husband, musician Eddy Brandt, filed a suit against Marshall for $250,000, charging "alienation of affections." Brandt accused the actor of stealing the love of his twenty-seven-year-old wife. An excerpt from the complaint was printed in the New York *American Journal*.

> Between January 1 and August 13, 1937, the defendant intentionally and wrongly consorted with Lee Russell Brandt with the intent and purpose of ... inducing her to transfer her affections to the defendant. That he did furnish her with comforts and luxuries and consort with her in private and public places ... .[257]

When asked for a comment, Marshall simply stated, "I don't know anything about it." The Brandt's 1932 marriage was dissolved in November 1937. Lee Russell filed for divorce that April, and won on a desertion charge.[258] Brandt rationalized the charge of desertion by saying that he had left Lee in Hollywood, because she wanted to try and get into the movies. "Then suddenly came a letter saying she attended a party at Edgar Selwyn's and had met Herbert Marshall. Three weeks later came another letter. She said she was not coming back, that there was no use in me coming out." A month after he filed charges against Marshall, Brandt dropped his suit, indicating that the actor had offered a cash settlement. *Variety* mentioned that Brandt had written a new song to honor the occasion, "Lovers Out of Love." Marshall refuted that there had been a payoff, telling reporters, "Nothing has been paid and you can rest assured that nothing *will* be paid."[259]

Summer of 1938 — Marshall and Lee Russell

Amid this soap-opera, Bart began his next tearjerker, *Always Goodbye*, opposite Barbara Stanwyck. The original story revolved around mother love and sacrifice—similar to Stanwyck's success *Stella Dallas* (1937). *Always Goodbye* was a remake of the highly successful, poignant *Gallant Lady* (1933), which had starred Ann Harding and Clive Brook. Unfortunately, *Always Goodbye* was tampered with beyond recognition. Charles Boyer was set to play the lead, but hated the new script, which fell into the hands of Marshall, who lacked the foresight to make the same decision.

Always Goodbye was peppered with situations that worked against compelling drama. At the outset, Marshall, a bacteriologist, saves Stanwyck from jumping into the East River, arranges for the adoption of her illegitimate child, and finds her employment in an upscale dress shop. This takes place in the film's first ten minutes. What is established as a "tearjerker," begins to shift tone in a parade of *haute couture* (Stanwyck is adorned in 24 designer frocks), and the annoying antics of Count Corini (Cesar Romero). Publicity for the film indicated that the film carried "a throbbing message for today's womanhood."

In the final six minutes, Stanwyck faces the problem of choosing between the man she loves, Marshall, or marrying her son's adoptive father (Ian Hunter), thereby becoming her own child's stepmother. Marshall reassures Stanwyck that her son comes first, telling her, "There isn't room for anyone else." He kisses her. They kiss again. "Ah!" Marshall sighs, "That's enough for me for the rest of my life!"

Marshall reteams with Stanwyck for an odd mix of pathos and screwball comedy in *Always Goodbye* (20th Century-Fox)

Arthur Pollock, for the *Brooklyn Daily Eagle*, complained "the story has a wide streak of nonsense." The *New York Post* lamented, "That Sidney Lanfield, director of robust musicals, should have been at this helm is a surprise and not a pleasant one." *Variety* acknowledged, "Miss Stanwyck and Marshall turn in fine performances in the face of the material they have to work with." Stanwyck does have her moments, managing to pull a reluctant tear from the viewer amid all the whimsy. In 2012, Stanwyck biographer Dan Callahan, summed up, "Though *Always Goodbye* has to count as one of the worst scripts Stanwyck ever played, it has a kind of lunatic confidence in itself that makes it a minor pleasure."[260]

As filming wrapped on *Always Goodbye*, Marshall was bitten about an inch from his right eye by a friend's chow dog. Clever makeup allowed him to complete the film. By mid-summer he was still making weekly trips to an eye doctor. Sheilah Graham also reported that Marshall was having problems with his "wounded leg"—she offered no specifics.

After obtaining a release from playing Deanna Durbin's father in *That Certain Age*, Marshall signed for the male lead in *Zaza* (from the French play), a remake of a 1923 silent film that had bolstered the career of Gloria Swanson. Claudette Colbert took on the role of a sassy, boudoir-hopping, music hall singer, who meets a married aristocrat named Dufresne (Marshall). Following their affair, she becomes the toast of the *Folies Bergere*. "I suppose I ought to say it's hot stuff," director George Cukor said during production, "but we're not trying to make a shocker." After a November 1938 preview in San Francisco, the completed film ran into trouble. "It was a story of adultery," Cukor later reflected," and after we finished the picture it got an absolute turndown by the Hays Office. It was terribly French, of course, that endless exploration of unfaithfulness and the suffering of love."[261]

The Hays Office denied *Zaza* their seal of purity. Two weeks of retakes were scheduled. Large portions of Colbert's riotous Can-Can dance bit the dust—deemed "too suggestive." The happy ending was tossed out—those indulging in sin must be punished. PCA chief Joseph Breen instructed that Colbert had to be left "behind the eight-ball." Director

Cukor faced the challenge, and did an admirable job by simply relying on innuendo.

Zaza kicks off with a rollicking mix of characters. We see Helen Westley as the brandy-imbibing step-mother, Bert Lahr as Zaza's devoted stage-partner, Genevieve Tobin as her bitchy rival, and Rex O'Malley as an easy-going songwriter. When O'Malley coaxes Marshall backstage to meet Zaza, Marshall hesitates. "Your Zaza attracts me too much," he admits. "I have a very good reason for seeing her only from this side of the footlights." He finally relents, amused at Zaza's attempt to lure him into her arms. Colbert caresses Marshall's hair, cooing, "You have a *lovely* voice!" (Marshall chortles at this inside joke.) His glimpses of her "bare necessities" during a costume change, adds to the hilarity. Cukor creates a memorable moment when Marshall unexpectedly appears behind stage with flowers. He takes Colbert in his arms, clasps her hand, and says, "Oh, Zaza, where are these hands going to lead us?"

Before long, Zaza puts her career on hold to live in a fantasy world. That is, until she finds out that Marshall has a wife and child. After a poignant encounter with his sweet-natured little girl, and unduly reserved wife, Zaza begins to understand Marshall better than he does himself. In Colbert's hands, Zaza matures. She can see what is best for Marshall. More importantly, she knows what is best for herself. The ending doesn't place Colbert "behind the eight ball" as Breen demanded—she moves forward, in full charge.

Los Angeles critic Harrison Carroll complimented Colbert's "moving portrayal," and Marshall for not making a cad "too unsympathetic." Louella Parsons thought *Zaza* still tugged at the heart and entertained with a "frou-frou naughtiness." She thought Colbert "breath-taking," and Marshall "excellent," but pointed out that the "almost ruthless censorship" wreaked more havoc on his role than on Claudette's. Hedda Hopper fumed, "If they're not careful the Hays office will whittle us right out of the picture business."[262]

In retrospect, Cukor created an admirable and effective screen event. From the moment he meets Colbert's dazzling Zaza, Marshall displays the necessary inner conflict to create a sympathetic character. His decorum is complemented by his bemusement. It is easy to see why Zaza's head was turned by his debonair dash and good looks. Despite retakes and cuts lessening the impact of Marshall's role, he offers a commendable performance.

Fall 1938 — Dance director Andre Charlot joins Marshall for a cup of tea on the set of *Zaza* (Paramount)

1938 had been a busy year for leading man Marshall. Upon his return to the screen a year later, he found himself fourth-billed (his lowest screen billing to date). Had Bart's ongoing romance with Lee Russell taken precedence over career? Or, was he ready for transition—an opportunity to *redefine* his career? Apparently, it was a combination of the two.

Marshall at home in Beverly Hills

CHAPTER 8
Adventure in Transition

"Any actor can appear in far too many pictures. When this happens, the public gets so tired of the sight of your face that you take a neat little nosedive."[263] This remark was made by Marshall in the fall of 1938. He also deduced, "The die is cast as far as I am concerned. As the Hollywood saying goes, I have been 'typed.'" To reverse being typecast, Marshall campaigned for the role of Tom Ransome in the up-coming Darryl Zanuck production, *The Rains Came*. The film was based on Louis Bromfield's best-selling novel. Marshall's attraction to the role was understandable. Ransome was a middle-aged artist, and ex-pat, wasting away in colonial India—more prone to grab a bottle of gin than a paintbrush. Ransome may have been a gentleman, but he was a very dissipated one. Marshall had a long conference with Zanuck, prior to the producer's departure for Europe in June 1938.

Louella Parsons pushed for Marshall to play Ransome, a role for which Bart's chum Ronald Colman was also being considered. "Many letters have been received suggesting Marshall as the ideal Ransome," she reported, "and it's a toss-up between the two English gentlemen." In November, *Variety* announced that Colman was in the top spot for the role, "with Herbert Marshall also in the running." Hedda Hopper offered an inside scoop that Marshall had asked Colman if he was intent on doing it. "Not at all," cheered Colman. "Go ahead, old man, it's all yours." Colman, who was on his honeymoon with second wife Benita Hume, had other priorities. He would later admit, "I just didn't like the part for myself."[264]

The Rains Came began filming in April 1939. George Brent, fourteen years Marshall's junior, faced the camera as Tom Ransome. *Photoplay*'s editor thought the performance "the very finest of Brent's career." The closest Marshall ever came to working with Bromfield was when they were guests together on *Information Please!* (NBC) in 1940. Margaret Mitchell's *Gone With the Wind* also had columnists predicting who would be cast for the leads. Theater critic Elinor Hughes, of the *Boston Herald*, suggested Marshall, or Leslie Howard for the role of Ashley Wilkes. "Herbert Marshall would be an ideal Ashley," wrote Hughes, "sweet, kind, patient ... sensitive enough and blind enough for that pathetic but wooden gentleman."[265] Marshall, despite this backhanded compliment, never indicated any interest in the role, which went to Howard.

With his screen career on hold, Bart took the opportunity to play opposite new leading ladies on radio: Olivia de Havilland in *Under Two Flags*, Joan Bennett in *History is Made at Night*, and Ginger Rogers in *I Met Him in Paris*. He tackled leads in *The Petrified Forest*, *Berkeley Square*, and *Bulldog Drummond*. NBC paged Marshall to portray Lawrence of Arabia for a potential series. "Marshall's voice is declared by those who knew the famous British adventurer to be uncannily like his," declared one report. Apparently, NBC was unable to find a sponsor.

During the fall of 1938, Marshall signed on as emcee for radio's popular *Hollywood Hotel*. Following this, he joined Leslie Howard and Mary Astor for a broadcast of *Interference* for *Lux Theater*. This allowed Bart to repeat his 1927 stage role as Philip Voaze, the "dead husband" who returns from war to discover that his wife has remarried. An Ohio critic raved, "Herbert Marshall ... stole the drama from the smooth Leslie Howard. Marshall played an exceptionally strong Philip Voaze." For Christmas Eve, Marshall lent his talent to a progressive slant on the nativity scene, *Christmas for One-Third of a Nation* (NBC). Instead of Bethlehem, the story took place, on location, at a migratory work camp in the San Joaquin Valley. Migrant workers from varying ethnic backgrounds, participated in scenes that depicted living conditions not unlike those of Joseph and Mary in *The New Testament*. Melvyn Douglas, Edward G. Robinson, Virginia Bruce, and Jackie Cooper, among others, participated in this call for attention to rural poverty, and the 250,000 migrant workers in California.[266]

November 28, 1938 Mary Astor and Leslie Howard join Marshall for a broadcast of *Interference* (CBS)

"What has happened to Herbert Marshall's movie career?" snipped gossiper Sheilah Graham. "Film offers are conspicuously absent." Graham concluded that Marshall was "blasted out of the film scene with *Zaza*." Her snide remarks didn't faze Bart in the least. He was intent on returning to the stage. In May 1939, Broadway producer Gilbert Miller asked Marshall to co-star with Helen Hayes in *Ladies and Gentlemen*, a Hungarian play adapted by Hayes' husband, Charles MacArthur, and Ben Hecht. Bart and Lee celebrated the good news with Doug Fairbanks Jr. and his new bride Mary. The newlyweds gave their first dinner party, exclusively for Bart, Lee and the Ronald Colmans. After celebrating his forty-ninth birthday, Bart headed east for rehearsals at Broadway's Empire Theatre.

During rehearsals, Marshall was subpoenaed in the highly publicized trial of William P. Buckner Jr., an international playboy and stock broker. Buckner had approached several motion picture stars, unfamiliar with his scams, to raise cash for defaulted Philippine railroad bonds. It was purported to be a million dollar fraud. Summons were also issued to Ronald Colman, Miriam Hopkins, Cary Grant, and Frank Morgan. On June 21, the New York Federal Court was overflowing with female spectators the day of Marshall's appearance. Once they got over the shock of his horn-rimmed glasses, "the women ... gave him their undivided attention."[267]

Marshall explained to the judge, that two of Buckner's associates had visited his home in the summer of 1938. "I think I said something about having an appointment for some wardrobe fittings. I asked them to have a spot of tea and then I left." Marshall had his secretary, Helen Dawson, take notes. Miss Dawson took to the stand, indicating that Buckner was requesting $6,000 from the actor, which would reap him "huge profits." "There are no risks," promised the promoters. "It is one of those unbelievable things." Apparently, Marshall agreed with the last statement. He gave Miss Dawson a memorandum to "turn the deal down ... I think they're crazy."[268] A typical news headline read, "Tea Was All Buckner Got From Film Actor." MGM contract player Frank Morgan confirmed in court his own refusal to "bite the tempting bait," and profit an implausibly promised $60,000 for a $6,000 investment.

Buckner's romance with Loretta Young was also under investigation. Several candid letters he had written her were read aloud in court—with the "saltier phrases," censored.[269] Young had been hounded by federal agents ever since she and Marshall co-starred in a *Screen Guild Theater* radio presentation in January 1939. At the bitter finish, Buckner's attempt to get Loretta, and innocent Hollywood money, backfired. On July 6, he was sentenced to two-years imprisonment, and fined $2,500 for mail fraud and conspiracy.

October 1939 - Playbill for *Ladies and Gentlemen*.

Marshall and Hayes read telegrams during west-coast tryout

Following the Buckner Trial, Marshall found himself back in court, and romancing Helen Hayes. They were cast as jurors in *Ladies and Gentlemen*—a satire on the American jury system. Marshall, a Bostonian architect, and Hayes, secretary to a Hollywood big shot, become locked in romance during a six-week murder trial. West Coast tryouts included San Francisco's Curran Theater, where S.R.O. crowds out-grossed Hayes' success in *Victoria Regina*. At the Los Angeles Biltmore, *Ladies and Gentlemen* rang the curtain after a highly profitable two weeks. The play was touted as the most important Pacific Coast theatrical event of 1939.

A critic for the *Oregonian*, lauded the trademark MacArthur-Hecht sarcasm that generated "prolonged laughter," and "brought the show to a standstill on three separate occasions." The hotel balcony scene between Hayes and Marshall was deemed, "a modern Romeo and Juliet, poignant and dramatic." San Francisco critic John Hobart, praised, "Mr. Marshall plays with the finesse, gentlemanly manners, and shrewd understatement that make his return to the stage altogether welcome." Hobart found the play a "lively theater-piece that mixes gayety and seriousness judiciously," but concurred with the *Oregonian* review that the ending was "a letdown." *Variety* surmised, "... before Broadway sees it, it can be fixed up."

Critic Hobart arranged an interview with Bart during the San Francisco run. The actor stated that he "slipped easily enough" into being back on stage "without being especially nervous." He couldn't get over the enthusiastic audience response to his performance. "And I'm not saying it to be pleasant," he emphasized. "I mean it. That balcony scene is a marvel, isn't it? I could spend a lifetime playing that one scene. It's so good I'd gladly make a career of it."270 The scene in question, between Marshall and Hayes, had little dialogue. "It is repressed emotion," he emphasized, "the suggestion of fire held in check, that is most stirring."271 Hobart was curious as to which of Marshall's films he was the most fond. Marshall selected *Trouble in Paradise* and *Mad About Music*.

While Bart was busy with the play, Edna arrived from England for a role as Leslie Howard's wife in David O. Selznick's production of *Intermezzo*. She made it clear to the press that Hollywood held "nothing" for her, and was anxious to return home. "It would be silly to attempt transplanting myself," she said.272 Unexpectedly, she waylaid her return home for a respite at Lake Arrowhead. The distraction? Her Hollywood agent, Nat Wolff, who also managed Bart's radio contracts. During their rendezvous, the future was sealed with a kiss, and a proposal of marriage. Best announced that she would bring Sarah Lynn back to the U.S. for the "benefit of California sunshine."273 Bart joined Edna at the Trocadero, where they talked over her future plans. The fact that his daughter was coming to live on the west coast, may have contributed to Marshall's decision to drop out of the Broadway opening of *Ladies and Gentleman*. Producer

Miller had fiddled with the play's ending, and rumor had it that Marshall was not pleased. In the fall, *Ladies and Gentlemen* would enjoy a successful three months at the Martin Beck Theatre.

Bart and Sarah Lynn enjoy some California sunshine

In mid-August 1939, as German armies prepared to invade Poland, the panic was on. Bart and Nat Wolff attended a cocktail party where they spent most of their time on the phone talking to Edna in London. She told them that she, Sarah, and the twins were sailing on the *New Amsterdam*. The only reservations she could obtain were mattresses strewn about the deck. All ships were filled to capacity. She wasn't even sure that the ship would clear the port at Southampton. Wolff was told to wait for a radiogram once Edna, Sarah, and the boys were at sea.[274] Once he got word, Wolff rushed to New York for their arrival on September 1. On September 3, England and France declared war on Germany. The first casualties of the war took place hours later. The British liner *Athenia*, with 1400 aboard, was torpedoed by a German U-boat just northwest of Ireland. The ship sank with a loss of 112 passengers and crew.

Hollywood producers frantically cabled a number of stars traveling in Europe, demanding they return home. Robert Montgomery abandoned a film assignment in London. Tyrone Power cut short his honeymoon in France. Norma Shearer, rendezvousing with lover George Raft, found herself stranded in Antibes—all the trains to Paris were booked solid. She managed to taxi across France to Le Havre, and board just as her boat was departing.[275] The United Press underscored the main reason producers urged the return of their high-salaried talent: fear that "the stars might be kept abroad and cause thousands of dollars delay in already-scheduled pictures."[276]

Edna Best, chin in hand, watches her almost ex-husband and Lee Russell at the Trocadero

Once they disembarked, Edna's eighteen-year-old twins opted to stay with friends in New York. Wolff escorted Edna and Sarah back to Los Angeles. On September 6, Marshall enjoyed a touching reunion with his little daughter at the Beverly Hills Hotel.[277] Edna contracted with RKO for the mother role in *Swiss Family Robinson*, co-starring Thomas Mitchell. Ironically, the first stars to be offered these roles were Lillian Gish and Herbert Marshall. When Best replaced Gish, she and Bart decided not to run the risk of sticky publicity about their relationship, and Bart bowed out. By mid-November, Edna, wearing a new engagement ring, announced her intention for divorce. She opted for the six-week wait for legal residency in Las Vegas. Prior to Vegas, she and Nat Wolff enjoyed chummy evenings out on the town with Bart and Lee Russell. "Nice to know that they are all such good friends," needled Sheilah Graham. The Marshalls celebrated the upcoming dissolution of their marriage by co-starring in a broadcast of their stage hit, *There's Always Juliet.*

In the Fall of 1939, Bart hosted *Hollywood Playhouse* (NBC) for two months. Kay Francis joined him for two broadcasts, including the fast-moving comedy, *She Married an Artist.* Ohio radio critic, Robert Stephan nodded, "Marshall bowed out last night in a very clever comedy, capably supported by Kay Francis. It was Marshall's best effort in weeks." NBC was so enthused by the Marshall-Francis combination, the two stars recorded an audition in mid-December for a potential radio series based on *The Saint* detective stories.[278] Sadly, the series wouldn't air until 1945, minus Marshall and Francis. And, when Marshall finally managed to make a film "comeback," it barely caused a ripple.

Marshall, fourth-billed, with Fay Bainter in
A Bill of Divorcement (RKO)

A Bill of Divorcement offered Marshall little opportunity. In a 1929 London production, he had played the lead of an emotionally unstable war veteran, Hilary Fairfield. George Cukor directed a 1932 film version starring John Barrymore as Fairfield. Katharine Hepburn (in her screen debut) played his daughter, who assumes she has inherited her father's disorder. In the 1940 remake, Adolphe Menjou was assigned the lead role. Marshall, fourth billed, was limited to a few, but effective scenes, as the fiancé of Fairfield's ex-wife (Fay Bainter). Maureen O'Hara offered a forthright interpretation as the daughter. Despite John Farrow's delicate direction, reviews were tepid. *Photoplay* concluded, "The film's preachments ... are dated." *A Bill of Divorcement* flopped at a $104,000 loss.[279] Richard B. Jewell's *The RKO Story* (1982) diagnosed that the story had "yellowed with age." Fortunately, directors Alfred Hitchcock and William Wyler would come to Marshall's rescue.

February 27, 1940 — Bart and Lee Russell marry in Las Vegas

CHAPTER EIGHT

Long in the mood for "divorcement" himself, Bart got his wish. For five years columnists had volleyed between reconciliation or divorce for the Marshalls. Edna resolved the matter in a Las Vegas court. On February 7, 1940, Judge Roger Foley accepted her complaint of "cruelty and desertion." She specified that Marshall deserted her in January 1934 (the month Marshall met Gloria Swanson). Minutes later, Edna, who was granted custody of daughter Sarah, also present, became Mrs. Nat Wolff. On February 27, Bart and Lee Russell, accompanied by their witnesses Rod La Rocque and wife Vilma Banky, arrived in Las Vegas to exchange vows—Judge Foley presiding. After three years of romancing, marital bliss was at hand ... for the time being. Their first congratulatory telegram was from Edna and Nat, who were honeymooning in Buffalo. The new Mr. and Mrs. Marshall cancelled plans to visit Boulder Dam, and boarded a train back to 1707 Tropical Avenue in Beverly Hills, which Marshall was renting from actor Ricardo Cortez (who was gearing up for a divorce from his second wife).[280] Bart had a date with Alfred Hitchcock. Production for the film *Foreign Correspondent* was to start immediately.

Hitchcock thought it crucial to contribute to the British war effort, and had resolved to make a film with a pro-Britain statement. Marshall no doubt felt the same, and for the first time on screen, played the heavy—a German with an English veneer. In *Foreign Correspondent*, he was the wealthy leader of a peace organization—a façade, that was actually a front for a Nazi spy ring. Joel McCrea, in the title role, played an American reporter in Europe investigating the chaotic political situation. During a series of nerve-wracking escapes, McCrea teams with an English reporter (George Sanders), and learns the truth about Marshall's organization. Chill specialist Hitchcock has the self-conflicted Marshall sacrifice his life in order to save his daughter (Laraine Day) from seeing him apprehended and put on trial. *Foreign Correspondent* comes to a close during a London air-raid, while hero McCrea broadcasts a stirring appeal to America to fortify and stay strong.

Bart stays in character as the villain by practicing darts between takes. *Foreign Correspondent* (1940) (UA)

"Mr. Marshall wears his years lightly," observed a Dallas critic. "Nor has his speech lost its sensational velocity." The *San Francisco Chronicle*, enthused, "Herbert Marshall will surprise you in this film. Every minute of the film reflects the Hitchcock genius." *Foreign Correspondent* was nominated for six Academy Awards, including Best Picture. *Film Daily* named it one of the 10 Best Films of 1940. Ironically, Hitler's Minister of Propaganda, Joseph Goebbels, thought *Foreign Correspondent* a masterpiece, and "viewed it frequently."[281]

In author Robert McLaughlin's *We'll Always Have the Movies: American Cinema During WWII* (2006), he points to the crucial decision of Hitchcock selecting Marshall to play the villain. "In a wonderful performance by Herbert Marshall, this man at the center of a bloody conspiracy is the most human person in the film."[282] Marshall underscores his subtle duplicity when he warns McCrea about the conspirators, "They're fanatics. They combine a mad love of country with an equally mad indifference to life, their own as well as others'. They're cunning, unscrupulous—and inspired." Marshall effectively strips away the viewers sense of security.

The filming of *Foreign Correspondent* proved to be a timely decision. Upon the film's U.S. release, the German Luftwaffe filled skies over London with 350 bombers in the first major daytime raids. Over the next month, nearly 6,000 people were killed, one-third of the city laid to waste. President Roosevelt promptly signed an executive agreement involving the transfer of 50 destroyers to Great Britain, as well as the first peacetime draft in U.S. history.

Marshall and Hitchcock also teamed for a radio adaptation of Hitchcock's Jack the Ripper thriller, *The Lodger* (1927). Marshall not only narrated, but effectively pitched his voice to a higher key to play the "religiously inclined" (as Marshall's narration explains) serial killer. Walter Winchell thought it "had enough chills to break the heat wave. Herbert Marshall was aces as the fiend." *Variety* was impressed with Marshall's "vivid and versatile reading," which helped create, "the 'My-God-I-can't-stand-anymore' school of dramatic intensity." Marshall's performance in *The Lodger*, is credited for ushering in radio's long-running series *Suspense*.

The Letter (1940) with Bette Davis (Warner Bros.)
(Courtesy of Larry Smith)

Following his fling with villainy, Marshall reverted to "type" as the betrayed husband of Bette Davis in William Wyler's remake of W. Somerset Maugham's *The Letter*. Davis was a logical choice to play Leslie Crosbie. She had a huge success in Maugham's *Of Human Bondage* (1934), regarded by critics as the film that made her a star. *The Letter* was Marshall's debut film for Warner Bros. The role of the husband was first offered to studio contract player George Brent, who refused, thinking that it wouldn't give him a chance to act. Brent told Louella Parsons that his bosses were delighted he turned it down. "You see," said Brent, "I hear they have Herbert Marshall, and he will be much better."[283]

In Wyler's version of *The Letter*, the role of the lover, played by Marshall in 1929, is killed off without saying a line. Fortunately, the husband role was developed into something more substantial. Due to the Production Code, censors now demanded a bloody ending for the unfaithful wife. Davis acquiesced to director Wyler's every demand. "After *Jezebel*," she said, "I would have jumped into the Hudson River if he had told me to."[284] Instead of the Hudson River, Davis was stabbed to death.

Marshall registered the utter despair of a man relinquished of his money and his wife. *Variety* commented that Marshall "never falters" in demonstrating his character's struggle amid the brooding atmosphere that Wyler creates. D.C. critic, Jay Carmody, felt that Wyler evoked "completely finished performances from all his players … Herbert Marshall, of course, could not miss as the imposed-upon husband." Carmody assessed that Wyler's remake was more sinister than the 1929 version, and concluded his review with, "Boy, another Oscar for Miss Davis."

Years later, Robert Osborne sat by Davis at a Hollywood screening of *The Letter*. Davis acknowledged that Wyler as the *real* star. Osborne overheard her say, "Oh, look at how Wyler is moving the camera. Brilliant, brilliant!" Or, upon noticing a minor player, say, "Look at him! Perfectly cast. That was Wyler's idea." "It was always about the movie," said Osborne, "never about herself." Davis' nuanced performance was one of her finest. She received her fifth Academy Award nomination as Best Actress. *The Letter* received a total of seven nominations, including Best Picture and Best Director. Marshall was overlooked. A Best Supporting Actor nomination was given to James Stephenson, the lawyer who compromised his professional integrity to set Davis free. Clive Hirschhorn's *The Warner Bros. Story* (1979), praised the "brilliant support" of both Marshall and Stephenson.

As the war in Europe escalated, Marshall became involved with British War Relief. Hollywood's El Capitan Theater hosted a fundraiser involving mostly British actors. The event raised over $100,000. Noel Coward's one-act plays from *Tonight at 8:30*, were presented for a three-night run in August 1940. Rosalind Russell joined Bart on stage. They both received high praise for their interpretation of *Still Life*, a mature, romantic drama about two individuals, trapped by their respective conventional marriages. *Still Life* would translate on film as the acclaimed David Lean production *Brief Encounter* (1945).

Whatever slack there was in Bart's film career, was compensated by a deluge of radio work. He co-starred with Ingrid Bergman in *Intermezzo*, Olivia de Havilland in *Vigil in the Night*, and Rosalind Russell in *Craig's Wife*. *Love Affair* paired Marshall for the first time with Myrna Loy. Campbell Playhouse featured Marshall with the lovely Alice Faye in *If Only You Could Cook*, which Bart had done for the screen in 1935. Humphrey Bogart joined in the fun as the bootlegger mobster.

Marshall substituted as host for the Jack Benny Show, while Jack was in New York. The *Milwaukee Journal* nodded, "Marshall more than filled the comedian's shoes." "The perfect Benny program—minus Benny," wagged another critic. Upon his return, Benny complained to audiences, "I'd like to thank Mr. Herbert Marshall for stealing my show last Sunday." In 2016, Larry Smith, Nitrate Film Specialist for the Library of Congress, understood Benny's reaction. "Marshall was cool, dignified," praised Smith. "Everybody loved him and best of all he was *funny!*"[285] From November 1941-April 1942, Marshall had his own radio program, *The New Old Gold Show*. Lucille Ball made a guest appearance, stole the show, and was added to the cast (Marshall's comeuppance for stealing Benny's thunder). Marshall-Ball did a husband-wife routine, a precursor to *I Love Lucy*—in which Marshall braved the question, "*Where* did you get that hat?"

In between radio commitments, Bart traveled to Seattle, Vancouver, and Toronto on behalf of such groups as Friends of Britain. His participa-

CHAPTER EIGHT

tion was always gratis. A fundraiser in Seattle positioned Bart as a livestock auctioneer, a little out of his line, but the event raised $65,000 towards a flying ambulance to rescue British airmen shot down at sea. Bart shook hundreds of hands, signed autographs, and answered the same questions over and over. He attended a stag dinner party at the Rainier Club, and a separate champagne cocktail party for female members. Wearing a sprig of lily-of-the-valley in his lapel, Marshall exuded ample charm for the ladies, as Scottish bagpipers played in the background. Appropriate music for the former "Lady from Hell."

1940 - Cocoanut Grove benefit for crippled children. Bart, Eddie Sutherland and Spencer Tracy model ladies hats. Tracy won the competition.

When asked about his goodwill missions, Bart maintained a dry sense of humor. "For some obscure reason," he explained, "people think those of us from Hollywood have a bit more appeal than other speakers. The programs are to inspire enthusiasm and good-will for England. They are violently anti-Nazi and a little pro-British, too."[286] His work wasn't without controversy. The Seattle event was picketed by demonstrators carrying signs to protest American war aid to England. Bart's commitment to war relief was fortified by a book he carried with him—an advance copy of *Random Harvest* by English author James Hilton. The protagonist, Charles Rainier, invalided out of the army during WWI, deals with shellshock and subsequent memory loss. Hilton draws a parallel between Rainier's struggle, and England's own paralysis in dealing with Hitler's maneuvers prior to the outbreak of WWII.

※

Bart was given one of his last romantic leads in the Columbia film *Adventure in Washington*. The studio hoped for a follow-up to the Frank Capra hit *Mr. Smith Goes to Washington* (1939). Using the same sets as Capra's Oscar-nominated film, director Alfred E. Green offered what *The New York Times* described as "pleasant and chucklesome entertainment." Marshall played John Coleridge, a U.S. Senator who pushes to fund defense programs in order "to meet unforeseen needs." Coleridge reflected the premonitions of many Americans in 1941. But overall, *Adventure in Washington* struck a lighter, more humanistic note.

Senator Coleridge, refuses to allow female reporters into his private press conferences. A catty Capitol Hill radio reporter, Jane Scott (Virginia Bruce), challenges his policy. Before long, their feud blossoms into romance. The heavy in all of this is a political war-profiteer named Conroy (Pierre Watkin). Conroy, a stockbroker, wants to "clean up" on a billion dollar defense contract. Both Marshall and Bruce loathe the man. "If you ever fall for *his* racket," Bruce tells Marshall, "you let me be the gentleman who hits you on the head first, and write your obituary second." They laugh, they connect, and become an item.

The primary focus is on Coleridge's unruly Senate page (Gene Reynolds), who is maneuvered into selling Senate secrets to Conroy. In so doing, Reynolds puts Marshall's career at risk. At the finish, Marshall suggests that the other pages give Reynolds a mock trial. With eyes and heart wide open, Reynolds responds with a rendition of "The American Creed" that is rich in feeling, and brings a climactic lump to the viewer's throat. Reynolds does an admirable job of metamorphosing from hoodlum to a conscientious champion of human rights. The *New York Evening Post* thought Marshall to be "surprisingly at home" in his role, and observed that the audience "enormously enjoyed the picture." Although not on the scale of *Mr. Smith Goes to Washington*, *Adventure in Washington* hits its target, and is worth re-discovering.

Adventure in Washington - with Gene Reynolds and Virginia Bruce (Columbia)

Adventure in Washington offered Virginia Bruce an aside about stock manipulator Conroy: "His party's the most expensive party." The Republicans had a reputation of being the "wealthy man's party." Bruce, a Democrat, always championed what she referred to as "the little guy." She had spoken on behalf of the Hollywood Anti-Nazi League, and voiced her support, like Marshall, for migrant workers. Although Marshall's Draft Registration listed him as an "alien," he participated in Democratic causes.[287] When Secretary of Agriculture Claude Wickard (Democrat) visited Los Angeles, he was honored by several stars. News reports included Marshall on the list, along with Bette Davis, Doug Fairbanks Jr., Edward G. Robinson, Melvyn Douglas and his wife, future Congresswoman, Helen Gahagan Douglas.

In May 1941, *Variety* announced that producer Samuel Goldwyn and director William Wyler had chosen Marshall for the plum assignment of Bette Davis' husband in *The Little Foxes*. Numerous stage and screen actors tested for the role. Wyler didn't tamper with playwright Lillian Hellman's chilling account of a ruthless, predatory Southern family, the Hubbards, who connive to make millions from a cotton mill. They'll stop at nothing: the exploitation of poor white and African-American labor, embezzlement, and murder. The Hubbard sister, Regina (Bette Davis), accomplishes the latter, by refusing to fetch a bottle of medicine that could save her husband Horace (Marshall) from a deadly heart attack. While he gropes in agony, climbing the stairs, she stares on with icy indifference. Horace, you see, had refused her pleas to help the Hubbard clan finance their "get rich quick" scheme. With Horace out of the way, Regina intends to blackmail her brothers into giving her the lion's share of the business.

Marshall, as Horace Giddens, was in his element as the stricken husband. One of the film's most powerful moments has Horace confronting Regina, after she gloats about his certain death. "I hope you *die*!" she tells him. Marshall grips the screen, as Horace lets go of built-up resentment. "It's easy for the dying to be honest," he declares.

> I'm sick of you ... sick of this house. Sick of my unhappy life with you. I'm sick of your brothers and their dirty tricks to make a dime. There must be better ways than

building sweat shops ... pounding the bones of the town to make dividends for you to spend. You'll wreck the town, you and your brothers. You'll wreck the country, you and your *kind*, if they let you. But not me. I'll die in my own way and I'll do it without making the world any worse. I'm leaving *that* for you."

The Little Foxes (1941) with Teresa Wright and Bette Davis (RKO)

Despite Goldwyn's concern that the film might be interpreted as a leftist attack on capitalism, the film scored nine Academy Award nominations.[288] The *San Francisco Chronicle* thought Marshall "just the man to strike the note of gallantry and honesty." Ohio film critic W. Ward Marsh praised, "Herbert Marshall ... is again at his best—in a role tailored to his talents and power." *Hollywood Citizen News* rated it the best performance of Marshall's career. *Variety* agreed that Marshall turned in one of his "top performances." The review noted, "Miss Davis is gambling again, with a decidedly unsympathetic role, but again her great talent wins out. Wyler has handled every detail with an acutely dramatic touch."

For the screen, Hellman amplified the role of Horace and Regina's daughter Alexandra, played winningly by Teresa Wright (nominated for Best Supporting Actress). It was the young, impressionable daughter, who inspired Marshall's poignant moment as he pondered aloud the meaning of the Biblical verse, "Take us the foxes, the little foxes, that spoil the vines: for our vines have tender grapes." Horace recognized that Regina and her ilk were the ruination of future generations.

Academy Award nominations also included: Best Picture, Best Director and Best Actress for Davis. Marshall deserved a nomination, but had to content himself with rave reviews. Understandably, many would claim that Davis offered the definitive performance of Regina. Prior to filming, it had been rumored that Ruth Chatterton had been offered the role. Chatterton ended up doing yearly revivals of *The Little Foxes* from 1947-1958. Christopher Plummer co-starred with her in a 1952 production. "Her Regina," reflected Plummer in 2008, "[was] so deadly frightening and so very much her own. Lillian Hellman told me ... that of all the Reginas, Ruth's was by far the best." Plummer added that Chatterton, "brought things out of us we didn't know we had."[289]

Years later, biographer Whitney Stine asked Davis about Marshall. She offered a helpless gesture and replied, "Bart was far more assertive off camera than on, and quite a ladies' man. He was a past master at portraying the sensitive type of man and was wonderful in *The Letter* and *Foxes*. He was such an old pro that nothing bothered him. Even Wyler, with all his retakes, didn't faze him one bit. 'I'd be happy to do it again, Mr. Wyler,' he'd say in his clipped English accent, which got Willie's goat."[290]

᎗

MGM paged Marshall for a film remake of Rachel Crothers' play, *When Ladies Meet*, which offered an unusual twist on the love triangle. Despite the heavily conversational tone, the film builds to a powerful scene where Greer Garson (a publisher's wife) and Joan Crawford (a novelist, and the publisher's mistress), meet for the first time. Garson talks about her philandering husband (Marshall), and Crawford offers details about her new novel—the plot, mirroring her affair with the publisher. The real jolt comes when they realize they are talking about the same man. Marshall did fine work as the publisher, exemplifying a man who is neither honest with himself, or the women in his life. Robert Taylor, also on board, was Crawford's love struck beau who knowingly brings the two women together. The stellar cast failed to improve upon MGM's 1933 version. An additional twenty minutes in length didn't help matters.

Chatting with Joan Crawford on the set of *When Ladies Meet* (1941) (MGM)

The Hollywood Reporter deduced, "Greer Garson ... stands out above the others." *Variety* concurred, "Miss Garson is outstanding as the wife, catching major honors. Marshall grooves neatly into the portrayal of the wandering husband." *The Boston Globe* concurred that Marshall "was smooth and plausible." Frank Morgan, who played the publisher in the 1933 version, was less sympathetic. The revamped screenplay allowed Marshall a wakeup call for his final scene. "I've never been honest with a single soul in my whole life," he says, with genuine discernment. "I was too selfish and too self-centered."

Garson, like Ann Harding in the original film, gives the story dramatic weight and poignancy. Crawford's slant on the young novelist differed from that of Myrna Loy. Loy carried a sense of naivety in matters of love. No one could accuse Crawford of lacking experience. Her performance relied on fluster and fantasy. As the *Boston Globe* put it, "Crawford is a little too strained and intense ... all [her] concentrated emotion would be more suitable to a tragedy." Years later, when Crawford was asked about *When Ladies Meet*, she fumed, "Terrible story, terrible script, and I doubt that any actress could have made the goddamned thing believable."[291] Nonetheless, *When Ladies Meet* grossed $1,846,000.

Marshall was alerted by MGM that he had the title role in their version of J. P. Marquand's best-selling novel, *H.M. Pulham, Esq.*[292] He would play opposite the luscious Hedy Lamarr. For whatever reason, he was replaced by Robert Young. Instead, Marshall was delegated to be the proud papa of Shirley Temple in her "comeback" picture, *Kathleen*. Upon meeting him, Temple discovered that Marshall's daughter Sarah Lynn was her schoolmate at West Lake School for Girls. "That makes us sisters, sort of," she exclaimed. The two "sisters" would soon be joined by a third. Upon completing *Kathleen*, Marshall flew to New York on business where he learned that Lee was expecting. He told Sheilah Graham, "I saw yesterday in a Hollywood gossip column that my wife is expecting a visit from the stork, much to my surprise. So I sent her a telegram asking 'Is it true?' As a matter of fact, I think it is."[293] The back-story to Lee Russell Marshall, to put it mildly, was *full* of surprises.

CHAPTER EIGHT

Bart and Lee at the Copa for British War Relief

December 1943 — Bart and Lee at the Mocambo

Marshall in *The Man Called X*

CHAPTER 9
Mrs. Marshall and The Man Called X

Shirley Temple's dressing room was filled with roses the first day of filming MGM's *Kathleen*, courtesy of Herbert Marshall. "Shirley's the most uncomplex child I've met," he said. "She's a natural, simple kid, giggles a little, just like anyone else her age." He watched her dash around between scenes trying to cram facts and figures into her head to keep up with her studies at Westlake School for Girls. Temple biographer Anne Edwards noted that Shirley's grades in her first year at Westlake were "barely passing," and that her favorite topic was "boys, boys, boys!"[294] Classmate, Sarah Lynn Marshall, was five years younger. "Sarah Lynn adores Shirley," said Marshall. When his daughter asked to visit the set, Shirley made one condition. She didn't want Sarah there on the day she had to cry before the camera.

Fans had waited over a year for Temple to blossom into adolescence and return to the screen. The scenario for *Kathleen* was similar to Bart's 1936 effort *Make Way for a Lady*—a neglected daughter's dislike for her dad's girlfriend, propels her to find him a more suitable match. In this case, oddly enough, it was twenty-year-old Laraine Day who had recently played Marshall's daughter in *Foreign Correspondent*. What's even more baffling was fifty-one-year-old Marshall's comment, "I decided to become a father in films. This meant a salary cut of 50 percent. But I was sick to death of making love to girls young enough to be my daughter." Day herself said years later, "Marshall ... was too old to be playing a love story with me ... and I was much too young to be playing a psychologist for Shirley."[295] (Day turned twenty-one soon after filming completed.)

Kathleen (1942) with Shirley Temple

In her 1988 autobiography, *Child Star*, Temple recalled a scene in a car where Marshall rolls over on his hip to reach Laraine Day's puckered lips. A rattling noise from his prosthesis ruined a take. (It was actually Gail Patrick, *not* Day in the passenger seat.) Marshall grasped the steering wheel, "white-knuckled in embarrassment," as Temple put it. She thought it hilarious. Temple also felt that "*Kathleen* was destined to bomb."[296] Per *Variety*, *Kathleen* "did not tee off auspiciously" for thirteen-year-old Temple. *The New York Times* deduced that Shirley came across as "a pucker-faced little brat, full of sugary daydreams," and that "Mr. Marshall seems pretty melancholy about the whole thing." Due to an unfortunate script with cardboard characters, *Kathleen* quickly bit the dust. Released

CHAPTER NINE

only a few weeks after the U.S. entered WWII, Marshall suddenly found himself with other priorities than his film career. He would make only one film in 1942.

※

Despite his feelings about making screen-love to young girls, the twenty years difference between Bart and Lee wasn't an issue. Photos of the couple frequently appeared in the media, but very little was mentioned about Lee Marshall herself. *Variety* indicated that Lee was the sister of Rosalind Russell. This fabrication from 1938, was published after Lee's ex-husband Eddy Brandt, sued Marshall for alienation of affections.[297] Over the next few years several columnists repeated the rumor of sisterhood for Rosalind and Lee. In 1942, gossip columnist John Truesdell concocted a story, "Roz Russell Is Jealous," claiming that Russell envied her sister (Mrs. Herbert Marshall) who was awaiting a "British Bundle From Heaven." Although Roz and Lee never refuted being siblings, nothing could have been further from the truth. Lee, whose real name was Elizabeth, took the surname of her mother when she decided on a modeling career.

Elizabeth Roberta Bloomfield, was born July 3, 1910, in New York. The 1910 census lists her parents James and Catherine Russell Bloomfield, and an older sister Irene, residing on South Lexington Avenue in White Plains. By 1925, the Bloomfield household, living on Long Island, included two sons, James and Russell. James Sr., born in New York, was a chauffeur. Catherine was born in Ireland, immigrating to the U.S. in 1900. If there was a connection between Catherine Russell and Rosalind Russell, whose family resided in Connecticut, it was a very distant one. In 1930, Elizabeth and her *only* sister, Irene, were employed as "mannequins" in a dress shop.[298] On April 29, 1932, Elizabeth married musician Edward Brandt. They headed to Hollywood soon afterward, but returned to New York, where he began forming an orchestra. In the Fall of 1934, Elizabeth, now going by "Lee," went to see a Garbo film. Purportedly, her life was never the same.

In a 1942 interview, Lee claimed that she first fell for Marshall upon seeing him in *The Painted Veil* (1934). She was taken with his fine looks and sympathetic eyes. And that voice! "That's for me!" she had told herself. If her story is to be believed, she sat through the picture twice, much to her husband's annoyance. Lee followed *The Painted Veil* around town, seeing it four more times. She decided that she was destined to marry Mr. Marshall. Lee bought every fan magazine on the newsstands. "I read every word I could find printed about Bart," she said. "And I must say he sounded as if he would be as dull as ditch water."[299]

Lee indicated that it was during a modeling stint at 5th Avenue's Bergdorf Goodman, that an MGM talent scout offered her a contract as a stock player. Husband Brandt drove Lee to Hollywood, and dropped her off to pursue a film career. At last, Lee was breathing the same air as her "Dream Prince," who had recently terminated his romance with Gloria Swanson. In 1937, Lee's husband told reporters that she had met Marshall at a party at producer Edgar Selwyn's. In Lee's 1942 version, she and Bart met in Palm Springs at a soirée thrown by director Eddie Goulding. She maneuvered herself next to Marshall, who began conversation by correcting her mispronunciation of the word "mischievous." She answered back, "I don't see that it makes any difference." Bart explained to her that he only corrected the speech of those he liked very much.

For all the press mention of Lee playing small parts in the movies, she frankly admitted that she had no screen ambitions and was perfectly content being Mrs. Herbert Marshall. She was defensive of her man. "I get furious now," she said, "when I read articles in magazines ... that make you think Bart is staid and stuffy. Why, he's the funniest man I've ever met." Lee talked about Bart's tendency to clutter the bathroom with hair tonic; his passion for polishing his shoes with the kit she had given him; and, their drives to the beach in his 1936 convertible roadster. "'Let's go for a blow,' he'll say." Lee softened a bit to emphasize, "Bart is so quiet and gentle and sympathetic you just can't help but love him." On one occasion he chastised a carpet sweeper salesman who called early one morning, waking him up. Over breakfast, Bart regretted his behavior, and told Lee,

"That poor soul had a hard day ahead of him. Don't you think we need a new carpet sweeper?" He and Lee argued over money. "If I didn't watch him," said Lee, "he'd give everything away."

A typical evening at the Marshall residence, included drinks and conversation with Bart's good pals: Ronald Colman, Rod La Rocque, Roland Young, Reginald Gardiner—a steady group. On occasion, Kay Francis would drop in.[300] Bart acted as bartender. After dinner they played gin rummy while listening to music. Marshall's favorite jazz orchestra was Duke Ellington, and the current hit, "I've Got it Bad and That Ain't Good." Bart's avocation was drawing sketches, some of which he, using a pseudonym, sent to the *New Yorker*. "But they always come back to him," said Lee.

August 29, 1942 Virginia Field chats with Bart and godmother Kay Francis

Things remained copasetic between Lee, Bart, Edna and Nat Wolfe. The two couples met frequently and Sarah Lynn had grown fond of Lee, whom she affectionately called "Leitzel."[301] Due to Sarah's fondness for her father, he was turning heads at the Mocambo, proudly displaying the Mickey Mouse watch his daughter had given him. In return, Sarah Lynn was gifted a half-sister. On May 13, 1942, Ann Marshall, weighing in at 9-pounds, was born at Cedars of Lebanon Hospital. Bart told reporters that Ann was his "lucky baby"—as his favorite number was "9." He asked Kay Francis to be the designated godmother of little Ann—a very "lucky baby," indeed.[302] The maternity ward was filled with on-lookers. On display with Ann Marshall, were the baby daughters of Alice Faye, and director William Wyler.

WWII

Four months after the bombing of Pearl Harbor, the Selective Service System began a fourth draft registration (males ages 45-64). Marshall signed his papers with the registrar in Beverly Hills on April 25, 1942. He was designated as an "Alien, age 51." The purpose of this particular draft was to assess the manpower in the U.S. Famed war correspondent Quentin Reynolds detailed Bart's own intentions to enter combat zones. In August 1942, Reynolds was aboard the destroyer *H.M.S. Calpe* headed toward the German-occupied port of Dieppe. A Wing Commander of the Royal Air Force brought up the name Herbert Marshall. He had met the actor, and had nothing but praise for the *man*.

> A good man—Bart. He's tried everything to get over here. He knocks himself out raising money for British War Relief and now he's selling bonds, but he's still trying to get over here. One of our chaps just got back from Washington. He said that Bart went down there asking their help to get a visa. Our chap said to him, "After all, Mr. Marshall, you got half-killed in the last war serving in France. Do you

want to lose the other half of your life in this war? Marshall just said simply, "Yes." He's a hell of a citizen, and some people think he's just another film actor.³⁰³

The Wing Commander asked if Reynolds knew Marshall, and he answered without hesitation: "My God, he's the best friend I have in Hollywood." Reynolds was in a strategic position to appraise what came to be known as the (controversial) Raid on Dieppe, which went badly for the Allies. In 1943, his recollections were published in a book, *Dress Rehearsal*.

As the war escalated, so did Marshall's commitment to helping the wounded and disabled. He wasn't alone on this score. Kay Francis spent countless hours in hospital units for the Naval Aid Auxiliary. An oral history from Corona Naval Hospital details a story from an intern who watched the actress work a miracle. A wounded veteran, dying in anguish, looked up and saw Kay, just as she took hold of his hand. "He calmed right down," recalled the intern. "She talked to him for hours. Her friends, the other stars, came in to get her, but they just sat down. They all just sat there till that son-of-a-bitch died."³⁰⁴ In an inspired move, Kay asked Bart to join her on several occasions. For this, he was more candid about himself, and made a tremendous hit with the men.³⁰⁵ In 1943, Marshall penned an "open letter" reassuring those in the armed forces that they would be welcomed back, regardless of disabilities.

> It's a letter I've been meaning to write you ever since Pearl Harbor. A message that will hearten you while you carry out the grim business at hand. I know you've been worried about this. I know, because I was worried too, back on the Argonne. Well boys, ... take the case I know best, because it's my own. I've never forgotten it.³⁰⁶

Marshall detailed his year of agony "being patched up" in a hospital, before fate intervened inside a pub, with the offer from actor-manager N. Carter Slaughter. Marshall mentioned his closest friend in the London

Scottish, a young bank-teller, severely wounded. "I thought he too was a goner," wrote Marshall. "But a few years after the war he suddenly appeared backstage in my dressing room looking sleek and successful"—the manager of a big bank. Marshall concluded his optimistic message by saying that things would "pick up where they left off." Unfortunately, many returning vets did not receive what Marshall described as "a helping hand when soldiers come marching home." William Wyler's Academy Award-winning film *The Best Years of Our Lives* (1946) would offer a more accurate assessment of the grim realities facing veterans in the aftermath of WWII.

Bart found himself lying in Rudolph Valentino's antique bed while filming W. Somerset Maugham's 1919 novel, *The Moon and Sixpence*. The producers rented "The Great Lover's" dream-wagon for the opening scene involving a British novelist, patterned after Maugham, and played by Marshall. The press made a brouhaha about the 8' X 11' Chinese teakwood monstrosity, but Marshall put reporters in their place, saying, "Any comments from me on such an occasion as this would be superfluous, except to say that as an article of furniture it is amazingly adapted to its purpose ... which is functional."[307]

The Moon and Sixpence, a minor classic in English fiction, was long overdue for a film version. Warner Bros. had purchased the rights, then gave up on the idea, considering it too daring. In 1942, it was independently produced and distributed by United Artists. *The Moon and Sixpence* was the fourth time Bart bedded down on screen with novelist Maugham, whose wide and complex world view was, as biographer Jeffrey Meyers put it, "a struggle between sexual repression and artistic expression."[308] The focus in this strictly adult film was on George Sanders, who filled the shoes of a middle-class London stockbroker named Charles Strickland. Without warning, Strickland abandons his wife and children to live in Paris, where he pursues the pagan life, and his dream of being an

The Moon and Sixpence (1942) (above) with George Sanders; (below) with Doris Dudley, Steven Geray (UA) (Courtesy of Larry Smith)

artist. In the novel, Maugham promoted his view that creativity is smothered by domesticity.[309] Strickland's relationships are compromised by his boundless ego, and brutal honesty. While fulfilling his destiny, he makes everyone miserable, including himself.

Strickland was modeled after French businessman-turned-artist Paul Gauguin, who passed away in 1903. Maugham's fascination with Gauguin had motivated the author to take a voyage to Tahiti in 1917. Maugham contacted several individuals who knew Gauguin. Marshall, as Maugham-like novelist Geoffrey Wolfe, narrates the film and appears intermittently as an acquaintance of the aloof Strickland. Their relationship is a testy one. With barbs and admiration, they edge towards tolerating one another. Once the scenario locates to Tahiti, the film's arresting sepia tones are unable to compensate for a slow, drawn-out conclusion. Also in the cast was Bart's pal Eric Blore, as an ex-pat thriving in the tropics. Their scene together is engaging—a capstone to their lifelong friendship off screen.

Producer David L. Loew and director Albert Lewin included a postscript to appease the Production Code, and reassure audiences that Strickland got his just desserts. Begrudgingly, the Hays office went along with the idea. In a letter to Lewin, Maugham assessed the screenplay as "a brilliant piece of work ... and adhered very honestly to the theme of the story."[310] The Roman Catholic Legion of Decency, nonetheless, was gravely taken aback by the nude images that graced the Technicolor finale: female breasts, buttocks, and male genitalia (God forbid). *The Moon and Sixpence* was one of the top-grossing ($1,200,000) films of 1942.[311]

Life magazine designated *The Moon and Sixpence* "Movie of the Week," and found Sanders "remarkably convincing." New York critic Jane Corby observed of Sanders, "What if he does overact? Mr. Marshall is, in his tendency to underact, the anecdote that suits the Sanders case." Marshall capably mirrored the image that Maugham had of himself—the priggish personification of insight, dry humor, and a dash of rancor. What doesn't hold up in 1942's *The Moon and Sixpence*, or in Maugham's novel, is the rampant misogyny that fuels the perception of virtually every female character. "Women have small minds," complains Strickland. "They try to imprison a man."

CHAPTER NINE

During a summer heat wave in 1942, *The Moon and Sixpence* held its premiere on the island of Martha's Vineyard. Maugham in attendance. Several months later, Paramount was negotiating for Marshall to play a role in Maugham's recently published *The Hour Before the Dawn*. The story of a pacifist-turned-bomber pilot (Franchot Tone) is mostly known for the beginning of the end of Veronica Lake's career. The role Marshall reneged on was that of Tone's brother. He would wait another three years before he tackled playing Maugham himself, in *The Razor's Edge*.

Marshall 1942 portrait. 1941 caricature by James Montgomery Flagg

American artist James Montgomery Flagg, known for his iconic 1917 recruitment poster of Uncle Sam, "I Want YOU for the U.S. Army," asked Bart to pose for him—not as Uncle Sam, but as himself. The Associated Press released the result, accompanied by Flagg's impressions of the actor.

> What's the first thing about Herbert Marshall that impresses you? It's the expression in his eyes—kind, sympathetic, eyes that have had a round trip to hell—and still love his fellow man. Men like and respect him, I find. Bart

isn't handsome—he's fine looking. As I studied him—and he's no open book—I found his features were blunt and his head round. And a bit of the bulldog is there. There would have to be! Of course his drag on the screen is women. They want to console him. Not an inconsiderable factor in his popularity with the tough but high heeled sex is that deep cello voice with which he charms 'em."[312]

Flagg continued to churn out patriotic posters during WWII, while Bart focused on War Bond Drives. In May 1943 he and Lee found themselves in Ottawa for a Victory Loan Booster. It had been twenty-one years since Bart was last there, touring with Marie Lohr—a memory etched in time due to her reprimanding audiences who were unaware of his disability. Marshall was cheered once again, by thousands at Ottawa's Confederation Square, as he addressed officials and employees at the Hughes-Owen Plant.[313] His participation contributed significantly to the $12.5 billion dollar Victory Loan campaigns. Along with former co-stars Norma Shearer, Kay Francis, and Barbara Stanwyck, Marshall was awarded a medal from the Canadian government. He and Lee made a point to greet Francis (February 20, 1943) upon her return from combat zones, entertaining for the USO.[314] Ann Marshall's godmother, was indeed a courageous soul. At one point, Kay found herself inside a foxhole during an air raid in Algiers, bombs bursting all around her.[315]

❧

After a decade living in Hollywood, Marshall held to the idea of returning to England, perhaps to retire. He always rented his domiciles in the Los Angeles area. His feeling was, "Why buy a house if I'm returning to England?" "I like it here in Hollywood," he said. "I'll stay here as long as they want me in pictures. But somehow, I could never feel that I'm not going back to England, someday."[316] His next film, *Forever and a Day* (1943), was a patriotic tribute to his homeland.

CHAPTER NINE

In an effort to bolster wartime sentiment, Hollywood's British film community produced *Forever and a Day*. The film used the metaphor of a 19th-century London home and those who dwelt within it (the Trimble family) to mirror the struggles of a nation. It was patterned after director Frank Lloyd's film success *Cavalcade* (1933). *Forever and a Day* begins in March 1941, following the Luftwaffe bombing of London. An American war correspondent (Kent Smith), a descendent of the Trimble clan, arrives at the family homestead. He is greeted by an attractive, albeit distant relative (Ruth Warrick), who leads him into the basement, an air-raid shelter filled to capacity. We see Herbert Marshall, a curate, leading a chorus of the old British pub song, "Down at the Old Bull and Bush." He engagingly chastises one gent, "You sang that song with *much* more feeling than you ever sang in church." In his brief moment, Marshall is convincing as a clergyman with heart and humor. It is at this juncture that flashback details several generations of Trimble households. An excess of pride, and apparently brandy, were the keys that fortified the family as well as the nation.

Forever and a Day (1943) air raid shelter scene with Billy Bevan, Aubrey Mather, Marshall, Ruth Warrick and Kent Smith (RKO)

Issues of class and racial boundaries were touched upon lightly, in favor of cultural cohesion and national belonging. Near the film's finish, the old Trimble structure is hit by a Nazi bomb. It takes an Anglo-American effort, two descendents (Warrick and Smith)— to rebuild the old homestead brick by brick, so that it may stand "forever and a day." A print of the film was presented to President Roosevelt at the White House.

Forever and a Day raised a million dollars for British War Relief.[317] Publicity touted seventy-eight British (and American) actors in the cast— all of whom performed gratis. Seven directors and twenty-one writers were also involved. Frank Lloyd directed the opening and closing scenes featuring Marshall.[318] *Film Daily* enthused, "Everyone connected with the film has covered himself with glory. Acting, writing, direction, photography are of the finest." The *Boston Herald* recognized that the film was a "labor of love," but found the overall pageant "dull." "Too much for one film," concluded D.C.'s *Evening Star*. In hindsight (1995), critic Leonard Maltin felt that the film was "uneven," but well-worth watching due to the "many fine moments and star-gazing galore."

During the release of *Forever and a Day*, "Herbert Marshall" also showed up in Warner Bros.' *This is the Army*, a flag-waving Irving Berlin musical that featured enlisted men with theatrical backgrounds. Private James MacColl offered impersonations of Ethel Barrymore, Noel Coward, Charles Boyer, but saved his best for last. He captured the nuance and facial expressions of Herbert Marshall to a "T." When asked if he likes hamburgers, MacColl (as Marshall) answers:

> Many people ask my opinion of hamburgers. Ladies and gentlemen, its more than an opinion it's an *adoration*. But hamburgers throw themselves away in this frantic desperation to do something, and in the end, does anyone love hamburgers? Do *they* love anyone? No. But *do I love them*, why you silly little things, of course I love them. What a question.

A critic for *The Sacramento Bee* nodded, "In this writer's opinion, Private James MacColl impersonating Herbert Marshall in mellifluous discourse ... more Herbert Marshallish than Herbert Marshall himself could do it, is the masterwork of the whole show."

Flight For Freedom — wartime propaganda with Fred MacMurray and Rosalind Russell (RKO)

Up next for Marshall was a fanciful piece of propaganda from RKO, *Flight for Freedom*, based on a theory concerning Amelia Earhart's 1937 flight and disappearance over the Pacific. A beautifully coiffed and gowned Rosalind Russell was assigned to play Tonie Carter, an ace flyer who becomes a decoy for the U.S. Navy. (For legal reasons Earhart's name was not used.) The effort to pull a glamorized Russell from a rut of "unsatisfactory romances" before she lifts off into "oblivion," felt routine. The amorous advances were supplied by Fred MacMurray, a daredevil pilot, and plane designer Herbert Marshall.

Ads featured Russell-MacMurray in a love-clinch, and asked, "Did These Two Strike The First U.S. Blow At The Japs?" In the film's attempt to demonize the enemy, a sinister-looking Japanese hotel clerk was on hand to push the propaganda forward. "The story is badly overwritten," said *The New York Times*, "the characters only superficially sketched and the great sacrificial climax ... is confused." At the finish, the starry-eyed aviatrix willingly takes a suicide-dive into the Pacific so that the Navy can investigate Japanese mandated islands. A *Dallas Morning News* critic concluded: "the mock heroics fall flat." Apparently Marshall wasn't impressed either, and skipped the film's premier. He preferred doing a thirteen-hour stretch of radio broadcasts, plugging war bonds.[319]

In the summer of 1943, Bart stopped in New York following a Canadian Victory Loan drive. While *Flight for Freedom* was being screened nationwide, he voiced his opinion on war movies. He did not want to make any more. Using war for box-office revenue felt unethical. "I am not against them, you know, but I had enough of it." His experience with the London Scottish haunted him, and always would. "I'm not trying to tell Hollywood what to do, but I think that only about 6 percent of the total output ... should be war pictures ... enough to give a good nudge to persons letting down on war efforts. I think *Bataan* is a good example of that, and the first good war picture we have had."[320] Film historian Jeanine Basinger confirms Marshall's opinion, designating *Bataan* (1943) as having an "eerie power ... sure of its task." The film, unlike *Flight for Freedom*, is an unpretentious, racially-integrated tribute to U.S. and Filipino forces who surrendered to Japan, before facing the heinous Bataan Death March. Basinger concluded, "What *Citizen Kane* did for form and narrative, *Bataan* does for the history of the combat genre."[321]

While in New York, Bart was seen at various bistros with Myrna Loy and her new husband John Hertz, Jr. Loy put her film career on hold to focus on marriage and politics, and to set up entertainments for military hospitals on the East Coast. She saw it all: burn victims wrapped in bandages, blind vets asking to touch her nose ("Yup, that's her," they'd declare). "I would have fun with them for a little while," said Loy, "and then go to the ladies' room and cry. It would infuriate me when after a stretch on the wards I'd go to some fancy restaurant and hear a lot of well-dressed people bitching about the butter shortage or gasoline rationing."[322] Marshall himself spoke at Madison Square Garden on behalf of Greek War Relief. An audience of 18,000 sat spellbound as he read an open letter to Adolf Hitler. It was written in Athens prior to the Nazi invasion of 1941, and surrender of the Greek Army. The message underscored the courage of a little nation showing "the world how to live—and how to die."[323]

Marshall and Astor battle the younger set in *Young Ideas* (MGM)

In lieu of another war-themed movie, Marshall completed a lightsome frolic at MGM, *Young Ideas*. In this he was paired with his friend Mary Astor. Astor and husband Manuel Del Campo were frequent guests of Bart and Lee. When Astor filed for divorce in 1942, Lee was on hand as a corroborating witness to Del Campo's frequent bouts with intoxication. Another bond between Marshall and Astor was her involvement teaching occupational therapy at Birmingham Veterans Hospital in Van Nuys.

Young Ideas was designed to boost the stardom of Susan Peters, who played Astor's precocious daughter. When Astor, a writer-lecturer, marries a serious-minded college professor (Marshall), Peters and her brother (Elliot Reid), horrible as they are amusing, determine to untie the marital knot. Astor biographer Joseph Egan told this author, "I like Astor and Marshall in this film. It was more about 'the kids,' but they came across as an intelligent adult couple and that was refreshing."[324] *Variety* concurred, "Mary Astor and Herbert Marshall team effectively as the elder newlyweds." *Young Ideas* didn't take itself too seriously. Bart's newly acquired skill with the bass fiddle was on display during a rowdy night club scene. Professor Marshall, after several rounds of scotch whiskey, hops on stage to "slap a mean bass." His "spontaneity," observed one critic, made "the laughs come fast and furious."

Andy Hardy's Blonde Trouble (1944) Rooney and Marshall lock horns (MGM) (Courtesy of Larry Smith)

Marshall signed again with MGM for Oscar Wilde's *The Picture of Dorian Gray*. He was set for the role of Basil, the artist who does a portrait of decadent young Gray (Hurd Hatfield). After doing screen tests with Hatfield, filming was put on hold. Marshall then agreed to play stooge for

Mickey Rooney. *Andy Hardy's Blonde Trouble*, one of the studio's weaker Andy Hardy entries, had Rooney attempting a college education, only to be distracted by pretty Bonita Granville, who has a crush on the college dean (Marshall). Marshall, who admits being tempted by the soulful looks of female students, locks horns with Rooney. *The Boston Herald* found Marshall's presence, "pleasant but startling." Next to Marshall's thankless assignment, was Rooney displaying all the impish antics associated with Andy Hardy. In real life he had recently divorced cinema's love goddess Ava Gardner. Rooney remarked, "It didn't take genius to realize that the studio wasn't going to let Andy Hardy grow up."[325]

It would be over a year before Bart made another film. In December 1943, following another Canadian Victory Loan Drive, he reneged on doing *The Picture of Dorian Gray*, and contented himself with radio guests spots. In January, he and Kay Francis broadcast a fun-filled frolic for the Armed Forces Radio Service, *Soldiers With Wings*. Marshall enjoyed himself, and let loose. On *The Eddie Cantor Show* Bart offered his version of "Pistol Packin' Mama." It was a hit with audiences. Before long, he was singing "Mairzy Doats" on the air. Bart was introduced as "The English Sinatra" on radio's popular *Duffy's Tavern*, crooning, "Leave Us Face It, We're In Love." Marshall also scored on *Duffy's* doing a Brooklyn taxi driver routine, accent and all.

THE MAN CALLED X

The world of radio continued to intrigue Bart when he contracted for his own series, *The Man Called X* (CBS). As secret agent Ken Thurston, Marshall circled the globe on dangerous missions. *Variety* complained that the premier broadcast lacked suspense. "The fault wasn't Marshall's," said the review, "for the vet film actor turned in his usual smooth performance." The series quickly moved to NBC, and became a huge hit—grabbing sixth place in the "Hooper Ratings"—radio's charmed circle of audience participation measuring systems. Bart jested with columnist Bob Thomas that the plots were influenced by whatever sponsor was backing the show. "When we worked for an airplane sponsor [Lockheed] we used to zoom through the air with a great speed. But now that we're on for a toothpaste concern [Pepsodent], we just squeeze our way along."

An episode titled "Strange Gal Kisses" had a typical plotline. While in New York, Mr. X mills around a theater lobby when a strange woman comes up and smothers him with kisses. During their smooch-fest, Mr. X notices an item of jewelry she is wearing. He suspects it to be the famous *fleur-de-lys*, part of a Rotterdam collection bombed by the Nazis. He follows her to Paris. During a *tête-à-tête* at the hotel Grand Palais, her fiancé shows up—the man behind the jewel heist. The plot thickens with a mix of "I love yous" and "I hate yous," before Mr. X invites the gendarmes to step in and haul the bad guys away. There was enough intrigue and humor to keep *The Man Called X* on air from 1944-1952.

Marshall faced cameras again for *The Enchanted Cottage* at RKO, and Paramount's noir-ish chiller, *The Unseen*. After these films were released in 1945, the Marshall household was in transition. In October, Lee Marshall announced her intentions for divorce. Bart's next wife, Boots Mallory, filed for divorce the previous month from producer-husband William Cagney, brother of James Cagney. While Bart was "going places" with Boots, he and Lee still lived together under the same roof. The housing shortage necessitated this cozy situation.[326] To make things more interesting, Lee began seeing actor Robert Walker, who recently divorced actress Jennifer Jones, who would soon play Marshall's daughter in producer David O. Selznick's *Duel in the Sun* (1946). It was Jones' affair with Selznick that broke up her marriage to Walker. Marshall and Co. unwittingly provided their fair share of fodder to fuel the Hollywood gossip columns.

CHAPTER NINE

Sisters — Sarah Lynn and Ann Marshall (1943)

Marshall played W. Somerset Maugham in *The Razor's Edge* (20th Century-Fox)

CHAPTER 10
Marshall & Maugham

"I call him Willie and he calls me Bart"
(Herbert Marshall, 1946)

Marshall's on-going hospital and bond tours received recognition all the way to the top—Allied Commander Dwight Eisenhower. During the final months of WWII, Eisenhower met with Violet Kochendoerfer, who worked with the American Red Cross in Berlin. "We talked about movie stars," wrote Kochendoerfer in her memoirs. "Of those he had met ... Ike thought Herbert Marshall and Madeleine Carroll were tops."[327] Carroll worked on troop trains for the Red Cross in Italy—in the line of fire. Bay Area writer Patty De Roulf penned an article, "The Untold Story of Herbert Marshall." The story confirmed Marshall's ability to lift the spirits of veterans who returned home from battle, minus arms and legs. His concern, understandably, had deep roots. Hundreds were inspired by his sound advice. De Roulf wrote that as soon as the war in Europe began, "Bart went around quietly contacting and making arrangements with veterans' hospitals. Then, on his own time, with his own money, he visited boys who returned from overseas with amputations. Bart looks on these visits as a personal matter which concerns only the veterans and himself."[328] A lieutenant in the Army Air Forces, had this to say,

> Herbert Marshall gave me back my life. When I found out I had a metal claw instead of a hand, I was completely broken. What employer would hire me? How

could I ever face my friends again and bear their pitying glances? I tell you I wished the Jerries had done a g o o d job instead of just shooting up part of me. Mr. Marshall talked real sense into us. He followed it up with demonstrations, actually showing us what he could do. Before he left, we were convinced that if he had been able to lead a normal life, we could do the same.

1944 — Colman and Marshall "lifting spirits" of GIs at the Hollywood Canteen

De Roulf's article was inspired following her encounter with an African-American ("a short, dark chap"), a former dancer, who had lost his left leg and right foot in the Pacific. She asked if he had heard of Herbert Marshall. "Hear about him?" he repeated, "He's practically my Ten Commandments! How can a guy dance without feet? Well, Herbert

CHAPTER TEN

Marshall showed me how. And I know that if he can accomplish what he has, that I should be able to get along all right, too." De Roulf indicated that her article was written without Marshall's permission. De Roulf wanted the world to know: "Herbert Marshall is doing one of the finest war jobs any human being can do." Marshall's next film assignment carried a similar message—a blinded WWI veteran who provides a symbol of hope for the newly wounded in the aftermath of WWII.

The Enchanted Cottage, by Arthur Wing Pinero, was written to provide solace for shell-shocked British veterans of WWI. The 1945 film was relocated to New England and WWII. Marshall easily held the screen as a composer, blinded in battle during the previous war. He is the catalyst for helping an embittered, disfigured WWII pilot (Robert Young) regain faith in himself. Upon their meeting, Young begs the question, "How in the name of *heaven* have you stood it all these years?" The composer responds philosophically, "In place of these two eyes that are gone, I have a hundred invisible ones that see things as they *really* are."

Young marries a girl (Dorothy McGuire) with emotional scars, finding herself unattractive. As love blossoms, the reclusive duo watch their physical imperfections disappear. They decide that their home, which once served as a honeymoon cottage, must be "enchanted." Marshall's character has the insight to spare them the truth, and encourage them to embrace what has happened. In so doing, they soon recognize that it's love that created the "miracle." Like the blind composer, they "see things as they *really* are." No longer isolating themselves, they begin to mingle with other people.

During the shoot at RKO, Marshall explained that his character wasn't supposed to see McGuire and Young. "And after they get through giving me that glazed look I almost can't," he moaned. "All day long I wander around in a glassy haze." Contact lenses were inserted into his bloodshot eyes with a suction cup. It took over an hour to refocus after the lens were removed. Marshall also did an impressive job at the keyboard. (Concert pianist Max Rabinowitz was on hand to coach him, and to act as his double on screen.)

The Enchanted Cottage — Glassy-eyed Marshall as the blinded composer (with Alec Englander) (RKO)

The Enchanted Cottage was an opportunity for filmgoers to look deeper than the surface of things. *Film Daily* underscored the film's "capacity to fill the soul with courage ... humanity and warmth." *Variety* wagered that the timely drama would encourage tolerance for crippled and disabled vets, and "make rehabilitation of the boys easier." Reviews invariably singled out Dorothy McGuire's standout performance. Marshall deserved kudos for establishing and sustaining the story's ethereal tone. His sensitivity melds beautifully into the heart-warming tale. D.C. critic Jay Carmody referred to Marshall as "one of the greatest craftsman in the business."[329]

CHAPTER TEN

As WWII came to a close, a columnist for *Variety* cornered Marshall at Sunset Blvd.'s Colony House. Bart was his usual cordial self, but carried the weight of recollection—the wounded, disfigured veterans he counseled. "I'm trying not to take the world at its face value," he said sarcastically. "Sometimes plastic surgery is *not* so entrancing."[330]

The Unseen (1945) film noir with Gail Russell and Joel McCrea (Paramount)

Paramount's *The Unseen* (1945) allowed Marshall to play against type and step into the world of film noir. In the top spot, Joel McCrea played a brooding widower whose wife had died mysteriously. He lives with his two children and their new governess (the lovely Gail Russell). Sinister influences seem to dominate the children, who carry the burden of dark secrets—similar to the themes in Henry James' *The Turn of the Screw*. McCrea puns that his kids "belong behind bars." When a series of murders take place near the abandoned house next door, Russell takes it upon herself to investigate. Suspicion is thrown at several characters, including McCrea. Marshall shows up as Dr. Charles Evans, the family physician—the real culprit, who covers his crimes by paying McCrea's son "hush money."

While the early portions of *The Unseen* succeed in creating atmosphere and suspense, the film lapses into a monotonous mix of chatter and shadows. Following a preview, *Film Daily* complained, "Failure to work out its story clearly and coherently serves to make *The Unseen* ... disappointing. Blame goes to those who did the screenplay, Hagar Wilde and Raymond Chandler." The lethal pen of scenarist Raymond Chandler (*Double Indemnity*) attempted to salvage a previous script by Hagar Wilde, who had fallen ill.[331] Chandler admitted to producer John Houseman that he did his best work when he was drunk.[332] D.C. critic Jay Carmody felt that Chandler's "best work" lacked "a tinge of realism to hold up the suspense." Carmody added, "Both McCrea and Herbert Marshall turn in customarily convincing performances." Cleveland critic, W. Ward Marsh, observed, "Herbert Marshall ... cuts his character sharply." The critic for *The New York Post* barbed, "*The Unseen* had better stay that way."

As filming wrapped on *The Unseen*, Bart and Lee invited Kay Francis over to celebrate July 4th, with cocktails and "dinner in the kitchen," after Kay (according to her diary) had been, "lazing around all day."[333] Francis was resting up before taking on the task of associate producer (and star) for the low-budget Monogram feature, *Divorce*. One reporter had the gall to ask, "Has anyone mentioned the embarrassing fact that you are well qualified to work on a picture titled *Divorce*?" Kay (who had chalked up four or five marriages) all but swallowed her coffee cup. "Yes, you rat," she laughed, "but I've been avoiding it."[334] It wouldn't be long before Bart's matrimonial score caught up with Kay's.

Five years into their marriage, Bart and Lee began to feel tremors in their relationship. The back-story involved James Cagney's sister-in-law, Boots Mallory, the wife of film-producer William Cagney. In September 1945, Boots filed for divorce. A few weeks later, Lee Marshall announced that she and Bart had separated. She told reporters, "But I'm young and I don't intend to let this smash my life."[335] In October, Cagney denied his wife's charge of "cruelty," and asked for divorce on the same grounds. He also demanded custody of their three-year-old twins. By March 1946,

CHAPTER TEN

Louella Parsons let the "cat out of the bag" revealing that Bart and Boots were "seen everywhere together." Had Boots been seeing Bart prior to her filing for divorce? "Naturally, Lee and I were separated before I met Boots," he informed Parsons. "So she's no way involved."[336] Parsons credited this considerate, if dubious, response to "That Marshall charm!"

April 1946 — Bart and Boots join Reginald Gardiner and his wife Nadia at the Mocambo

Crack-Up (1946) Marshall sleuthing for Scotland Yard, with Dean Harens, Erskine Sanford and Ray Collins (RKO) (Courtesy of Larry Smith)

During the upheaval in his marriage, Bart signed for the RKO noir *Crack-Up* (1946), a tale of corruption and forgery in the art world. In this, Marshall did some sleuthing for Scotland Yard. Imaginative cinematography (Robert De Grasse) creates a visually stunning film, despite a colorless performance by leading man Pat O'Brien—miscast as an art lecturer for a Manhattan museum. Marshall, working incognito, arrives on the scene after a traumatized O'Brien, an ex-G.I., breaks into the museum late one night. Earlier that day, he had offended an elite crowd of affluent art patrons. O'Brien believes art is for the masses, a view which annoys the museum supervisor and his wealthy cronies. Later in the film, it is speculated that O'Brien is under the stress of shell shock. He is fired from his position. Before long, a curator at the museum is murdered.

Crack-Up plods along until we learn that there is a scam to replace prestigious art masterpieces with forgeries—engineered by Dr. Lowell (Ray Collins), an art fanatic, and private collector. As a ploy to prevent O'Brien from displaying museum art behind X-Ray machines, Collins had injected him with a narcotic (most likely sodium thiopental, which was being used to treat shell shock victims). Drug-induced flashbacks are included to enhance the plot.

Scenarist John Paxton (*Murder, My Sweet*), who co-wrote *Crack-Up*, empathized with the plight of the working class. When Marshall trails O'Brien into a penny arcade, he eyeballs a cross section of average people, hard-working, and law-abiding. "The human pursuit here," Marshall observes, "is reduced to the simplest terms. You change a half-dollar for a hand full of hope. Five shots of happiness for a nickel." While in the arcade, Marshall reveals to O'Brien that he kept him from being arrested. "My fairy godfather," scoffs O'Brien, unconvinced. Besides, Marshall is a little too chummy with his gal (Claire Trevor). *Crack-Up* definitely has its moments.

As he shadows O'Brien, Marshall displays caution not to reveal his professional interest in all the goings-on. A Philadelphia critic deemed *Crack-Up* "a foggily conceived thriller," but discerned, "Herbert Marshall, so smooth he aroused our suspicions"—which is exactly what the script called for. *Variety* echoed the view of many critics, saying, "O'Brien is not too aptly cast as the lecturer. Claire Trevor as his girlfriend fares better. Marshall ... also shows up well. Irving Reis' direction ... lacks extra drive to punch the material over solidly." Following Marshall's so-so dive into film noir, W. Somerset Maugham provided him a much needed a career boost.

William Somerset Maugham was born in 1874, in Paris, where his father handled legal affairs for the British Embassy. Orphaned at the age of ten, Willie was sent to England to live with his reverend uncle, a somber, severe man. There was no love. Willie became withdrawn, finding contentment in books and solitude. He developed a bad stammer, which added to his self-consciousness. At sixteen, Maugham was sent to Heidelberg to study. He regained self-confidence. Fellow students appreciated his sharp wit. He also lost his virginity to a handsome pianist. Biographer Selina Hastings noted that at sixteen, Maugham was "an impressionable and highly sexed adolescent." Hastings emphasized, however, that Maugham's sexuality was kept an open secret. He was twenty-one during the 1895 trial of Irish playwright Oscar Wilde, charged with "gross indecency with men." Wilde was convicted and imprisoned for two years. The trial traumatized generations of homosexual men. Although Maugham took a wife at age forty-three, he described himself as "almost continuously in love" throughout the ordeal of marriage.

Marshall retained a sense of humor in regard to human sexuality. While staying at the Ritz in New York in 1938, he made reference to Wilde, finding him to be a perfect choice for actors seeking the limelight.

> In order to click, it seems you have to at least guide your country to safety, in the manner of Abraham Lincoln, or suffer for sinning against society as the late Oscar Wilde did. All of which is quite gratifying to us "hams."[337]

c. 1900 - W. Somerset Maugham

In another interview, Bart indicated that his favorite author was British novelist Lytton Strachey (*Eminent Victorians*). Strachey, noted for his irreverence and wit, was a pacifist, and also gay.[338] He was more forthcoming regarding his sexuality than Maugham. For his conscientious objection in 1916, Strachey was called before the Hampstead tribunal. A military representative interrogated him with the question: "What would you do if you saw a German soldier attempting to rape your sister?" Strachey answered, "I should try to interpose my own body."[339] The board was not amused. Strachey was determined unfit for military duty.

While Marshall kept his own privacy intact, he had allowed that he and Edna Best followed "inclination, not convention." Maugham, despite writing sexually explicit novels, and taking intermittent "vacations" from *his* marriage, was intent on appearing every inch the conventional English gentleman. "There was a great deal he was determined to keep hidden," wrote biographer Hastings. Much of Maugham's personal story, however, is revealed in the autobiographical tone of his books.

Marshall and Maugham both experienced repercussions from serving in The Great War. Maugham was an ambulance driver for the Red Cross, transporting troops from battlefield to hospitals. He dressed wounds and tied bandages. He recalled one German prisoner, who had his leg cut off, being adamant that the amputation would not have happened if he were French. "The dresser asked me to explain to him that it was necessary," said Maugham, "and with graphic detail." The bitter impact of war was reflected in Maugham's controversial play *For Services Rendered* (1932), which painted a bleak picture of postwar chaos, and the "incompetent fools who ruled the nations." Maugham stated that he wrote the play, "to protect the new youth of today from dying in the trenches."[340] Even so, prior to Pearl Harbor, Maugham accepted an assignment from British Intelligence to relocate to the U.S. and promote the British cause.

※

In February 1946, Louella Parsons announced that W. Somerset Maugham had personally selected Herbert Marshall to portray him in producer Darryl Zanuck's *The Razor's Edge*, based on the author's 1944 novel. Maugham explained to Zanuck that besides Marshall's talent as an actor, he favored his speaking voice. It was an ironic choice—Maugham choosing Marshall, whose eloquence with the spoken word was in direct contrast to Maugham's stubborn stammer. Scenarist Lenore Coffee recalled meeting Maugham in 1919—"his face twitching as the mangled words were forced out."[341] Coffee, who had a stammer of her own, froze up, terrified to speak to him. Maugham understood.

Marshall had been an acquaintance of Maugham's for several years. Both carried a sense of dry wit and a tinge of melancholy. "I call him Willy," Marshall told columnist Gene Handsaker, "and he calls me Bart. Knowing him, makes it more difficult to play the role. I hope he'll be tolerant."[342] Maugham didn't exactly have a high opinion of actors. In his 1938 memoirs, he stated, "I have never been able to look upon actors as human beings." An exception, were the Marx Bros. Marshall qualified that he and Maugham were not intimate, but casual friends. "About once a year we bump into each other," said Bart. "In *The Razor's Edge* I didn't try to impersonate Maugham. I simply played him as he wrote himself into the novel ... but I was a bit fearful lest I displease him."[343]

Maugham integrated his personal experience and insights into *The Razor's Edge*. After losing faith in the Anglican Church, he was absorbed in finding a purpose for life—enlightenment. Maugham's three-month journey to India in 1938, focused on Hindu philosophy and religion. He avoided British government officials and their ilk, and was repelled by the superior attitude that colonists had toward the Indian people. Biographer Hastings notes that "Maugham was unprepared for the impact of India." Whether it be a Hindu, Sufi, or Muslim, he kept hearing the same message. It was liberating, and exhausting. Maugham found pleasure in writing *The Razor's Edge* and didn't care whether or not anyone liked it. "I got it off my chest," he said, "and that is all that matters to me."[344] Upon release, the response was overwhelming. A half-million copies sold by the end of the first month.

On screen, Marshall, as Maugham, weaved in and out of *The Razor's Edge*, commenting on his own creations, his main focus being the protagonist, Larry Darrell (Tyrone Power). As the film opens, Darrell has returned from The Great War, in which a comrade had lost his life in order to save him. As a result, Darrell struggles with the meaning of existence, and is compelled to find answers. He postpones his marriage to a Chicago society girl, Isabel (Gene Tierney). A year later, the two meet in Paris. Isabel is repelled by Darrell's meager lifestyle, and returns home to marry his best friend, Gray (John Payne), who can provide her with luxuries. Isabel's rich uncle Elliott (Clifton Webb), a pretentious social climber, had had an obvious effect on her. In direct contrast was her friend Sophie (Anne Baxter, in a sensitive performance), who Darrell (toward the finish) attempts to rescue from prostitution and alcoholism. Darrell's search eventually takes him to India where he finds, not answers, but an abiding inner peace that had always been with him. Marshall closes the narrative, with a nod to Darrell: "Goodness, after all, is the greatest force in the world, and he's got it!"

CHAPTER TEN

The Razor's Edge (1946) with John Payne, Gene Tierney, Tyrone Power (20th Century-Fox)

The Razor's Edge Marshall, as Maugham, eyes characters for his next novel: Anne Baxter, John Payne, Gene Tierney, Clifton Webb (20th Century-Fox) (Courtesy of Larry Smith)

George Cukor was originally assigned to direct *The Razor's Edge*. Cukor, unimpressed with Lamar Trotti's script, suggested to Zanuck that Maugham write one. Zanuck consented, but was dissatisfied with the result, finding it "too verbose and lacking visual appeal." "It was a disappointment to Maugham," said Cukor, "and to me ... so I dropped out."³⁴⁵ Cukor had even planned to change the original ending, and have Darrell teach at a prestigious university. In the book, Darrell's visionary belonged to the working class, not the world of verbosity and academics. In hindsight, it was good that Edmund Goulding took over as director. This was Goulding's third outing with Marshall (whom he called "Bartlet"). The cast may have scoffed whenever Goulding attempted to "act out their parts" for them, but he was able to coax "superb performances from the actors, whose interpretations reveal full and rich characters."³⁴⁶ Both Baxter and Webb received Academy Award nominations.

Upon release, *The Razor's Edge* was a blockbuster, nominated for four Academy Awards, including Best Picture. *Life* magazine pointed out, "The movie ... shows an absorbing interplay of characters ... natural, human adults. Because of this it is as exciting as any Hitchcock thriller but deeper and more rewarding." As Larry Darrell, Tyrone Power offered a distinct presence and mystique. Power's recent assignment for the Marine Air Corps, often under enemy fire, had allowed him to witness, like Darrell, the carnage of war. Seattle critic Nat Lund observed an "added maturity and understanding" in Power's acting. "As Maugham himself," added Lund, "Herbert Marshall is properly unobtrusive, playing the part of an intensely interested spectator"—exactly what Marshall intended. A subtle reference to Maugham's sexuality surfaces with Tierney's line, "I always get the queerest feeling from Mr. Maugham."

In 2014, author Cliff Aliperti wrote, "Herbert Marshall was the perfect embodiment of characters hatched from the mind of W. Somerset Maugham. Not only was Marshall the perfect fit for some of Maugham's fictional creations, but he was the perfect screen representation of Maugham's own fictionalized version of himself."³⁴⁷

Marshall signed for another ambitious blockbuster prior to filming *The Razor's Edge*. David O. Selznick's *Duel in the Sun* (1946) was intended to rival the producer's *Gone With the Wind* (1939). Columnist Harold Heffernan was on the set. "For *Duel in the Sun*," he reported, "the once impeccable Herbert Marshall is a man to steer clear of. He drinks, gambles and fools around with women. You won't know your old friend Herbie."

CHAPTER TEN

Marshall as gamblin' man Chavez in *Duel in the Sun* (1946) (Selznick)

Duel in the Sun had a turbulent production history. Studio strikes, a jumble of rewrites and reshoots, delayed completion for two years. Numerous directors were behind the camera, with King Vidor receiving sole credit. Marshall originally was to narrate the story with no on-screen role.[348] Selznick added new opening scenes, casting Marshall as Scott Chavez, father of Pearl Chavez (Jennifer Jones), who white settlers have deemed a heathen, a "half-breed." Selznick felt their scenes together would explain Pearl's background and behavior. Marshall's brief appearance captured the spirit of a former Southern aristocrat, a renegade, who tries his luck at gambling and love, and fails at both. During a card game, we watch one bourbon-soaked opponent blow smoke in his face. "Would you mind?" asks Marshall. "That *weed* ... I find it rather repulsive." He throws in his cards. The game is over. Before long, so is his life.

Chavez, who bears the racially charged epitaph "Squaw Man," trails his adulterous wife, who is a native woman, and her lover. He shoots them both. Chavez had long decided that his wife was a bad influence on young

Pearl. Marshall holds the screen, when Chavez, on trial for murder, calmly sentences himself.

> I plead no mitigating circumstances. They deserved to die, as I deserve to die. For I long since killed a person much superior to either of them — myself. I killed that person the day I gave my family's name to the woman who became my wife. And since I believe the punishment should fit the crime ... I suggest you hang me by the neck until I am dead.

There follows a tender interlude between Chavez and Pearl inside a jail. He has arranged for her to live on Texas cattle ranch with his cousin (and former sweetheart) Laura Belle (Lillian Gish). "Your mother and I can't hurt you any longer," he says reassuringly. Upon her arrival, the sexually-charged Pearl wastes no time in seducing both of Gish's sons (Gregory Peck and Joseph Cotten). A frontier evangelist (Walter Huston) divines that Pearl was "built by the devil to drive men crazy." He advises her, "Pray till you sweat!" From there on, the overwrought, if fascinating film, serves as an excuse for erotic interludes, and gunfights. Testosterone played a key role in plot development. Poor Pearl comes to the conclusion, "I guess I'm just trash, like my ma!" It's no wonder that wags in Hollywood derisively referred to the film as "Lust in the Dust."

Duel in the Sun had its world premier before an audience of 2,000 wounded veterans at Birmingham Hospital in Van Nuys—Marshall and cast in attendance.[349] Selznick announced that the film would have a "veterans first" policy throughout the country. Perhaps the erotic spectacle would prove therapeutic. *Motion Picture Daily* underscored that it was "very, very hot stuff." *The New York Times* saw "flashes of brilliance" amid a "clutter of clichés," noting that "bad boy" Peck offered the best performance. *Film Daily* pointed out, "Walter Huston ... and Herbert Marshall make much of smaller parts." However, it was Jones and Gish who received Academy Award nominations.

CHAPTER TEN

Duel in the Sun — a.k.a."Lust in the Dust," with Jennifer Jones as Pearl, who was "built by the devil to drive men crazy" (Selznick)

On the other side of the big pond, London critics were inclined toward barbs. "Spasm in the chasm," summed up Leonard Mosley. "Lusts of the flesh ... ludicrous and grotesque," complained Roger Manvell. "Only the simplest will be had for suckers and believe in it all."[350] Campbell Dixon for London's *Daily Telegraph* qualified that the Selznick opus revealed the producer's "qualities and shortcomings to a nicety." "Technically, the film is superb," wrote Dixon. "This gigantic spectacle of sand, sex and sadism ... is just a pleasant charade at the vicarage." Indeed, church leaders were horrified. The Legion of Decency pounced upon *Duel in the Sun*, condemning it.

As if to compensate for the racist overtones in *Duel in the Sun*, Marshall narrated a twelve-minute documentary paying homage to the culture of Native Americans. German cinematographer Carl Junghans produced *Monuments of the Past* (1946), based on a sacred Navajo chant about the vanished cliff dwellers, who lived in the mist-shrouded temples of the Grand Canyon. "Their ghosts still whisper in the ruins," explained Marshall. "The towering monuments are still alive ... the stone arch of

Rainbow Bridge for the Navajo, still is the path to infinite beauty." The camerawork of Junghans, said one review, "paints a breath-taking picture in color."

※

While Selznick occupied himself with cuts and retakes for *Duel in the Sun*, Marshall completed another film for RKO. *Ivy* (1947), directed by Sam Wood, detailed the amorous affairs of a turn-of-the-century *femme fatale* and English beauty (Joan Fontaine). After spending the inheritance of her husband (Richard Ney), and tiring of her lover (Patrick Knowles), Ivy meets another victim, Miles Rushforth (Marshall), a millionaire with a yacht. Unfortunately, Rushforth is an honorable man. He escapes her conniving clutches, and sails to South Africa. Ivy determines to be the loveliest widow in London by the time Rushforth returns. To accomplish this, she poisons her husband.

Fontaine did a good job of making herself appear appealing and helpless. Her trademark searching glances before the camera fit the character. Marshall, competently defined his own role. *The New York Times* cautioned, "While Miss Fontaine gives a worthwhile performance, there are times where she literally chews the scenery." Nonetheless, Fontaine received her share of praise, while *Ivy* received mixed reviews. She later recalled one embarrassing moment on the deck of Rushforth's yacht. Marshall tripped over a coiled rope while walking along the deck. As Fontaine went over to help him, she noticed Sheilah Graham walking towards them. Fontaine whispered, "Don't look now, Bart. If she joins us, she'll talk your leg off."[351]

CHAPTER TEN

Ivy (1947) with Joan Fontaine (Universal)

During the shoot of *The Razor's Edge*, Edna Best (whose twin son had recently made her a grandmother) was working on an adjoining soundstage, playing Ronald Colman's wife in *The Late George Apley*. Bart occasionally joined them for tea. Sarah Lynn had a "bit" in the picture, and was basking in praise for her appearance on Mutual radio's *Casebook of Gregory Hood*. In the episode "Murder in Celluloid" she played a child star, who helps solve the mystery of a missing map. Sarah's voice easily registers a precocious infatuation with detective Hood (Gale Gordon). When she asks why he hasn't married, Hood explains that he is waiting to find the "right woman." With the fade-out line, she begs, "*Please* keep on waiting!"[352] In three years, Sarah Lynn's talent would blossom into a career. She quit high school to join a road company starring the legendary team of Alfred Lunt and Lynn Fontanne.

In the summer of 1946, Bart moved into an apartment for a brief stay. He bemoaned the fact that he was paying up to $500 a month rent, and hadn't the foresight to by a home when he first came to Hollywood. His wife Lee was taking her time to file for divorce. Sheilah Graham's spies occasionally spotted the happy trio: Bart, Boots, and Lee, dining out. "These friendly divorces always puzzle me," she gibed. "I will never say anything against Bart," Lee insisted. "He is one of the most charming people I have ever known."[353] Rumor had it that Lee and actor Robert Walker, recently divorced from Jennifer Jones, were headed for matrimony. Their on-again-off-again romance made gossip columns for over a year. Walker's close friend, Jim Henaghan, recalled, "Bob loved Lee, and, with me, she witnessed much of his misery. Mrs. Marshall made few demands on Bob, nor he on her."[354] The emotionally distraught and gifted young Walker, never really recovered after his divorce, dying at the early age of thirty-two.

In the Spring of 1947, while completing MGM's *High Wall,* Marshall had a run-in with the law. He deemed it necessary to take "time out" ... for marriage, and was off the screen for over a year.

Bart and his beloved Boots; (*below*) August 5, 1947 - Newlyweds Bart and Boots slip out the backdoor of a Santa Barbara church to evade throngs of autograph seekers (Courtesy of Kevin Brownlow)

CHAPTER 11
"What the hell is going on here?"

Herbert Marshall

Sunday evening, April 27, 1947. Bart and Boots enjoyed a couple rounds of Scotch at Bart's residence on West Norton Avenue in Los Angeles. Following libations, they dined at a favorite restaurant. Both were in a good mood. Ex-wife Lee had obtained a Mexican divorce that January, and Bart made it clear that he and Boots would marry just as soon as her divorce from Cagney was final. They set a wedding date of August 1. "Boots and I both want to be married in Santa Barbara for sentimental reasons," he told reporters. "That's where I met her and where we fell in love."[355]

They left the restaurant rather late. It wasn't long before Boots, at the wheel of Bart's custom-made foreign sedan, was being followed by a patrol car. A red-light began flashing, then a siren. Boots refused to pull over. There ensued what was described as a "wild chase." One deputy testified, "There were no tail or headlights on the car Mrs. Cagney was driving when we saw them turn into Sunset Boulevard from Hollywood Drive." Patrol officers followed the couple until Boots stopped several feet from the curb of Marshall's home. She smelled of alcohol, and when questioned, her speech was slurred. Marshall, however, was more coherent and volunteered, "What the hell is going on here?"[356]

Shortly before midnight, Boots admitted that she and Marshall had had "three or four scotches" at his home and at the restaurant.[357] She was taken into custody on suspicion of drunk driving. At police headquarters,

Judge Cecil D. Holland granted Boots a continuance, ordering her to appear in court the following day.³⁵⁸ The press had a field day. Bart's new fiancée was *the* hot topic: "Ex-Follies Girl Is Held For Drunk Driving In Herbert Marshall's Car." Boots went to trial on a plea of "not guilty." "I have done nothing wrong," she told the press, "and I am sure I will be found guiltless." In court, Boots denied being under the influence. From there on, the hearing succumbed into what could best be described as, alternate facts. She testified that on the night of her arrest she was "suffering from hysterics brought on by fright, not liquor."³⁵⁹ On the witness stand, Marshall graciously corroborated Boots' testimony, telling the judge, "She was sober, perfectly sober."³⁶⁰ The judge was compliant. Due to "lack of evidence," Boots was released. Such was the prelude to what many considered Marshall's happiest marriage. With a sigh of relief, Bart resumed his three or four Scotch and sodas per evening, each "with a twist of lemon peel," he confirmed.³⁶¹

Marshall accepted a chairmanship for the Federation of the Handicapped, designed to launch a national campaign to raise $450,000. Following his meeting with the organization's president, Dr. Leo Mayer, Marshall said, "I believe with Dr. Mayer that we must not only offer medical treatment to the handicapped, we must help them to become self-supporting, independent men and women. If Federation of the Handicapped is to continue to train and place hundreds of disabled people each year, it must have funds."³⁶² Mayer, a prominent orthopedic surgeon, created numerous operative treatments for the rehabilitation of the physically challenged—an interest that he had pursued prior to the U.S. entry into WWI.

Marshall returned to his professional obligations, signing on for MGM's *High Wall* (1947)—a logical choice. In *Dark City: The Lost World of Film Noir*, author Eddie Muller aptly describes the film as "a specimen of shell-shocked noir." Scenarists Lester Cole and Sydney Boehm give an insider's view into what veterans were up against. When a brain-injured bomber pilot, Steve Kenet (Robert Taylor), ends up in a state mental hospital, he receives the bad news: "There are twenty-five hundred patients in this hospital and twelve doctors. We'll get to you when we can." In real life, Marshall was an eye-witness to the understaffed, underprepared hospitals in the aftermath of WWII. Shock treatments, lobotomies, and psychosurgery on veterans were commonplace, and only made matters worse.

Sinister, smooth-talking Marshall in *High Wall* (1947) with Moroni Olsen. (MGM) (Courtesy of Larry Smith)

On screen, Marshall played a sinister, smooth-talking publisher of religious periodicals. He uses Taylor's "psychological condition," to get away with murder. Taylor is under the delusion he strangled his wife, until a psychiatrist (Audrey Totter) gives him a shot of narco-synthesis (truth serum). Before long, he zeros in on the real culprit: Marshall. Marshall tells Taylor, "Any accusations you make against me will be ridiculed. The ravings of a lunatic. There's no possible way you can prove I killed your wife!" Marshall's romantic involvement with Mrs. Tenet had placed his career in jeopardy. The god-fearing people in the company he works for are considering him for a big promotion: Vice-President. A climactic flashback, induced by psychiatrist Totter injecting her needle into *Marshall*, saves the day for Taylor. Despite an obligatory happy ending and fade-out kiss, *High Wall* rates as topnotch noir.

In *The Films of Robert Taylor*, author Lawrence J. Quirk determined that while Taylor was "appropriately harried and tense ... Herbert Marshall almost steals the picture as the murderer." Critic Edith Lindeman praised Marshall's "consummate skill." "Suspense is generated," she confirmed, "from the first glimpse of Marshall gloomily huddled over a bar." Whenever Marshall shows up, and even when he doesn't, one is compelled to wonder what's going on in his twisted mind.

Cecelia Ager's review for the liberal-leaning *P.M. Daily*, paid tribute to the "outstanding script," whose co-writer, Lester Cole, was now under investigation by the HUAC. Ager offered a snide aside to the powers at MGM: "Out of professional loyalty to the House UnAmerican Activities Committee, Metro has recently decided to forget its contractual obligations to Mr. Cole and arbitrarily dispense with his services."[363] Contributing to the demise of Cole's professional career was the star of *High Wall*, Robert Taylor. Cole had provided the actor with one of his best roles, which Taylor played with consummate skill. When subpoenaed by the HUAC, Taylor blamed screenwriters for Communism infiltrating into the film industry, designating Cole as "reputedly Communist." Despite having worked with Cole, Taylor stated that he, personally, wouldn't work with a Communist.[364] Cole became one of the infamous "Hollywood Ten." He was blacklisted, and served time in prison for refusing to testify.

※

Sunday, August 5, 1947. The First Presbyterian Church in Santa Barbara was the venue for Bart and Boots' wedding. Reverend Joseph M. Ewing presided, while Nigel Bruce served as Best Man. The bride and groom remained in Santa Barbara for a honeymoon. Aside from working on stage and film together, Bart and Nigel had a special connection. Nigel had also served in France during WWI, receiving eleven bullets in his left leg. He was able to keep his leg, after spending two years in a wheelchair.

The back-story of Marshall's new wife, a native of New Orleans, sounded like something a publicist would dream up. For Patricia "Boots"

Mallory, however, it was the real thing. Her mother Myrtle Fiddler, from Mobile, Alabama, was only fifteen when her boyfriend Trachy Eslava took her across the state line to marry.[365] They hopped back on the train to Mobile, where Trachy was arrested. "Husband, 18, Jailed on His Wedding Day," read one headline. Trachy had lied about his wife's age. His own father, who was against the marriage, arranged his son's arrest. Myrtle's father quickly secured a bond for his new son-in-law's release.[366] It was a bumpy start. The couple relocated to New Orleans in time for the birth of their daughter, Lillian Patricia, on October 22, 1912.[367] "I think all Southern girls marry young," said Boots in a 1932 interview. "They mature so early."[368] She never knew her father.

c. 1931 - Ziegfeld girl Boots Mallory rhapsodized, "Southern girls ... mature so early."

Soon after her birth, Patricia's parents returned to Mobile, where they separated. "It was a runaway marriage based on infatuation," explained Boots. "My stepfather is exactly like a father to me—even nicer. I use his name. And he was the one who nicknamed me 'Boots.'" John Henry Mallory, a tugboat operator, proved to be a better match for Myrtle. During childhood, Boots joined her stepdad on tugboat runs from Mobile to various ports in Florida. Upon completing the 8th grade, Boots opted to quit school. After all, she knew how to play the ukulele. When an agent got a load of her talent—ash-blonde hair, big blue-gray eyes, and premature sex-appeal, Boots joined a vaudeville act. Producer George White happened to spot her in a New York nightclub. He quickly signed Boots to join the chorus of *George White's Scandals of 1928*. One musician in the orchestra pit, twenty-two-year-old Charles Bennett, got an eyeful of Boots, and asked her to engage in holy matrimony. Boots was fifteen. Like her mother, she had matured early. "We took an apartment ... and were very happy," said Boots. "I posed for a lot of commercial artists."

Broadway impresario Florenz Ziegfeld was next to latch onto Boots, for the *Ziegfeld Follies of 1931*. After the premier, Boots made news in the *Daily Star*. "Mr. and Mrs. Charles Bennett, Forty-Fifth street, are entertaining Mr. Bennett's sister from Cambridge, Ohio. Mrs. Bennett, whose stage name is Boots Mallory, is playing in the new Ziegfeld 'Follies.'"[369] Next up for Boots, was *Hot-Cha* (1932), also produced by Ziegfeld.[370] For a lark, she did a screen test for Fox. Before long, Boots and Bennett put their furniture in storage and headed West. In Hollywood, Boots ballyhooed that she had been married to Charles three-and-a-half years. "I wouldn't have come without him," she said. "I have to have someone to baby me." Before long, Boots was filing for divorce from a man she never married.

Boots was cast in Erich von Stroheim's *Walking Down Broadway*. The story involved young people in the big city, romance, streetwise sexuality, and lots of censorable material. It wasn't easy for Boots. She had no acting experience, and von Stroheim was a tough taskmaster. Walter Winchell reported that the director, trying to get Boots to cry, "smacked her one, blackening her eye and loosening her teeth."[371] One eyewitness thought von Stroheim "sadistic." "He slapped her, oh so hard ... the crew were ready to jump and pounce on him. That poor girl, her face almost black and blue, it 'swole' up the next day." Cast member Minna Gombell said that von Stroheim, prior to shooting love scenes, told actors to visit the studio lavatory and pleasure themselves "almost to the point of completion," prior to each take.[372] Filming, and von Stroheim abuse, wrapped in mid-October, 1932.

Hello Sister (1933) Boots and James Dunn co-star in a truncated version of von Stroheim's *Walking Down Broadway* (Fox)

Following a closed screening, Fox felt Boots had potential, but *Walking Down Broadway* ended up on the shelf. Fox executive Sol Wurtzel found the film "appalling." Leonard Spigelgass, who worked on the scenario, recalled, "I overheard someone say that it could only be shown to a convention of psychoanalysts." The film was released several months later as *Hello, Sister* (1933)—a patch-up job with new footage and only a few traces of von Stroheim. In her column for *Variety* Cecilia Ager, bluntly assessed Boot's performance.

> She learns the words of her lines very proficiently—and stops there. The moods, the emotions that evoke those

lines she'll have nothing to do with. So girls cry, do they—Miss Mallory makes crying sounds. They're glad? Miss Mallory smiles dutifully. Sometimes they're lonely. Miss Mallory hangs her head. There's really nothing to acting, Boots Mallory style.[373]

Boots made two more films for Fox, but failed to impress. It was no matter to her. Boots wasn't exactly hell-bent on a career. Instead, she signed her name to a marriage contract in Agua Caliente. She was now Mrs. William Cagney, brother of box-office champ James Cagney. Charles Bennett, was less fortunate. He was arrested the previous month, along with a chorus girl, for looting a lingerie shop on Hollywood Boulevard.[374]

1933 — Boots becomes Mrs. William Cagney

Prior to becoming Mrs. Cagney, Boots announced plans for a Mexican divorce from Charles Bennett. Bennett filed a complaint, testifying that on August 15, 1928, they had agreed to "a marital relationship permanent and exclusive of all others"—a common-law marriage. Boots subsequently stated in a superior court that while she "posed as his wife, she never considered that she was married to him."[375] The couple were prominently featured in a nationwide news article, "New York's Ban on the Common-Law Wife."[376] The decision was designed to curtail a popular form of racketeering among Broadway's "Gold-Diggers"—alimony.[377]

For a dozen years Boots and Bill Cagney were a good match. Bill's older brother James hired him to act as his business manager and producer. Bill was considered the "business brains of the family."[378] In 1942, Boots and Bill added to the Cagney clan. They adopted twins, Jill and Stephen. The twins had turned three when Boots filed for divorce.

As for her family back in Alabama, Boots' stepfather, now a shipyard foreman, was briefly mentioned in reports of her marriage to Herbert Marshall. In 1953, Bart and Boots would inadvertently make news, when her half-brother, Grady, told Mobile police that he killed a man with an ice pick. "Actor's In-Law Signs Slaying Confession," read one headline. "Grady Mallory, 24, brother-in-law of actor Herbert Marshall, signed a confession that he had killed a night watchman ... in a waterfront shack."[379] Both men had been drinking heavily. Grady, who was on probation for robbery, now faced first degree murder. Bart and Boots made no comment. At the time, they were considering a husband-wife TV series, *The Adventures of Bart and Boots*, which never materialized. Thenceforth, their adventures were kept strictly to themselves, and apparently they were very happy together.

※

Cleveland columnist Inez Wallace visited Marshall several weeks after his fourth marriage. Over a cup of tea, she noticed a distinct difference from the last time she saw him. She felt that his merriment was "forced." "The minute you came in the room I sensed a difference," she wrote him afterwards. "You are beating your wings against too much pressure." She warned him to "slow down."[380] At fifty-seven, it was time to curb the pressures of film, radio, and a busy social life. Perhaps it was just a coincidence, but Marshall did slow down after Wallace issued her epistle. After all, she had studied voodoo rituals in the West Indies, and knew all about the "walking dead." Her research culminated in a story for RKO, *I Walked With A Zombie* (1943). It would be over a year before Bart made another film.

Marshall assured Wallace that *The Man Called X*, now in its fourth season, was the most important thing to him at the moment. He also hosted and starred in radio's *Hollywood Star Time* for CBS. The show had a big budget and line-up of guest stars. Marshall had lead roles in *Lost Horizon*, *A Star is Born*, *One Way Passage*, *Ball of Fire*, and *Woman in the Window*, opposite Joan Bennett. He began 1948 co-starring with Irene Dunne in a *Screen Guild Theater* broadcast of *Brief Encounter*. In July, while maintaining his low profile, the Motion Picture Relief Fund awarded Marshall a scroll for donating all his income from *Screen Guild Theater*. Founded in 1921, the Relief Fund had recently completed a Motion Picture Country House and 40-room hospital. The facility was designed to assist those with limited resources, who had worked in the film industry.

Marshall watched the demise of the old guard in the British film community. In May of 1948, Dame May Whitty, who had co-starred on stage with Bart, died at the age of eighty-two. She became Dame Commander of the Order of the British Empire in recognition of her charitable work during The Great War. The feisty actress wanted *no* minister in attendance at her memorial service. So, close friends pitched in. C. Aubrey Smith read The Lord's Prayer. John Van Druten gave the eulogy, and Marshall offered the benediction. Later that year, C. Aubrey Smith, kingpin of the tea-and-crumpet set in Hollywood, passed away at his hilltop home overlooking the Pacific. The eighty-five-year-old actor was knighted in 1944 by King George VI. Smith and Marshall co-starred on stage in *The Ware Case* (1924), and on screen in *Trouble in Paradise*. Marshall and his pal Eric Blore, among many others, attended the memorial service in which Doug Fairbanks Jr. read a eulogy written by English author James Hilton (*Lost Horizon*).

CHAPTER ELEVEN

Margaret O'Brien, Brian Roper and Dean Stockwell meet Marshall in *The Secret Garden* (MGM)

In the Fall of 1948, Bart took a break. He and Boots headed to New York City for a holiday. Ex-wife Lee and six-year-old Ann Marshall were also visiting back East. This allowed Bart time with his daughter, prior to filming his final release of the decade, MGM's *The Secret Garden* (1949). Considered a classic of children's literature, *The Secret Garden* is set in Yorkshire, where an orphaned girl named Mary (Margaret O'Brien) lives with her wealthy, widower uncle, Lord Craven (Marshall). Bedridden inside Craven's dark, foreboding mansion, lies his invalid son Colin (Dean Stockwell), who suffers from a spinal condition, unable to walk. Both children are willful and demanding until they discover a long neglected garden, which Lord Craven has kept under lock and key since the death of his wife.

As the embittered uncle, Marshall minces no words upon meeting his young niece. He abruptly dismisses her with, "I hoped you might be beautiful." As for the gloomy surroundings, he advises her, "It's an excellent house for bitterness. I have books. I drink." He even admits to not being sure of his own sanity. The real catalysts for change in *The Secret Garden* are Marshall's housekeeper (Elsa Lanchester) and her younger brother (Brian Roper), both excellent in demonstrating the wisdom and integrity of common folk. It is they who encourage Mary and Colin to restore the secret garden, and "blossom" into human beings. A Technicolor finish provides a soulful reunion, inside the garden, between Lord Craven and his son, who gets up from a wheelchair to take his first steps. He walks toward his father for a tender embrace—and new beginnings.

August 17, 1948 - Bart and Boots attend a party for Jeanette MacDonald, following her recital at the Hollywood Bowl

Variety questioned the film's appeal to children. "It is a yarn about kids and ... it would appear designed to entice them. Yet the allegorical and psychological implications ... are clearly for the grownup trade." While some felt that the shrill dramatics of O'Brien and Stockwell could have been tempered to better advantage, Cleveland critic W. Ward Marsh thought Stockwell "superb," O'Brien "her 'old' talented self," Lanchester "quite perfect," and Marshall "cuts a sympathetic sorrowful figure." Marsh found *The Secret Garden* "a completely lovely and enchanting picture." The film "fared mildly at 1949 box-offices."[381]

Bart and Boots celebrated his fifty-ninth birthday at the Mocambo. Liberace entertained that evening with an elaborate version of "Happy Birthday." The pianist shared his concerns with Bart about critics who made "sour notes" about his piano playing and attachment to his mother. "Listen, my boy," replied Marshall, "every performer walks out on stage knowing that no matter what he does, at least four people in the audience will hate him for no reason at all."[382] Liberace considered Bart and Boots among his closest friends. "A lot of other people are nice to me," the pianist confirmed, "but ... I don't get around socially too much."[383]

Sarah Lynn made news in 1949, playing in Tennessee Williams' *This Property is Condemned*. She had also been property girl and extra at the La Jolla Playhouse. That fall, Sarah made her Broadway debut in Maurice Evans' *Double Bill* (two one-act plays) which also starred Edna Best. Sarah was allotted a walk-on. "I want her to work up from the bottom," said Edna, "and learn every phase of the theater."[384] A year later, Sarah was being singled out for her performance with the Lunts in *I Know My Love*. As far as acting lessons, Sarah would admit, "I did have a few classes with mummy, but they were never any good. We kept fighting. Working with Alfred Lunt and Lynn Fontanne for six months, is like spending twelve years in an acting class."[385]

Marshall himself made news by breaking a rib. He stumbled over some furniture at his new home on North Foothill Road in Beverly Hills. Unable to take time off, he was obligated to complete *The Underworld Story* for United Artists, before sailing to Europe September 8. He had contracted for a film to be shot in the Mediterranean, and directed by Julien Duvivier.

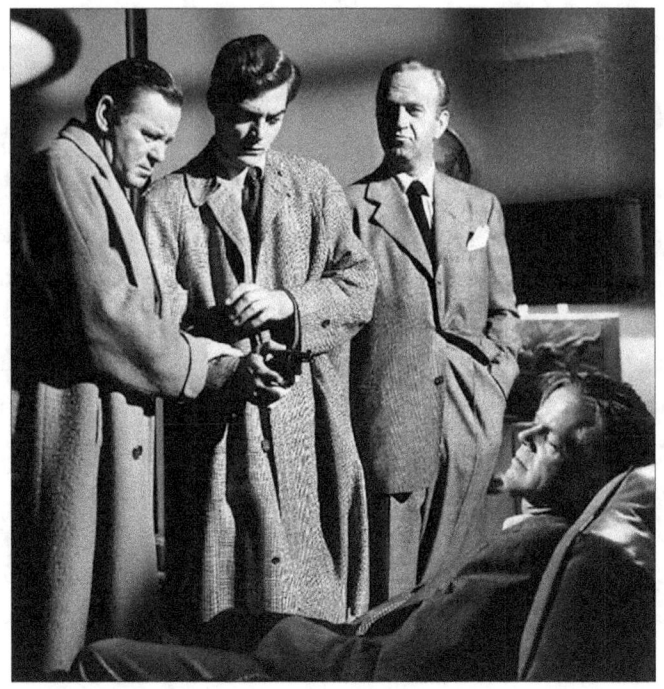

The Underworld Story — with Gar Moore, Howard Da Silva and Dan Duryea (UA)

The cynical plot of *The Underworld Story* (1950) presented Marshall as a New England news magnate. After his beloved daughter-in-law's body is found in the woods, Marshall's neurotic son (Gar Moore) admits to the crime, but blames his father. In Moore's eyes, his wife and Marshall were edging toward intimacy. His confession spurs Marshall toward giving him a well-deserved slap across the face. It's quite a riveting scene between the two. Upon hearing that the wife's African-American maid, Molly, is under suspicion, a reluctant Marshall and his anxious son agree to let the maid pay for the crime. They fund a $25,000 reward for her capture. Dan Duryea shows up as a unscrupulous newshound who encourages Molly to turn herself in (so he can get the reward). Duryea also plots to raise funds (which he plans to pilfer) for Molly's defense. Marshall helps quash efforts for a defense fund. Both men represent the press, at its very worst.

Even though Marshall is conflicted about subverting justice to protect his legacy, the twisted morality of the wealthy elite is displayed. Duryea serves justice only after his money schemes fail. Both men end up under the thumb of a mobster (Howard Da Silva). Marshall, who is coerced into dealing with Da Silva, asks him with disdain, "What *are* you?" Da Silva offers the rejoinder, "The same as you, only *smarter*." Director Cy Enfield's biographer noted that *The Underworld Story* was "emblematic of left-liberal concerns of the time."[386] From mobsters to lawyers to newspaper magnates, the money racket fueled the American economy and manipulated public opinion. The ploy of racial bigotry in a small town, however, wasn't exactly a progressive move in this case. The actress playing the role of Molly (Mary Anderson) was white, which necessitated the subtle use of lighting and shadow for her scenes.

It was no surprise that press reviews weren't favorable. Bosley Crowther, for *The New York Times*, called the film "haphazard and so full of detectable holes that it carries no impact or conviction." Crowther allowed that filmmakers were "free to proclaim that newspaper men are no good, we think the same of this film." The HUAC wasn't happy either. They subpoenaed scenarist Henry Blankfort, and director Cy Enfield for what was considered subversive subject matter. Blankfort, who had also been involved with the Anti-Nazi League, was blacklisted. Howard DaSilva was blacklisted. Enfield, branded a Communist sympathizer, fled to London and worked under assumed names.[387] In retrospect, *The Underworld Story*, as critic Leonard Maltin puts it, "is surprisingly effective"—a compelling account of how the road to democracy is compromised by unbridled wealth and greed.

※

Bart's sojourn to Europe was full of the unexpected. By the end of September 1949, he and Boots were residing at the Gran Hotel Mediterraneo on the island of Majorca. They were joined by co-star George Sanders and his new bride, Zsa Zsa Gabor. The intended eight-week shoot for *Black Jack*, dragged on for five months. Aside from director Duvivier, the men in charge of the production consisted of various princes, counts and diplomats. "I was filled with foreboding from the start," Sanders later recalled.[388] Day after day, the cast and crew of *Black Jack* cruised around the island, getting next to nothing accomplished. Zsa Zsa couldn't stand the monotony, and left for Paris. The second assistant director, Count Mezo, took time off to go fox-hunting. Rumor had it that Bart and Boots had split up. Bart told reporters in Spain that rumors of separation were, "Quite wrong." As everyone else was taking sabbaticals, the Marshalls headed to London. They arrived in January 1950, and stayed for a fortnight. It had been over thirteen years since Bart's last visit. He quipped that he had been "permanently homesick" ever since.

Black Jack (1950) — released in France as *Le Dernier Temoin* (Classic Pictures)

During the fifth month of production, with only a third of the film completed, Sanders gave notice. He told the producer that "if he did not finish the picture nobody would ever know how great a failure it was going to be." Gabor invited Bart and Boots to accompany them to the ship. "They accepted with alacrity," said Sanders, "and without questioning our actions, fell in with our mood." The quartet fortified their "mood of irrepressible gaiety" with champagne toasts. "We toasted freedom," Sanders cheered. "We toasted love ... absent friends, collectively and individually," until the ship's whistle blew.

After much pleading, Sanders and Gabor eventually returned to Majorca. Production sped up. The film was completed. The Marshalls decided to visit Paris and spent more time in London. They arrived in New York in March, aboard the *Queen Mary*. Aside from living expenses, the cast members of *Black Jack* were never paid. The deal was supposed to be that salaries would be paid out of box-office revenues. Sanders, Marshall and co-star Agnes Moorehead intended to sue, but financial losses precluded any compensation to the stars.

In *Black Jack*, Sanders, a dope smuggler, has a surprise reunion with his old buddy Marshall, a medical researcher, who is actually an investigator for the U.S. Federal Bureau of Narcotics. Also aboard this caper is a socialite drug dealer (Agnes Moorehead) posing as an undercover agent. The trio find themselves in Majorca, waiting for an opportune moment to fulfill their respective ambitions. As nobody is who they appear to be, the film is filled with unexpected twists and turns. For Marshall fans, his spontaneous homage to Shakespeare proved intoxicating, as he steps outside his hotel room, looks up to see Moorehead on the balcony above, and revels, "But soft! What light through yonder window breaks? It is the east, and Juliet is the sun ... ." His eloquence with the Bard's words undoubtedly would have made him one of theater's most memorable Romeos.

Black Jack is considered one of director Julien Duvivier's lesser efforts. It was finally released in the U.S. in 1952 as *Captain Black Jack*. *The New York Times* summed it up as an "absurd and trashy little melodrama." In hindsight, the combination of scams and sarcasm keep the film afloat. *Black Jack*, like James Bond movies, holds the attention despite the implausibility. Marshall waited another year before facing the big-screen camera. In the meantime, television beckoned.

On his way home to Los Angeles, Marshall visited Toronto. He was asked to narrate the United Nations broadcast of *Tomorrow for Two*, based on a true story of a young couple detained in an Austrian displacement camp. Eventually, they relocate to Canada with the help of the United Nations International Refugee Organization (IRO). At the time of the broadcast, the IRO was assisting close to 10 million refugees stranded in Europe. As narrator of the half-hour broadcast, Marshall offered the closing statement:

> It would take hours to tell of the thousands upon thousands of people hoping to be resettled. By understanding their problems, remembering their story, you can help the IRO and United Nations bring a brighter tomorrow not just to two but to thousands.

Following a hectic seven months, Bart and Boots arrived back in Hollywood, where he celebrated his sixtieth birthday in the hospital. Louella Parsons gave no specifics other than that Bart's daughter Ann paid him a visit. By October 1950, Marshall was ready to tackle television. He signed to star in a "live" production of *Airflyte Theatre* for CBS. Prior to the telecast, Bart made his TV debut in a dramatic segment for *The Ken Murray Show*. The *Airflyte* episode was based on O. Henry's *Municipal Report*, in which Marshall played a magazine editor who visits Nashville, only to become an accessory, after the fact, to murder.

Marshall was no fan of "live TV," especially after a presentation of *The Philadelphia Story*, in which he and Mary Astor played parents of bride-to-be Dorothy McGuire. McGuire, Marshall and John Payne muffed a few lines. Marshall concluded, "No one can give a good performance 'live.' The mechanical odds are too great." Bart's co-stars from the 1930's added to the chorus. George Brent told *TV Guide*, "I tried just one 'live' show, a *Climax!*, and that was my first and last one." Brent complained about the abundance of cameras and cables actors had to contend with. Kay Francis gave up her career after tripping over a dolly track on a "live" broadcast of *Strike it Rich* (CBS) in 1954. She sustained a fracture, and sued the producers $150,000.[389]

Anne of the Indies — A rum-sodden Marshall attends lady pirate Jean Peters (20th Century-Fox)

Marshall's first full-length feature in Technicolor, *Anne of the Indies* (1951), was about a swashbuckling lady pirate (Jean Peters). It was strictly for the younger set. Bart was aboard ship as a rum-sodden doctor who attends to his lady's physical and emotional wounds, or, as *The New York Times* put it, "clucks over her like a nervous hen." Bosley Crowther's review scoffed that Peters had "the swashbuckling airs of a lass in Miss Twitt's Finishing School." The reputable French director, Jacques Tourneur, made no special effort to make the proceedings believable. Off-screen, Marshall was being compensated by, not rum, but Schenley's Fine Whiskey, serving as their spokesperson. "For an enchanting evening ... I enjoy Schenley," Marshall enthused in numerous ads.

In April 1951, Marshall was back in the hospital. He checked in at Cedars of Lebanon for a minor hernia operation. Following surgery, he developed a blood clot and was placed in an oxygen tent. On May 7, Boots at his bedside, Marshall's condition was reported as "critical."[390] Two days later, he improved and was listed in "fair condition." After a few weeks, he was able to resume broadcasts for *The Man Called X*.

By November, Marshall felt well enough to co-star with daughter Sarah, on TV's popular *Robert Montgomery Presents*. The episode, *An Inspector Calls*, was based on the 1945 play by J.B Priestley. Marshall, an investigator, tries to solve the suicide of a young working-class factory girl. He discovers that she had been exploited and abused by several members of an upper-class British family. The play was a scathing critique of the hypocrisies of English society, and reflected Priestley's socialist political views. Long Island critic John Lester raved, "It was about as satisfying as anything I've seen on TV in a long time. Marshall was splendid ... and performed strongly."[391]

The Man Called X went off the air after eight years, but Marshall kept busy guest-starring in radio programs such as *Suspense*, in which he essayed the mad scientist in *Frankenstein*. He and Deborah Kerr did a *Screen Guild Theater* revival of *Michael and Mary*. Bart offered his professional swansong to Somerset Maugham, for *Theater of Romance* (CBS) in which he narrated the author's short story, *Red*—a reflection on idyllic love. For TV, Marshall committed himself to host a half-hour suspense drama series, *The Unexpected*. Critic John Crosby found the premier episode "horribly complicated and hopelessly dull." Even so, *The Unexpected* lasted for a total of 39 episodes.[392]

Friday, June 13, 1952. Wedding bells were ringing for Sarah Lynn Marshall and theatrical production designer Melvin Bourne, at New York City's Little Church Around the Corner. The church had tied the matrimonial knot for theatrical folk for over eighty years. The couple, had known each other for a few weeks. Following the ceremony, Bart and Edna beamed approvingly alongside the newlyweds. *The Brooklyn Eagle* captioned a photo of the happy quartet, "Love Laughs at Jinx"—as in Friday the 13th.

CHAPTER ELEVEN

June 13, 1952 — Edna and Bart join newlyweds Sarah and Melvin Bourne at New York's Little Church Around the Corner

Bart's next release for the big screen was Otto Preminger's sleek, celluloid misfire, *Angel Face* (1953). He played a British novelist, and father of a psychopathic daughter (Jean Simmons). Unwittingly, he sums up his daughter's character over a game of chess. "You little beast," he smiles. It's checkmate—his king is dead. Simmons is a disturbed young lady, who wants to murder her wealthy stepmother. Marshall himself had become lax with his writing, while spending his American wife's fortune. "Charles," she tells him, "at times your charm wears dangerously thin." The couple are put out of their misery after Simmons messes with the gearshift, which plunges the family car over the side of a cliff. Simmons, understandably, refers to her own sports car as a "broomstick."

Robert Mitchum, almost as unlikeable as Simmons, sees right through her, but hangs around for a few obligatory smooches in the moonlight. Why? No real reason except to keep the Freudian plot boiling. However, things remain at room temperature, even when they face a murder trial. Mitchum rides along on Simmons' broomstick, and pays the consequences. The only realistic character in *Angel Face* is Mona Freeman, who plays

Mitchum's girlfriend. Freeman recognizes Simmons' machinations, steps aside, and keeps her integrity, which makes her all the more interesting. As written, Simmons faced an impossible task to make her character believable.

Jean Simmons and Marshall play checkers in Otto Preminger's *Angel Face* (RKO)

More compelling than the film, was an incident that took place on the set. Mitchum was required to slap Simmons' face. After several takes, he refused. Preminger threw a fit. On the following take, Mitchum turned around and slapped Preminger, asking if that's the way he wanted it done. Preminger asked producer Howard Hughes to fire Mitchum. Hughes refused. *Angel Face* was based on an actual 1947 murder trial in Newport Beach. The scenarists (and Preminger) tampered with real events, and critics found the end result less than riveting. *The New York Times* mentioned the "fuzzy character motivations," and called the film "an exasperating blend of genuine talent … and turgid psychological claptrap." French director Jean-Luc Godard, on the other hand, included it among his top ten favorite American sound films.

※

In July 1952, Roberto Rossellini sent publicist Joe Steele to Hollywood to persuade Marshall to co-star with Ingrid Bergman in the film *Duo*. The project was scheduled to begin filming in October. Dorothy Manners reported that Steele returned to Rome with Marshall's terms, and "the deal was practically sealed." The story, by French novelist Colette, focused on a middle-aged man and his high-spirited, unfaithful wife.³⁹³ Before filming began, Rossellini learned that the rights to Colette's novel had been sold. More's the pity. Marshall surrendered his talent to make back-to-back exploitation films that catered to the science-fiction craze of the 1950's.

Marshall and astronaut son William Lundigan in *Riders to the Stars* (1954) (UA)

While the U.S. government was failing to send manned rockets into space, Ivan Tors Productions successfully launched three, Herbert Marshall in charge. *Riders to the Stars* (1954) focused on scientist Marshall's obsession to capture meteors and bring them back to earth. He's even willing to sacrifice the life of his astronaut son (William Lundigan). Lundigan's obsession is the female scientist involved with the project (Martha Hyer). The moment Lundigan sets eyes on her buxom figure, he remarks to a fellow astronaut, "Speaking of jets!" Hyer gets to serve coffee and reward hero Lundigan with inevitable fade-out kisses. *The New York Times* summed it all up as, "pseudo-scientific mumbo-jumbo." Final scenes for *Riders to the Stars* were held up when Marshall injured his good leg during filming. He fared better than a technician who had his hand amputated after an explosion, and the crew member who lost his life trying to save a space suit that caught on fire.³⁹⁴

Between films for Ivan Tors, Marshall created chilling momentum and suspense in Daphne du Maurier's *The Birds* for *Lux Radio Theater*. He played an English journalist who observes the skies of Dover becoming "alive with birds." "They were out there waiting ... waiting, for what?" he asks himself. Radio alerts answer his question, warning that flocks of black clouds were attacking people countrywide. In 2005, author Harry Heuser praised, "The 1953 production, starring Herbert Marshall, was probably one of the most imaginatively sound staged melodramas ever to be presented on the *Lux* program."[395] The success of the broadcast certainly motivated Alfred Hitchcock's great film successes, *The Birds* (1963). Marshall mused that he was "scarcely the star of the piece." "The gulls and the gannets," he quipped, "villains that they were, ran the whole show."

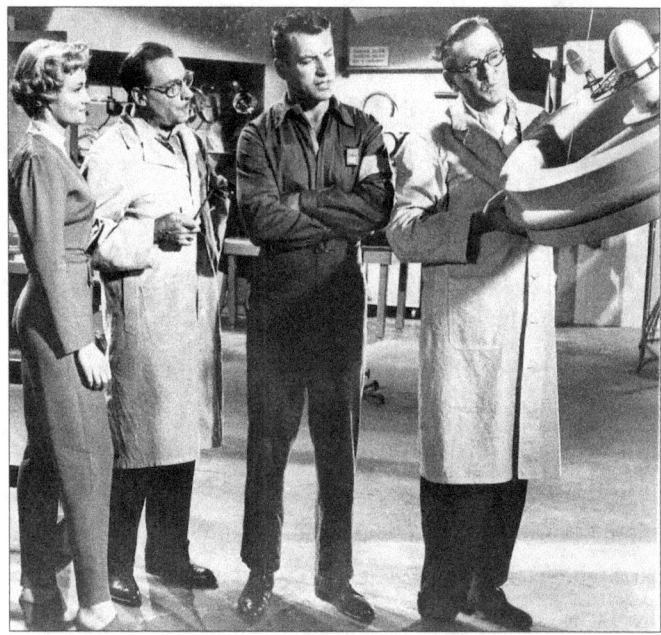

Marshall puckers up for *Gog* (1954), with Constance Dowling, Philip Van Zandt and Richard Egan (UA)

Marshall's second sci-fi film (shot in 15 days) may have been enhanced by 3-D, but suffered an overabundance of scientific gadgets and jargon. *Gog* (1954) takes place inside a secret underground lab in the Nevada desert. Marshall and six other scientific "brains" are usurped by their own radio-active creation, a computerized super-brain that monitors two robots, Gog and Magog—associated with Biblical prophesies of doom and danger. Richard Egan shows up as a scientific investigator from Washington D.C. He treats one hospitalized lab worker, overexposed to radium, as if she had a hangover. "The doctor says it isn't serious," he tells her, "just a little too much radiation." (In 1954, the Atomic Energy Commission dished out the same message, "There is no danger." Radioactive fallout left a legacy of leukemia, lymphoma, thyroid cancer, bone cancer, and brain tumors.)

Marshall discovers that the codes controlling the super-brain have been hacked by foreigners (albeit Russians). For a "feel good" ending, Marshall announces the launch of a satellite that would allow the almighty U.S. to conquer space and monitor all activity on earth. If anything, *Gog* helped reinforce the fear that fueled the Cold War. *The New York Times* summed up, "*Gog* is utter nonsense." Director Herbert L. Strock recalled an incident involving Marshall, who was concerned about his limp being too obvious. Strock, unaware that Marshall had an artificial leg, laughed it off, saying it was "a good gimmick." Marshall gave him a look. "Gimmick? With this pain, I'd hardly call it a gimmick." Strock agonized, "I will never forget that for as long as I live. I felt terrible, I apologized, and he, being the charming English gentleman he was, understood."[396]

The Marshall legacy moved into the next generation on September 16, 1954. Sarah Lynn gave birth to Timothy Marshall Bourne, in New York City. Bart told the good news to Louella Parsons, who promptly reported, "A happy Herbert Marshall telephoned to say that he is a grandfather."[397] In years to come, Timothy would carry on the family tradition in the performing arts, only this time, behind the camera.

Guest appearance on *What's My Line?*
November 28, 1954 (CBS)

CHAPTER 12
"Goodness, after all, is the greatest force in the world and he's got it"

- closing line from *The Razor's Edge* (1946)

On November 28, 1954, Marshall signed in as the "mystery guest" on TV's *What's My Line?* The panelists, all blindfolded, asked pertinent (or impertinent) questions to track down the identity of the celebrity visitor. When columnist Dorothy Kilgallen asked, "Would you describe yourself as a character man?" Marshall, cleared his throat, and hesitantly replied, "The day has come." Indeed, Marshall was relegated to fifth billing for his next two screen outings. Both "character" roles allowed him to step into Renaissance England.

The Black Shield of Falworth (1955) offered swashbuckling men in tights, and the courtly ladies who practiced the art of indifference to lure them into matrimony. Based on the 1891 novel *Men of Iron*, the film starred a youthful Tony Curtis and his charming wife Janet Leigh. Marshall, regally robed, was on hand as Leigh's father, The Earl of Mackworth, who enables Curtis to regain his family title, as well as the hand of Leigh. A Dallas critic aptly concluded that the film was designed "to make the younger set happy," then added, "There is still nobody better than Marshall when it comes to reading the King's English." Amid clashing swords and romantic swooning, one can detect a smirk lurking behind every well-spoken syllable that Marshall uttered. He appeared to be enjoying himself.

The Black Shield of Falworth (1955) with Tony Curtis (Universal)

Reunited with Bette Davis in *The Virgin Queen* (20th Century-Fox)

CHAPTER TWELVE

Bart recalled his first day on the set, when a young publicist dropped by. "I was just getting myself calmed down enough to go into the first scene," Marshall explained, "when a chap stuck his head in my dressing room. I wasn't quite in the mood ... but the fellow did have a job to do. I invited him in. 'Mr. Marshall,' he said, 'tell me have you thought at all about retiring?'" The actor was dumbfounded. "What kind of greeting is that," he asked, "for a man just starting a new picture?" Marshall never considered retirement as an option.

In February 1955, Marshall contracted for a role in *Sir Walter Raleigh* starring Richard Todd, which went through a sex-change to become *The Virgin Queen* starring Bette Davis. The script was altered to please the actress, who had been off screen for three years. Davis had previously played Elizabeth I in *The Private Lives of Elizabeth and Essex* (1939). She was ready to sink her teeth deeper into the role, as well as into anyone who got in her way. In 2015, Joan Collins (who played Elizabeth's lady-in-waiting) said of Davis, "She was horrible to work with."[398] In his memoirs, Richard Todd mentioned having to inform Davis that they would have to reshoot a scene due to an error on his part. "Bette ... shouted, 'You Bastard!'," said Todd. "I really loved working with her."[399]

Marshall lends a note of authenticity as Lord Leicester of the queen's court. He stands tall, regal, and his gait is solid and sure. Words easily trip off his tongue. "God help your pride should you find favor with the Queen," he warns Raleigh, who is determined to acquire ships to sail to the New World. Raleigh wins her majesty's favor, but when Elizabeth learns that he has impregnated her lady-in-waiting (Collins), she is consumed with rage and gives Raleigh a dressing down. It required no special effort on Davis' part. She later recalled that her husband Gary Merrill and son Michael visited the set. "Mikey turned to Gary with a puzzled face," said Davis, "and asked, 'Why is mummy yelling at that man instead of you?'"[400]

Dallas critic Frank Gagnard admitted to having "an enjoyable time watching Bette Davis chew up the CinemaScope screen." "*The Virgin Queen* takes a comic strip attitude toward history," advised Gagnard, "so suspend disbelief, ignore the facts." While the imperious Davis captured the spirit of Elizabeth I, Marshall, noted one Milwaukee critic, was "smooth as always in the role of an elder statesman." Another review pointed to "Herbert Marshall, suave as ever. You'll know him by his voice behind that face full of hair."

※

In the fall of 1955, it was a clean-shaven Bart, and a smiling Boots, who debarked from the *Queen Mary* at Southampton. A reporter for *The Sketch*, London's weekly journal, was inspired to ask the actor, "How have you remained so magnificently, implacably, unmistakably British?" Marshall responded pleasantly, "I *am* British." While visiting his homeland, Marshall moved up to third-billing in two low-budget films.

Wicked as They Come (1956) focused on the glamorous Arlene Dahl, who uses men like stepping stones as she reaches for diamonds and dry martinis. Marshall, an advertising executive, is easily compromised by Dahl's charms, and becomes her sugar daddy until she nabs his father-in-law—the company president. Dahl's luck runs out when she mistakes her elderly hubby for a blackmailer, and shoots him. She is charged with murder and sent to prison, where she offers, as one Boston critic discerned, "the pale and noble look of a woman ... suffering from a severe cold."[401] *Cue* magazine thought the film, "Rather ridiculous." Marshall's young wife in this noir-ish melodrama was actor Clive Brook's daughter, Faith.

Film historian Jeanine Basinger points out that while the males in *Wicked as They Come* use deception to gain power, it is deemed unacceptable for a woman to do the same. "Taking on power," writes Basinger, is "Dahl's real crime."[402] As Dahl's character puts it, "You men just don't like it, do you, when your dirty game is played back?" Dahl, in fact, sued Columbia Pictures for a million dollars after she saw the sexy, composite photos of her being used in promoting the film. She claimed she never posed for them.[403] The New York Supreme Court deemed Dahl as being "hypertensive." The case was dismissed. The "dirty game" of advertising remained intact.

Marshall went directly into *The Weapon* (1956), with Lizbeth Scott

CHAPTER TWELVE

and Steve Cochran. Scott portrayed a war-widow whose young son discovers a handgun among the ruins of post-war London. The boy accidentally shoots a playmate and runs away, weapon in hand. The bullet retrieved from the wounded child, provides a clue to a decade-old unsolved murder. The plot centered on investigators Cochran and Marshall getting to the boy, before the murderer does. *The Weapon* grips the attention, before taking too many twists and turns, including a contrived romantic interlude for Scott and Cochran. The *New York Post* concluded, "it goes haywire." *Harrison Reports* deemed it a "suitable supporting feature" for double-bills.

Marshall returned to England to make *The Weapon* with Lizabeth Scott, George Cole, and John Horsley (Republic)

Lizabeth Scott was undergoing her own private drama. England provided a brief respite after the scandal magazine *Confidential* ran a story about her being one of Hollywood's "baritone babes." On a trip to Paris, the report detailed, the actress "took up with Frede [Frédérique Baule], that city's most notorious Lesbian queen and the operator of a nightclub devoted exclusively to entertaining deviates like herself." In 1955, Scott and her attorney, Jerry Giesler, sued the tabloid for $2,500,000.[404] They lost on a technicality.[405] Film historian James Robert Parish points out, "The exposé ... nearly ended Lizabeth's professional career."

Bart was back in New York in time for the Broadway opening of *Ponder Heart*, in which daughter Sarah had an important role. "Daddy told me he was very pleased with me," cheered Sarah. "That's high praise in our family ... when everyone around is a pro." On stage, she played the naive child bride of an eccentric older man (David Wayne). Wayne voiced admiration for his young co-star. "She's the finest actress I've ever worked with," he admitted. Richard Watts Jr., for the *New York Post*, concurred. "There should be special praise for the credibility, sympathy and humor of Sarah Marshall. To capture one of these qualities would have been commendable; to combine them as she does is a notable accomplishment." Asked how she managed to capture the simple look of a child bride, Sarah answered, "I just let my jaw drop. My mother used to scold me for doing it. 'You look like an idiot,' she would say."[406] Sarah's relationship with her mother wasn't an easy one.

In September 1956, Edna and Sarah were to play mother and daughter in the British comedy *The Reluctant Debutante*, opening at Henry Miller's Theatre. Fresh from an Emmy-nominated performance with Noel Coward in *This Happy Breed* (CBS), Edna took charge during rehearsals. Sarah, understandably, was nervous at the prospect, and later recalled that when she made her grand entrance, the first thing she heard was Edna yell, "Okay, stop! *Darling* ... ." "Her eyes rolled to the heavens," said Sarah. "It was awful. I did not know what to do with my hands. I didn't know how to say ... probably the line was 'Good Morning, Mommy.' I couldn't do it. And, it was a hell-of-a-good chance for me."[407] When Best fell ill and dropped out, Sarah felt it best to follow suit. Producer Gilbert Miller pulled strings to get the actresses from the London production to fly to New York. Best never appeared on stage again. Her husband, Nat Wolfe, later volunteered, "She had an old-fashioned nervous breakdown."[408]

For the time being, Bart contented himself with television appearances. He charmed Spring Byington by appearing as himself on her popular series *December Bride*. For *Lux Video* he played the psychiatrist in *Now Voyager*, which Claude Rains portrayed in the classic Bette Davis film. Off-beat humor was the focus for Marshall's appearance on *The George Gobel Show*, in which he played a British submarine commander. Two of Bart's best TV offerings were for *The Alfred Hitchcock Hour*.

1958 — *Little White Frock* (Alfred Hitchcock) with Jacqueline Mayosee

Hitchcock introduced the episodes (directed by Herschel Daugherty): *Bottle of Wine* (1957) and *Little White Frock* (1958). In *Bottle of Wine*, Marshall played a middle-aged judge whose young wife opts to take a lover (Robert Horton). Marshall invites the boyfriend to share a bottle of sherry, then informs him that it has a secret ingredient: poison. In a surprise turn, the boyfriend unintentionally kills his host. *Little White Frock* was a *tour de force* for Marshall, as a veteran actor who invites a producer and his wife over for dinner. He announces his retirement, then involves them in a highly personal and tragic story, which they completely fall for until he confesses that it was his audition for a role in the producer's upcoming play. "Frankly," he tells them, "I want work." It was refreshing to see Marshall take center stage at this point in his career—a testament to his talent—a break from minor roles and films that that are easily forgotten.

Not long after *Bottle of Wine* aired, Marshall headed to New York where Sarah's play *Visit to a Small Planet*, by Gore Vidal, was getting raves. She had the role of a college student who studies art, but majors in sex. Bart and Sarah were dining out one evening with Philip Coolidge, who played her on-stage father. Sarah brought up a scene where she is being kissed by co-star Conrad Janis. "I curl my toes during the kiss, and moan a bit," she explained, before turning to Coolidge and warning, "if you don't come on stage sooner than you've been doing, I won't be responsible for what happens."[409] Coolidge turned a deaf ear. It wasn't long before Sarah left her husband Mel Bourne, and relocated to Essex House, a luxury hotel on Central Park South. On June 13, their fifth wedding anniversary, Bourne sued for divorce on grounds of adultery.

In Manhattan Supreme Court, Bourne testified that between scenes in *Visit to a Small Planet*, Sarah and Janis had tête-à-têtes in her dressing room—behind a locked door. She may have been trying to stay in character, but Bourne was having none of it, and named Janis as co-respondent. News reports made a point of saying, "Sarah's father is film star Herbert Marshall." While Sarah and Conrad never married, they remained lifelong friends.

✾

While in New York, Marshall filmed *Stage Struck* (1958), a remake of the Katharine Hepburn film, *Morning Glory* (1933). He essayed the veteran English actor previously played by C. Aubrey Smith. Susan Strasberg, daughter of legendary drama coach Lee Strasberg, took the role of a young Broadway hopeful. The opening scene has Marshall offering Strasberg his undivided attention inside a producer's office. He is amused by and sensitive to her euphoria for "the theater"—as well as the stage name she has selected for herself: Eva Lovelace. "I'm in favor of anything that gives you confidence," he says reassuringly. At an opening night party Lovelace determines (after too much champagne) to climb the stairs and do the balcony scene from *Romeo & Juliet*. Marshall comes to her rescue, on cue, as Romeo, encouraging her to complete the scene, and impress onlookers. Henry Fonda, as the producer, and Christopher Plummer (making his screen debut), a playwright, share romantic feelings for Lovelace.

Stage Struck (1958) with stage struck Susan Strasberg, and producer Henry Fonda (RKO)

While the plot was nothing new, director Sidney Lumet and veteran photographer Franz Planer offer a virtual love-letter to New York City. Strasberg's enthusiasm frequently oozes over the top, but, like her character, she was still maturing. Marshall received high praise as the understanding elder. *Commonweal* magazine thought him "first-rate." D.C.'s *Evening Star* complimented Marshall's ability to "shed warmth on every corner of *Stage Struck* he occupies." In his 2008 autobiography Christopher Plummer recalled, "I remember how impressed I was with Herbert 'Bart' Marshall's smoothness as an actor, his effortless technique and his very great personal charm." Plummer mentioned Marshall's amputation and resulting nerve damage. "What courage he exhibited," wrote Plummer, "never letting us be aware for an instant that he was suffering permanent pain."[410]

Bart and Boots headed to Washington D.C., where he narrated a thirteen-part television series about the Federal Civil Defense Administration (FCDA). The agency, a Cold War program, was designed to prepare citizens for nuclear attack. A private luncheon was held in Marshall's honor, attended by British Ambassador Harold Caccia. Many felt the FCDA misled the public into believing they could survive a nuclear war. School children were drilled to hide under desks in case of a nuclear bomb. They became known as the "Duck and Cover" generation. In his suite at D.C.'s Woodner Hotel, Marshall explained that he was no longer fighting to stay on top. If he had a pet peeve, it was TV's teleprompters. He preferred learning his lines beforehand. In one instance, (Hitchcock's *Bottle of Wine*) he had no choice. "It fell to me," he complained, "to deliver some long soliloquies from Aristotle and Sophocles, a couple of the boys I'm not particularly friendly with."[411]

Marshall offers a smashing performance in *The Fly* with Vincent Price (20th Century-Fox)

It seems incongruous for someone like Marshall, that his best remembered film from the 1950's would be the science-fiction cult classic, *The Fly* (1958). The film, in Cinemascope and Technicolor, with class-A production values, was an unexpected hit for 20th Century-Fox, reaping over three million dollars profit. While *The Fly* may be remembered for its camp appeal, James Clavell's screenplay was a thought-provoking query into the ethical ramifications of scientific exploration. As Police Inspector Charas, Marshall helps investigate the purported death of Andre Delambre, a scientist who experimented with teleportation. Charas learns that Delambre had accidently merged his body parts with that of a common fly. As the fly's brain begins to take over, Delambre talks his wife into a mercy killing. One memorable scene, near the end, has Charas and Delambre's brother, Francois (Vincent Price), observe the human-headed fly caught in a spider web, crying for help. Price later recalled,

> So here we were, Herbert Marshall and I co-starring with a talking fly, and trying to speak our lines while staring at a spider's web. We'd start to play the scene, and I'd say, "Well, Inspector." And, the little voice would say, "Help me!" Then, Herbert would say, "Well, Monsieur, I think that we should .... ." "Help me! Help me!" Well, finally Herbert said, "Help you? The Hell with you, help *us*." Herbert and I kept ruining the takes by ... laughing ourselves sick.[412]

Marshall had the satisfaction of lifting a heavy rock and smashing the human fly, before a ravenous spider gulps it down. *The New York Times* recognized the film's adult appeal, rating *The Fly* as "one of the better, more restrained entries of the 'shock' school. Most appealing is the compassion blended in with the suspense." Dallas critic Tony Zoppi acknowledged that the inspector was "beautifully underplayed by Herbert Marshall." While *The Fly* did little for Marshall's career, it firmly established Vincent Price's identification with the horror genre. Marshall was paged to repeat his role in a less-impressive sequel, *Return of the Fly* (1959). He was too ill, emotionally and physically, to participate. Tragedy had struck home on December 1, 1958, when Bart's beloved Boots passed away at the age of forty-six.

※

In May 1958, one of Marshall's dearest friends, Ronald Colman, had died of pneumonia. Marshall attended the funeral in Santa Barbara, and confided to reporters, "His death will mean a great loss."[413] Boots was in ill health herself, suffering from a chronic throat condition. On the afternoon of November 30, her condition suddenly became worse, and she was admitted to St. John's Hospital in Santa Monica. Throughout the night, her physician and a throat specialist "worked feverishly to save her life." She died the following day, Bart at her bedside. His only comment at the time was, "Thank God, she died peacefully."[414] Funeral services were held privately at Pierce Brothers in Beverly Hills. News reports mentioned that her adopted twins, Jill and Stephen Cagney, were living with the Marshalls on North Foothill Road.

Later that December, Bart received an offer to return to the Broadway stage. Producer Harold Bromley approached the actor about starring as the British Prime Minister in a political satire by Harry Tarvin, *Goodwill Ambassador*. Bart signed for the role, and was preparing to fly to Ireland for rehearsals and a scheduled premier. A few days before departure, Marshall ended up in the same hospital where Boots passed away. He was reported in fair condition, and spent ten days recovering from pneumonia and pleurisy. In the meantime, Dennis King took the role in *Goodwill Ambassador*, which never reached Broadway.

More sadness entered Bart's life when Eric Blore—his friend of fifty years—died of a heart attack on March 2, 1959. Blore had been retired since 1956, following a stroke. Tragedy struck once again in May, when Edna Best suffered a heart attack and was listed in critical condition. Following the death of her husband that March, she had been living in a

CHAPTER TWELVE

New York sanatorium. Major surgery for a brain tumor was required, and it wasn't until October that Edna felt well enough to chat on the phone. Before long, she opted to return to England to reside in a convalescent home near her twin sons who were in the advertising business.[415]

Amid Marshall's marathon of grief, he was asked to be a pallbearer for friend and director Edmund Goulding, who passed away in December 1959. A heavy, mahogany coffin was to be hoisted by Bart, and fellow actors David Niven and Reginald Gardiner. Other pallbearers included one gigantic fellow who Niven described as having "Tarzanesque proportions" and a lisp. As they proceeded to carry the casket 300 yards *uphill*, Bart bent over to adjust his prosthesis, jesting, "Just shifting into 'climb'."[416] Before arriving at the designated spot, Marshall and Gardiner could take no more. The coffin was set down. More mishaps ensued. Niven wagered, that Goulding's "wild and wooly sense of the ridiculous" would have appreciated the unintentional antics of his handpicked pallbearers.

⁂

Marshall returned to acting, guest-starring in two 1960 episodes of *Adventures in Paradise* (ABC). In the detective series *Michael Shayne*, he played a former silent film director, who wraps up the hour by admitting to murder and taking his own life or, as his character defines it, "a permanent cure for heart trouble." Jack Kruschen, as a film producer, chimes in to say, "Beautiful, the way that man speaks!"

Marshall's screen appearances in 1960 were minor roles in *College Confidential*, and the Doris Day drama *Midnight Lace*. For these, he received 7th and 6th billing, respectively. Louella Parsons told fans, "After seeing Herbert Marshall dining alone and looking unhappy recently, I'm delighted that Bart is taking a key role in *College Confidential*. For a long time it seemed as though he couldn't get over the death of his wife, Boots. They had found such wonderful companionship in their marriage." By the time the film was released, Bart had a new companion and wife. On April 25, 1960, he married Dee Anne Cummings Kahmann, a thirty-eight-year old buyer for a department store. The couple opted for a quiet ceremony in the chambers of Los Angeles Judge LeRoy Dawson. Dee Anne, a Montana native, had two previous marriages.

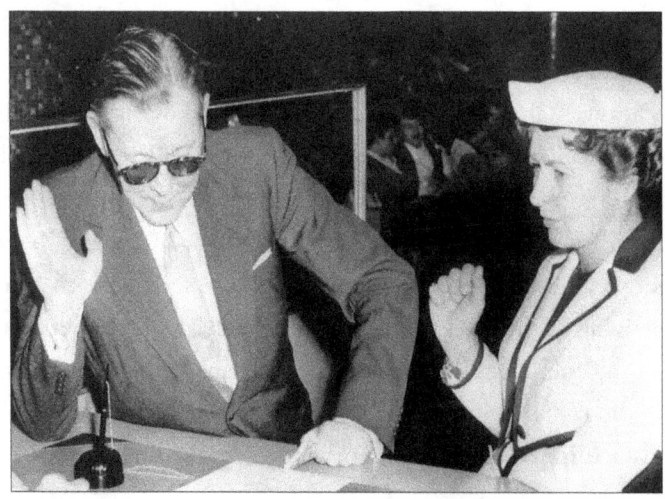

April 25, 1960 — Marshall marries Dee Anne Cummings Kahmann

College Confidential — low-budget exploiter with Steve Allen and Jayne Meadows (far left) (Universal)

CHAPTER TWELVE

On the set of *College Confidential* director Albert Zugsmith brought out a magnum of champagne to celebrate Bart's 50th year as an actor, as well as his first (and last) dive into cinematic sexploitation, replete with buxom babes. Steve Allen starred as a sociology professor conducting a controversial campus sex survey. As department head, Marshall comes to Allen's defense after he inadvertently had shown students a porn flick. Allen ends up in court, pleading for academic freedom. *The New York Times* summed it all up as "movie claptrap." Director Zugsmith, money in pocket, followed this opus with *Sex Kittens Go to College* (1960). In a 2002 career article about Marshall, writer Brad Richards acknowledged that the film "marked the nadir of his film career."[417] For Marshall there was no place to go but up.

Midnight Lace Marshall escorts Doris Day to the dance floor in this taut thriller. Rex Harrison and Myrna Loy look on (UI)

In the fall of 1960, Marshall co-starred with his daughter Sarah in ABC's *Hong Kong*, starring Rod Taylor. The episode *Colonel Cat*, filled with blackmail and murder, involved a wealthy banker (Marshall), who is reluctant to reveal that his son is a traitor and renegade. The opening scene has a lighter touch, as Marshall jests, to a group of party guests, that Sarah is "a shameless creature ... no subtlety, no mystery at all!" The father-daughter duo play well off of each other. In subsequent scenes, Sarah empathizes with the dilemma her father faces and encourages him to come forth with the brutal facts.

Midnight Lace (1960) on the set with Myrna Loy

It was Marshall's good fortune to be cast in producer Ross Hunter's slick thriller *Midnight Lace*. London was the film's locale, but cameras were confined to Universal studios where the film was shot during the Spring of 1960. A menacing pea-soup London fog surrounds Doris Day while she is tormented by death threats. Her husband (Rex Harrison) puts in a call to Scotland Yard. The line-up of suspects included John Gavin, Roddy McDowall, and Marshall. As treasurer for Harrison's firm, Marshall is suspected of embezzlement in order to pay off his bookie. The one bright spot is Myrna Loy, a middle-aged swinger, who plays Day's Aunt Bea, *and* Marshall's former love interest. *The New York Times* found Marshall to be "smooth," and enjoyed Loy dropping in to "drop a few glittering gags." Pundits over the years have unfairly focused on Day's elaborate wardrobe in lieu of appreciating her emotionally honest portrayal. In 2014, film critic Glenn Erickson acknowledged: "That *Midnight Lace* works as well as it does is due to Ms. Day's committed performance."

Loy recalled in her 1987 autobiography, "That was the last time I saw Herbert Marshall, a most charming man, who had been part of the British crowd that came to my Hidden Valley house." She mentioned Marshall's suave performances—his handicap—"you would never have known it, even in *Midnight Lace*, when he had become somewhat feeble. It was terribly sad to see, as it is with so many friends as one gets on."[418] For his next film, Marshall was confined to a wheelchair. *Fever in the Blood* (1961) was a rambling mixture of murder and political corruption behind a gubernatorial race. Marshall played an ex-governor who, as one critic put it, "is dragged into the story for no particular reason and one gets the impression that Marshall thinks so too."[419]

※

Marshall got out of his wheel-chair and proceeded to do a strenuous three-month east-coast tour of the Broadway hit, *A Majority of One*—his first stage role in twenty-one years. Prior to that, he filmed a TV pilot, *An Evening with Herbert Marshall*. Bette Davis agreed to be his first guest star, and took a day off from filming *Pocketful of Miracles* to bolster the first episode.[420] The pilot failed to find a sponsor. While celebrating his seventy-first birthday in New York, Marshall said that his "best gift" was visiting his daughter Sarah, who had been nominated for a Tony award for her role in *Goodbye, Charlie*.

A Majority of One involved Mrs. Jacoby, a Jewish widow, and her romance with Mr. Asano (Marshall), a wealthy Japanese widower (and Buddhist) from Tokyo. Both had experienced losses in the hands of "the enemy" during WWII—Asano lost his daughter to Hiroshima. The focus was on two individuals from different cultures, overcoming their own prejudices, and finding common ground. Dora Weissman, of the

American Yiddish theater, joined Marshall for the company tour, which opened on June 5, 1961, at Philadelphia's Playhouse in the Park. A review for the *Philadelphia Inquirer* noted that it was "warmly received by a capacity audience. Making a welcome return after a long absence ... Herbert Marshall is both quietly charming and belligerently forthright as Mr. Asano." It was pointed out that Marshall relied more on "demeanor" than make-up for the role of the Japanese businessman.

Summer 1961 tour of *A Majority of One*

There were unexpected challenges. Playhouse in the Park was built along experimental theater designs, a circular stage, and when the play reached Pocono Playhouse the cast faced restaging. One reporter noted, "Marshall worked under a handicap. His little known and nearly forgotten leg prosthesis was the cause for some concern during the re-rehearsals."[421] Throughout July and August *A Majority of One* toured New England, before closing at the Cape Playhouse in Dennis, Massachusetts. Author James Robert Parish was prop master during the production at the Cape. In 2016, Parish recalled assisting Marshall in the star cottage. Marshall shared with Parish what he thought to be an amusing anecdote. "Marshall told me that he was having dinner at home one night, when he heard his voice coming over the TV set. He had to look up to see which of his films it might be." Parish added,

CHAPTER TWELVE

One of my duties at the Cape Playhouse, besides props, was to help out Marshall when he wanted anything backstage. I can still visualize being in the star dressing room, bringing Marshall his drink, Scotch (I believe it was), each night before performance. He said he still got pain in his missing leg. At the end of the week of *Majority of One*, Marshall called me into his star dressing room and said, "Would you do me the honor of accepting this?" (It was a check for $10 — which back then was "real" money).[422]

In July, Marshall and Kay Francis had a reunion at Popponesset Beach. Parish recalled that aside from the gray highlights in Kay's hair, she was easily recognizable—fit, tall and regal. "She looked much the same as in her Warner Bros. days."[423] In my 2003 conversation with Kay's close friend Jetti Ames, she mentioned, "Kay used to go to Popponesset in the summertime. We'd stop and see her on our way to Nantucket. She liked to be by the sea, and salt air. She was close to Hilda Coppage [owner of the Popponesset Inn]."[424]

Television personality Irene Hennessy mentioned in one of her July columns for the *Boston American*, that she had watched Francis and Marshall lunching at Popponesset. Bart had just finished playing at Falmouth Playhouse. His meeting up with Kay made sense. When I visited Jetti Ames at her home on Nantucket, she told me that Kay held a special fondness for Marshall, with whom she had stayed in touch. It's unlikely the duo reminisced about Hollywood. Kay remained embittered about her treatment from Warner Bros. Author Parish made a point of saying that during his conversations with Francis, "She went on about not wanting to talk about the past." Jetti Ames also confirmed, "Kay lived in the *present*." No doubt Bart brought Kay up-to-date on her goddaughter Ann Marshall, a green-eyed beauty who had just turned nineteen. Both MGM and Columbia studios had shown interest in Ann, who was more interested in the art and music scene in Los Angeles. She was currently dating Phil Everly of the rock and roll duo, The Everly Brothers.

A Majority of One was a befitting stage swansong for Marshall. The play's theme reflected the compassion of the man himself. The culture clash of a Jewish woman from Brooklyn and a Japanese gentleman from the other side of the world, culminated in human understanding and love. Leonard Spigelgass, who wrote the play, had intimate knowledge and experience with these kinds of issues. In William J. Mann's *Behind The Screen: How Gays and Lesbians Shaped Hollywood 1910-1969*, he points out that "Spigelgass' scripts were ... a little different from most, a filtering of the world through the eyes of a gay Jew." [425]

※

Louella Parsons welcomed Marshall home following tour, reporting that he was back at his favorite table at the elegant French restaurant La Rue on Sunset Boulevard. After a six-month respite, Bart signed for an appearance in *Five Weeks in a Balloon* (1962). Producer Irwin Allen, nicknamed "The Master of Disaster," was at the helm of this cliché-ridden "disaster." It was loosely based on Jules Verne's 1863 yarn about an attempt to plant the British flag in West Africa and defeat a convoy of slave traders. As British Prime Minister, Marshall reroutes the expedition. While the *Dallas Morning News* thought Marshall "outstanding" in his cameo role, the film was a waste of time. Critic Glenn Erikson concluded in his 2006 review, "Human slavery is just too serious of an issue to be the subject of light-hearted adventure."[426]

In June 1962, Bart went directly into *The Caretakers* (1963), a heavy-handed melodrama in which he was the superintendent of a mental hospital. His headstrong head-nurse (Joan Crawford), teaches the art of judo to her underlings, in order that they may protect themselves from resident psychotics. The recently hired Robert Stack, has a more compassionate approach to mental illness. The bulk of the film consists of Crawford and Stack making proclamations while patient Polly Bergen runs the emotional gamut. An American Psychiatric publication from 1999 found that *The*

CHAPTER TWELVE

Caretakers "exploits the sensational aspects ... and was a strangely inappropriate film."[427] *The New York Times* found the result, "shallow, showy and cheap ... a badly commercial exploitation of very sensitive material." The "commercial exploitation" included hospital staff members drinking Pepsi-Cola, at Crawford's insistence. She was on the company's board of directors.

Judo expert Joan Crawford enjoys cocktails with Marshall in *The Caretakers* (1963) (UA)

Crawford later claimed that she allowed her old friend Bart to film close-ups before she did, as he was rather feeble. That way, Joan explained, he could go home early.[428] The *Boston Traveler* remarked, "Herbert Marshall, former film star, seems a bit tired of it all." While Marshall tolerated the on-screen bickering between Stack and Crawford, his diplomatic approach on sensitive issues made perfect sense. When he reflects upon his own youthful ambitions, it is touching. In Lawrence J. Quirk's biography of Crawford, he mentioned *The Caretakers* "dime-store psychology," but acknowledged, "[Marshall] plays very well with Joan and retains his excellent delivery, always with that impish twinkle in his eye." Marshall went directly into his next film, maneuvering around the set with no problems—looking fit and alert. Most likely, Marshall found relief working in a much better film under the helm of director John Huston. Crawford, herself, began shooting her hugely successful comeback with Bette Davis in *Whatever Happened to Baby Jane?*

John Huston paged Bart for *The List of Adrian Messenger* (1963), a clever whodunit, starring George C. Scott. Marshall's role as the head of Scotland Yard offered what one critic referred to as "sterling support." The focus was on investigator Scott's linking a series of "accidental" deaths to a specific perpetrator. Also on display was Huston's passion for fox-hunting, during the climactic scene shot on location in Ireland, where Huston lived at the time. The film boasted a list of "guest mystery stars" who were disguised by make-up artist Bud Westmore. Included in this charade were Robert Mitchum, Tony Curtis, Frank Sinatra, and Burt Lancaster. Huston later admitted, "It was basically only Mitchum who did any acting among the cameo appearances ... the rest of them had a mask made of the actor who played them. It wasn't grand theft, but it was pretty close to it."[429] Unaware of Huston's deceptive ploy, critics and audiences were entertained by what D.C. critic Harry MacArthur championed as "corking entertainment ... played with a winning tongue-and-cheek flair by a top-notch cast."[430]

In the fall of 1963, while doing a guest-spot for TV's long-running *77 Sunset Strip*, Marshall gave one of his last interviews to veteran Hollywood reporter Bob Thomas. The wit and sophistication that had catapulted Marshall to screen stardom was now passé. As he relaxed at home in red silk pajamas, scotch and soda in hand, Bart waxed nostalgic. "Somehow I miss those days. They don't seem to make my type of picture anymore." Marshall also lamented the passing of his old chums Colman, Blore, Nigel Bruce and C. Aubrey Smith, adding that, "Aubrey was the epitome of the British Empire. That is, the Empire as it was in his time, not the one that seems to have been taken over by Christine Keeler. I remember once he introduced me at a cricket game as Capt. Marshall. I don't know where on earth he got that. I was a private, a plain G.I."[431] Keeler, a topless showgirl prone to sexual shenanigans with prominent British officials, was making headlines in the infamous "Profumo affair," a scandal which rocked the British empire. As far as TV, Bart admitted, "I wouldn't want to work hard enough to carry a series."

Sarah Marshall, at the age of thirty, was also monitoring her work schedule. Following her Broadway success, *Come Blow Your Horn* (1961-62), she relocated to California. For awhile, Sarah shared a home in Encino with her sister Ann, who was following her mother Lee's footsteps as a fashion model. Sarah preferred television and movies to long Broadway runs, "because I'm lazy," she admitted. For their father, it was more a matter of managing physical pain, an arduous task as he approached his seventy-fourth year. As the amount of alcohol to ease his pain increased, so did depression. This affected Bart's ability to work, as well as his marriage. Reporter Alex Freeman divulged in March 1964, "Old-timer Herbert Marshall and his wife ... are hassling and she's gone home to momma to think things over."[432] Apparently, things were patched up before Marshall flew to New York in September to participate in a CBS TV special *The Presidency: A Splendid Misery*, in which he essayed the role of George Washington.

New York critic Rex Reed visited the CBS production center on 57th Street just as Robert Ryan arrived in a taxi to be greeted by Herbert Marshall. But, Reed put it this way,

> A strange thing happened: Abraham Lincoln stepped out of a taxi and shook hands with George Washington. The two gentlemen entered the lobby ... and into a room marked Studio B where they were joined ... by Thomas Jefferson. This illustrious assemblage ... were actors arriving for the first rehearsal of one of the new season's hour-long specials, *The Presidency: A Splendid Misery*.[433]

The script consisted of words written by former Presidents regarding the burdens of being designated chief of state. The title was taken from a remark made by Thomas Jefferson. Producer Dick Siemanowski counted on the words to speak for themselves. "The liquid voice of Herbert Marshall, a stately choice for Washington," assessed Reed, after hearing the actor utter the statement, "My station is new—I walk on untrodden ground." Robert Ryan, as Abraham Lincoln in the early stages of smallpox, offered the humorous, "Now I've got something I can give everybody." Other U.S. Presidents were portrayed by E.G. Marshall, Jason Robards, Dana Andrews, et al. Fredric March narrated. Actor Charles Siebert was offered two lines in the production—his first professional assignment. In 2015, he recalled,

> I was in very distinguished company. The most notable thing about the experience was they wanted to tape it in one take. A problem arose with one actor, Herbert Marshall, ... who had lost a leg in WWI. He read George Washington and was to be seated at a desk on a platform perhaps 6-8' high ... having to climb up to that level every time we rehearsed, then down again, then up again, until we got that one take on tape. Well, the climbing seemed to tire and exasperate this 75 [sic] year-old man and he became increasingly rattled.[434]

Siebert noted that Marshall became so agitated he had problems reading his lines, let alone remembering them. The idea of doing it in "one take" had to be set aside in order for him to complete his segment. It seems unfathomable that producer Siemanowski hadn't the foresight to provide a set which would accommodate Marshall's limitations. Despite the circumstances, critic Rick Du Brow found the end result, "a provocative, worthwhile hour."

Director Edmund Goulding had mentioned that Herbert Marshall's success as an actor pivoted around one main ingredient. "It's in his voice," said Goulding. It is ironic that in his final screen performance, Marshall was voiceless. *The Third Day*, shot early in 1965, introduced Marshall as a paralyzed stroke victim. At a crucial moment, with determination and willpower, he manages to tap his forefinger indicating that he approves of a plan that his son-in-law (George Peppard) created to save a small town industry. Marshall

CHAPTER TWELVE

had founded the company, and his conniving nephew (Roddy McDowall) is hell-bent on selling out to a conglomerate, leaving 2,300 locals unemployed. Based on a novel by Joseph Hayes, *The Third Day* translated on screen into glossy soap opera. Hayes' intriguing subplot of how corporate greed can devastate entire communities, kept being pushed aside to display the love problems of Peppard and his wife (Elizabeth Ashley), Marshall's daughter. Long flashbacks of Peppard and his pleasure-seeking mistress (Sally Kellerman), a victim of manslaughter, become tiresome. Marshall, who leaves an indelible impression, and his sister-in-law (Mona Washbourne) were the only ones who kept their dignity in this implausible opus.

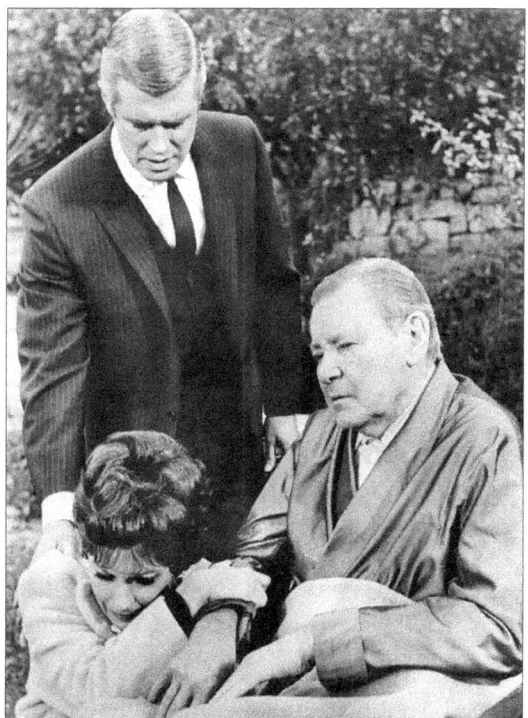

The Third Day (1965) a voiceless Marshall etches a touching farewell to his career - with George Peppard and Elizabeth Ashley (Warner Bros.)

The New York Times called *The Third Day* "... tiresome stuff. Poor Mr.

Peppard and Miss Ashley ... after suffering through this twaddle, they deserve to find another sterling script, like that of *The Carpetbaggers*." Ashley wrote in her 1979 autobiography, "I could tell from the script it was going to be a piece of Technicolor garbage, but I would be costarring with George."[435] Off screen, the Peppard-Ashley relationship blossomed into a marriage that didn't last. In 2013, film editor and critic Glenn Erickson wrote that *The Third Day* "comes alive" during the code tapping sequences between Peppard and Marshall, whose character is "brought back into the world." "It's such a great idea," said Erickson, "that we would have liked to see more of it, or at least see [Marshall] reconnecting with his wife and daughter in this way."[436]

※

Throughout the remainder of 1965 Marshall hit a downward spiral. In November, due to severe depression, he was admitted into the Motion Picture Country Hospital. Upon his release in mid-January, he returned to his home on Oakhurst Drive in Beverly Hills where he died eight days later, on Saturday, January 22, 1966. His death at 12:20 a.m. was attributed to a heart attack. Marshall's memorial service, conducted by Dr. J. Herbert Smith, pastor of All Saints Episcopal Church, was held the following Wednesday at nearby Pierce Brothers Mortuary. Pallbearers included London-born actors Reginald Gardiner, Robert Coote, Frederick Worlock, and lyricist Harold Adamson. In attendance were 150 mourners, including Raymond Massey, Charlie Ruggles, and Glynis Johns.[437] While Marshall's ashes were interred at Chapel of the Pines in Los Angeles, his spirit soared elsewhere. He had once admitted, "Somehow, I could never feel that I'm not going back to England, someday"[438]

Dallas drama critic John Rosenfield paid a lengthy tribute to Marshall the week following his death. "The motion picture lost some of its riches when Herbert Marshall died the other day," wrote Rosenfield. "He won no Academy Awards, but led a legion of imitators." Rosenfield pointed to Marshall's "fine-grained understatement," his precision of "restrained speech," and his "professional contribution to humanity." "Bart Marshall's influence on his chosen trade," concluded Rosenfield, "was as profound and historic as Charlie Chaplin's."[439] British historian Jeffrey Richards' *Visions of Yesterday* (2014) assessed:

> Herbert Marshall is one of the few actors who have ever convincingly portrayed 'goodness.' This is extremely hard to achieve. More often than not, pure 'goodness' comes out as either boring or sanctimonious. But Marshall managed to project 'goodness' and make it both sincere and likeable. It was something in the softness of his voice and his eyes. He could evoke audience sympathy even when playing villains.[440]

"Goodness, after all, is the greatest force in the world and he's got it." The words of W. Somerset Maugham were an appropriate fit for Bart Marshall. Coincidentally, Maugham passed away only a month prior to Marshall. In his last years, the author frequently thought about death. "I am like a passenger waiting for his ship at a war-time port," he wrote. "I do not know which day it will sail, but I'm ready to embark at a moment's notice."[441]

MAY 1, 1917

A twenty-six-year old soldier waited by the dock at Boulogne, "ready to embark at a moment's notice." Nearly a month had gone by since he was struck down in battle, unable to walk. His stay in an Abbeville military hospital had left him feeling numb, hopeless. Finally, the hospital ship *H. S. Jan Breydel* pulled into port. He was returning home, at last.

Top — 1943 shot of Marshall, the artist, doing a self portrait

Middle — 1935 sketch from *If You Could Only Cook* (unknown artist)

Left — 1938 sketch by caricaturist Henry Major

LEGACY
The Marshall Family

Herbert Marshall had one of the outstanding collections of illustrator/cartoonist Charles Addams, who is primarily known for *The Addams Family*. In 1950, author John O'Hara (*Pal Joey, Butterfield 8*) recalled visiting Marshall's home. "On my first visit to Bart Marshall's house I was delighted to see the many drawings he had. I said to Bart, who, by the way, draws very well himself, 'But you haven't got *my favorite* Addams.' Bart looked at me a moment, then, without asking me to tell him which drawing, he said, 'Dear John, come with me.'" O'Hara followed. "Yes, by God, he had the picture," the author marveled. O'Hara never divulged to which of Addams' drawings he was referring. Addams had created so many marvelous works since that afternoon at Marshall's home, that O'Hara could, as he put it, "no longer have a single favorite."[442] By 1957, columnist Hal Eaton reported, "Herbert Marshall owns the world's largest collection of Charles Addams originals."[443]

The wickedly funny drawings of Charles Addams, mirrors the type of irreverent wit that kept Bart Marshall in good humor. "I can always depend on them for a laugh when I need one," he confirmed.[444] In many ways, aside from a passion for drawing, the two men mirrored each other. Addams was described as a well-dressed, courtly man with back-combed hair and a gentle manner." A friend of Alfred Hitchcock, Addams was also somewhat of a lady-killer, seen accompanying Marshall's former co-stars Greta Garbo and Joan Fontaine to social functions.

When asked about her father, Sarah Marshall remarked that she never got to know him very well "until I was old enough to drink."[445] Opening up to his adult daughter over a glass of Scotch made sense for a man like Marshall, who, according to Sarah, kept his missing leg a secret from her until she was an adult. Perhaps he didn't want to cause her any worry. Ever since Bart's touring days with Marie Lohr, his war injury and amputation occasionally received news coverage. This had somehow escaped Sarah. She reminisced during a 2007 interview, "I never knew that my father had a war injury of any kind. I think that children are very brave ... if they had told me the truth it probably would have been a lot easier for me and my father."[446] Bart was very proud of Sarah's accomplishments and was an eyewitness to every play she appeared in. "Father's never missed me in anything I've ever done," Sarah reported to *Life* magazine in the fall of 1961.

The Long, Hot Summer (1958) Joanne Woodward with Sarah Marshall (20th Century Fox)

When asked about her parents, Sarah remarked, "They remained the best of friends, and I grew up almost as much a visitor at Bart's as at home with Edna."[447] Sarah found her mother to be more of a challenge. "I wanted to be an actress, I think because she was an actress. I put her on a pedestal. I never would have gone against anything she said .... And of course the resentment built and built and built. What happened was, I never could please my mother. And it's a big responsibility trying to please another human being. Huge. Especially when she was so damned right. Her way was the best way when we're talking about the theater." After Edna and Sarah's aborted plans to co-star together in 1956's *The Reluctant Debutante*, Sarah continued on Broadway through 1962. From thereon, she focused on television guest spots (*The Twilight Zone*, *Alfred Hitchcock Hour*, *Star Trek*). In 1982, Sarah carried forward her father's legacy with W. Somerset Maugham, as the attorney's wife in *The Letter*, starring Lee Remick. *The New York Times* found the TV film to be "sturdy stuff," and Sarah Marshall and the supporting cast to be "equally splendid." Sarah said that it was the combination of her famous parents and her own talent that contributed to her success. "Their names opened up a lot of doors," she admitted.

1988 — Sarah with husband Carl Held

Sarah's 1964 marriage to actor Carl Held (whom she met during the 1959-60 Broadway run of *The World of Suzie Wong*) remained a happy one. The couple lived in England from 1968-1980, doing plays and telefilms. Held had an eight year stint with the popular series *Falcon Crest*. The couple spent the 1980's dividing their time between England and Hollywood. After fifty years of marriage, Sarah, following a long battle with stomach cancer, died at the age of 80 on January 18, 2014.

Known for her flair and wit, Ann Marshall connected herself to the arts and music scene in the Los Angeles area. Early on, she was a friend of recording giant Phil Spector. Following her romance with Phil Everly, Ann's head was turned toward singer Scott MacKenzie, whose 1967 song *San Francisco-Be Sure to Wear Flowers in Your Hair* reflected the Love Generation of the 60's. Ann, called "Annie" by her friends, then fell in love with the other Everly Brother, Don. In 1970 the two were living in Don's Malibu home. In 2007, Ann reflected back. "Phil left me on my 20th birthday, and I left Don on my 30th. I sent their mother a telegram: 'Happy Mother's Day! And thank you for not having a third son.'"[448]

1970 — Ann Marshall with singer Don Everly

Ann became a lifelong friend of Michelle Phillips, who sang with the folk-rock group The Mamas and The Papas. They met while Ann was working at the trendy L.A. boutique Paraphernalia. Ann took Michelle to meet Phil Spector at his La Collina mansion in Beverly Hills. At one point Spector, "drunk as a sailor," as Phillips put it, held them both at gun point refusing to let them leave. "Don't worry about it," said Ann. "He does this all the time."[449] Keeping cool amid chaos was one of Ann's many talents, which didn't go unnoticed. Perhaps the most important connection for Ann's career was her enduring friendship with Jack Nicholson, who she met during Phillips' affair with the actor. Ann became Jack's personal secretary for close to thirty years. In her memoir, Anjelica Huston, who lived with Nicholson off and on from 1973-1990, recalled that Ann helped keep Jack's life "running smoothly." "He called his assistant, Annie Marshall, 'my staff,'" wrote Huston. "Annie was tall, dark, and pretty, brilliantly funny, neurotic, and smart as a whip."[450] Anjelica credited Annie for helping her through her relationship with Nicholson, and to finally "grow up."

Cannes 1974, Jack Nicholson, Angelica Huston, Ann Marshall, producer Gerald Ayres

Ann acted as gatekeeper for Nicholson. "No one got to Jack except through her," wrote Nicholson biographer Dennis McDougal.[451] In his memoirs, Gerald Ayres, who produced Nicholson's *The Last Detail* (1973), noted that he "adored" Ann, referring to her as, "Beautiful Ann Marshall ... she was highly effective as Jack's right hand."[452] Ann had the difficult task of keeping Jack on track. "Jack has a penchant for misplacing items," said Ann. "He can lose seven wallets in the space of a year, and it drives him out of his mind when he can't locate something."[453] Through the 1980's and early 90's Ann assisted Nicholson on such films as *Ironweed*, *Batman*, *Hoffa*, and *Wolf*. She was occasionally offered a bit role on screen. When she suffered a brain aneurism in the mid-90's and was forced to retire, Nicholson stood by and took care of her. She relocated to Aspen, Colorado, for several years. As of 2017, Ann resides in the Los Angeles area.

THE WIVES

Aside from Boots Mallory, Bart was outlived by his wives. Actress Mollie Maitland kept Marshall's name, going by Hilda "Mollie" Lloyd Marshall. Following a 1953 visit to Montreal, she listed her occupation as "Formerly on stage."[454] Mollie resided at the Stanhope Court Hotel, Kensington, London, and lived there until her death, December 24, 1973, at the age of 84.[455] Ex-wife Lee Russell remained on friendly terms with Bart and Boots. In 1952, she began dating wealthy mid-Westerner Peter J. Even. Following their 1957 marriage, Lee kept a low-profile. She went by her given name Elizabeth. The couple, who lived in Beverly Hills, would divorce in 1967. Elizabeth lived to be 91, passing away June 1, 2002 in Los Angeles. Bart's last wife, Dee Anne Marshall, never remarried, and returned to her pioneer roots near Medicine Hot Springs, Montana, to look after her mother. Dee Anne died February 27, 1983, at the age of 61.

Following his affair with Gloria Swanson, Marshall and Edna Best remained a team "in spirit" in the minds of their many fans. From 1920-1942, the couple costarred in thirteen stage productions, three films, and three radio broadcasts. As daughter Sarah mentioned, "they remained the best of friends." Best became a U.S. naturalized citizen in 1950. Following her stroke in 1959, Best returned to London. She eventually relocated to

Clinique le Mesnil, a nursing home in Geneva, Switzerland. A 1970 report stated that Edna preferred to be called Mrs. Marshall-Wolfe, never talked about her theatrical career, and rarely received guests.[456] She passed away in Geneva on September 18, 1974, at the age of 74.

Christmas 1962 — Bart surrounded by his family. Eight-year-old Timothy is next to his mother Sarah. Behind Marshall are his wife Dee Ann, son-in-law Carl Held, and daughter Ann

The legacy of Bart and Edna is now being carried forward by their grandson Timothy Marshall Bourne. "I was born, and literally stayed back stage a lot," recalled Bourne in 2013. "I have a memory of sitting at a bar at Sardi's. My mom was very close to Vincent Sardi. I remember being picked up and put on a stool and I would stay there while the show was going on. To this day I can walk on a stage and smell the old dusty duvetyne, and it brings me back."[457] The smell of duvetyne, used for creating theatrical scenes and curtains, failed to draw young Timothy into the profession. New York critic Ward Morehouse observed that at the age of five, Timothy was content to parade around in cowboy boots. His parents had joint custody and he appeared to be well adjusted.[458] "All my family was in theater," said Timothy in an 2016 interview with *Oz* magazine.

"My mom was an actress, and my grandparents were, too. I didn't want anything to do with film or theater. I felt like the people were nuts!" Bourne's remark mirrored the feelings of his grandfather Bart. "I am one actor who never wanted to be an actor," stated Marshall back in 1936. He referred to the hard work and heartache that he saw his parents endure.

Timothy's turnabout regarding "theater," took its own spin. "So, I cooked from a very early age until my early 20's," he explained. "I was a chef's apprentice in France." In 1981, Bourne was "personal chef" for Jack Nicholson, fixing him lamb chops during an on location shoot. In September of that year, he married Trixie Flynn, an assistant to Nicholson. By that time, Timothy had discovered other hidden talents. "I went to visit my dad on vacation," he said, "and found a location for a Woody Allen movie he was designing. I ended up working in Woody Allen's organization for many years ... as a location scout, then became a location manager. So there I was."[459] Bourne was designated as assistant and unit production manager for popular films like Woody Allen's *Radio Days* (1987), *Big* (1988) starring Tom Hanks, *The Prince of Tides* (1991) starring Barbara Streisand, and *A League of Their Own* (1992).

On a 1988 location trip to Wilmington, North Carolina, Bourne fell in love with the coastline and natural beauty surrounding the area. "And, I stayed," said Timothy. "We have generated over the years in Atlanta, in Wilmington and certain parts of Louisiana this wonderful film culture that has grown." Bourne praises the fact that the local film industry provides quality jobs and pay. "And I don't mean actors," he emphasizes. "I'm talking about carpenters, electricians, painters, cameramen, if you factor in extras, you're talking about several thousand jobs in the course of a four-month period." The assignment may be temporary, but work is always available. Bourne has five children from his three marriages. His eldest son Seamus Marshall Bourne teaches theater design at Berry College in Rome, Georgia.

Timothy Marshall Bourne has produced such films as *The Blind Side* (2009), *Joyful Noise* (2012) with Dolly Parton, and *The Bastards* (2017) with Glenn Close. Bourne is executive producer for the newly released *Love, Simon* (2018) in which a gay teenager defies the odds and creates a novel way of coming out to his classmates during the computer age. "I have always been a fan of the underdog," admitted Bourne in 2009. At the time he had recently completed *The Blind Side* (nominated for Best Picture), which detailed the true story of Michael Oher, a young, homeless African-American, who became an All American football star.

The Marshall legacy is in good hands.

Filmmaker Timothy Marshall Bourne

In February 1960, Herbert Marshall was honored with a star on the Hollywood Walk of Fame, which is located on the 6200 block of Hollywood Blvd. In 2014, Turner Classic Movies annual "Summer Under the Stars," paid tribute to Marshall with a twenty-four-hour salute that included ten of his noteworthy performances. "Few actors in films can boast as many high-octane leading ladies as Herbert Marshall," said host Robert Osborne, who underscored that Marshall "had one of the great speaking voices," and "worked with the finest directors: Hitchcock, Lubitsch, Cukor, Lumet, John Huston, King Vidor." As for Marshall's war injury, Osborne was impressed with the actor's "determination, and perseverance." "Marshall's personal story," said Osborne, "is a really fascinating one."[460]

Acknowledgements

Firstly, I should express gratitude to interviewers from the past who encouraged Bart Marshall to "sound off" about issues that meant something to him. He was proud of his middle-class roots and felt a certain disconnect from the well-born set. His complaining to scenarist Sada Cowan in 1936, about being called a "gentleman"—which to him meant entitlement, was an eye-opener. Cowan admitted that she was good at asking questions and making "a complete nuisance" of herself, ever since she began working in silent films with Cecil B. DeMille. Marshall's 1943 interview with actor-turned-sports editor Chip Royal, underscored his belief that the abundance of war films being made for box-office revenue was a mistake. War for profit didn't sit well with a man like Herbert Marshall. Aside from Hitchock's *Foreign Correspondent* (1940), Marshall only involved himself in one other war-themed film during WWII, *Forever and a Day* (1943), which was produced gratis by all parties involved, the profits going to British War Relief. In 1963, Marshall offered his last interview with columnist Bob Thomas, noted for bringing out the "real personality" of interviewees. Marshall made it clear to Thomas that during WWI he had been "a private, a plain G.I." He had no grandiose vision of himself, or the war that had left him with a legacy of pain, both physical and emotional.

The moment I mentioned my intention to write a biography about Herbert Marshall, author and film historian James Robert Parish was on board offering me access to his collection of Marshall films. Parish's contribution to film history is well-documented in his books (now available in ebook format), which offer insightful overviews of filmdom's classic stars: *The Debonaires*, *The Paramount Pretties*, *The MGM Stock Company*,

The RKO Gals, The Tough Guys, The Hollywood Beauties, et. al. Most importantly, I was delighted to hear Parish's personal recollections of meeting Marshall during the actor's 1961 summer tour (and final stage bow) in *A Majority of One*.

British historian/preservationist/filmmaker Kevin Brownlow provided a Foreword for Bart Marshall which is both concise and timely. He captures the essence of the actor with bite, humor and heart. Brownlow's remarkable contributions to film restoration and film history include the "granddaddy" of silent film books, the excellent *The Parade's Gone By* (1968), for which he gathered recollections of numerous film pioneers.

I extend my heartfelt thanks to Graceann Macleod, whose affinity for and knowledge of classic film is impressive. As a proofreader she has been a godsend. A narrative with a conversational tone is my preference, and Graceann's grammatical expertise has helped immensely in making the text a reader friendly experience. The delightful duo Jenny Paxson and Larry Smith have generously shared photos of Marshall from their own collection. Larry, who is a Nitrate Specialist for the Library of Congress, provided me with access to rare Marshall performances on *The Alfred Hitchcock Hour*. Jenny, an avid collector on Marshall's friend Douglas Fairbanks, Jr., has created an intimate and informative tribute to Fairbanks on Facebook.

Author Mark Alan Vieira (*Sin in Soft Focus: Pre-Code Hollywood*) who had been in contact with both Sarah and Ann Marshall, confirmed that Marshall's amputation was the left leg. Vieira's insightful comments on Marshall's amputation were particularly helpful. Vieira also contacted Ann on my behalf, but sadly related, "Ann Marshall did not answer my letter. I fear that she is very ill, since she didn't look well when I met her briefly in 2010."[461] In the fall of 2012, while researching my biography on Ruth Chatterton, I had written Sarah Marshall regarding her being cast with Chatterton in a Broadway revival of *Idiot's Delight* (1951). She never responded. I was unaware that she was undergoing a lengthy battle with cancer, which would take her life a year-and-a-half later. Sarah, despite her diagnosis of cancer, was an active participant in the project *Perfect*

ACKNOWLEDGEMENTS

Lover (www.perfectlover.com), a documentary about how her father dealt with disability during an era of secrecy and disguise. My friend and neighbor Ken Holybee (Director at Large, Vietnam Veterans of America) was generous with his time in discussing the still relevant struggles of disabled vets (and their families)—a hundred years after the saga of Herbert Marshall on the Western Front.

Stephen Michael Shearer, who wrote the definitive biography *Gloria Swanson - The Ultimate Star* (2013), was a great help in detailing Marshall's affair with the actress. Shearer had access to Swanson's personal papers/letters, and offered an insightful look into the dynamics of Bart and Gloria's three-year affair. Film archivist/author Brian Taves (*Robert Florey - The French Expressionist*) was generous with his research on Florey, who directed Marshall in *Till We Meet Again* (1936). Taves shared rare stills from the Florey estate, and commented about the friendship Florey established with Rod La Rocque, and, subsequently, Marshall himself.

My publisher Ben Ohmart was the one who suggested that I write Marshall's story. Ben is particularly fond of Bart's performance in the William Wyler film *The Good Fairy*. Ben connected me with Valerie Yaros, who works for the Screen Actors Guild (SAG). Valerie provided me correspondence between Marshall and Wyler. She shared her own extensive research on *The Good Fairy*. Yaros is working on the first biography of Frank Morgan (*The Wizard of Oz*) and his brother Ralph Morgan (first president of SAG). She has established a connection with their families and her book will be a most welcome contribution to the BearManor collection.

Marshall co-starred with each of my previous biographical subjects for BearManor: Kay Francis, Virginia Bruce, Ann Harding, Ruth Chatterton, George Brent and Sylvia Sidney. When publisher Ben Ohmart suggested I write about Marshall, it seemed a logical step. Marshall has always been a welcome presence on screen ever since he swept me away when I first saw him in a revival of *Trouble in Paradise* in the mid-1970's. Researching his back-story and documenting his talent was a privilege.

My "investigations" into the lives of filmdom's forgotten stars, wouldn't be nearly as enjoyable without the enthusiasm and support of my partner Joel Bellagio. Joel has been on board ever since we headed to Wesleyan University in 2004 to absorb the diaries of Kay Francis (which she kept from 1922-1953). Aside from witnessing almost every film these actors made, Joel reads each chapter after I complete it. His astute observations and advice have helped whittle away unnecessary verbiage. Less is more (thank you, Robert Browning). This is easily demonstrated in the acting style of Bart Marshall, whose nonchalant ease and fine nuance lent itself to whatever role he played—romantic leads, abused husbands, villains, private investigators, and W. Somerset Maugham, who inadvertently described Marshall's unique talent, when he wrote, "Every production of an artist should be the expression of an adventure of his soul."[462]

ENDNOTES

INTRODUCTION
1. David Hazen, "Herbert Marshall Knows War, Autograph Hunter Big Worry," *Oregonian*, August 30, 1936 (Hazen spent fourteen months in France and Belgium as a war correspondent with the army of occupation, during 1918-19)

CHAPTER ONE
2. review, *One of You Must Marry*, *The Theatre Magazine*, July 1, 1881
3. *The Bookseller*, London, 1871, pg. 6
4. review, *A Night Out*, *The Bristol Times and Mirror*, April 6, 1897
5. Gladys Hall (as Faith Service), "Why Bart Marshall Gets You!" *Modern Screen*, June 1936 (author Anthony Slide rates Hall, who dominated the fan magazine field, as both "prolific" and "good")
6. Chip Royal, "Marshall Turn to Cartoons as Best Way to Shoo Blues," *Reading Eagle*, June 27, 1943
7. Paul Harrison, "In Hollywood," *Trenton Evening Times*, June 15, 1937
8. Harold Heffernan, "'Talkies' Presented Problems, Too," *Long Island Star-Journal*, February 27, 1953
9. Ben Maddox, "Mayfair Charm," *Screenland*, May 1936
10. Ben Maddox, "Mayfair Charm," *Screenland*, May 1936 (Marshall told Maddox, "I was nineteen and ended up in the theatrical business as a last resort.")
11. review of *The Arcadians*, *The Era*, October 1, 1910
12. Gladys Hall (as Faith Service), "Why Bart Marshall Gets You!" *Modern Screen*, June 1936
13. Russell Ferguson, "What a Throat for a Razor!" *World Film News*, October 1937 (In this article about N. Carter "Tod" Slaughter, it mentions his 1910 production of *Second to None*, with Marshall and Colman in bit roles)
14. Hubbard Keavy, "Herbert Marshall Cuts Stays in Studio Short," *Evansville Courier*, November 20, 1932
15. Beckett, Ian, *The Great War*, Longman, c. 2007
16. Hubbard Keavy, "Marshall Cuts Short His Stay at Film Studios," *Omaha World-Herald*, November 27, 1932
17. Charles Darnton, "Hollywood's Hold on British Actors," *Screenland*, October 1936 (Darnton was a longtime theater critic and scenarist)
18. Mollie Marshall, Civil Registration Death Index, December 1973, lists her birth date as: October 7, 1889

19 review of *Grumpy*, *Duluth News-Tribune*, December 4, 1915

20 Percy Hammond, "News and Views of the Theater," *Evening Telegram*, February 11, 1922

21 Grace Kingsley, "When Hunches Saved the Stars," *Macon Telegraph*, May 10, 1936

22 John Keegan, *The First World War*, Pimlico, c. 1999, pg. 324

23 Mark Lloyd, *London Scottish in the Great War*, Pen and Sword, c. 2000, pg. 111

24 Author Mark Alan Vieira noted (May 2016) that a documentary filmmaker confirmed with both of Marshall's daughters that his left leg was amputated below the hip, *not* the right, as suggested by UPI and *Time Magazine* articles covering the actor's death in 1966. This error has been repeated in print numerous times since then.

25 Simon Robbins, *British Generalship on the Western* Front, Routledge, c. 2005, pg. 33

26 Les Carlyon, *The Great War*, 2006

27 Mayme Ober Peak, "'To Be Called Suave Gets on My Nerves,'" *Daily Boston Globe*, January 13, 1935

28 Herbert Marshall, "An Open Letter to Hollywood's Fighting Men," *Hollywood*, March 1943 (Marshall gave his age as twenty-five at the time he was hospitalized, he was actually a few weeks from his twenty-seventh birthday.)

29 Herbert Marshall, British Army WWI Service Records, 1914-1920, "Service and Causality Form," B 2512, Infantry Record Office, London

30 Herbert Marshall, "An Open Letter to Hollywood's Fighting Men," *Hollywood*, March 1943

31 Gladys Hall (as Faith Service), "Why Bart Marshall Gets You!" *Modern Screen*, June 1936

32 "The King's Wrong Guess," *The Irish Times*, July 30, 1928

33 *Supplement to the London Gazette*, November 7, 1918

34 Basil Rathbone to Edward R Murrow, *Person to Person* (CBS), January 11, 1957

35 Brian Aherne, *A Proper Job*, Houghton Mifflin, 1969, pg 288

36 Laurence Stallings, *Plumes*, University of South Carolina Pr., c. 2006, pg. 146

37 Dorothy Manners, "Herbert Marshall - Just the Opposite of Gable," *Movie Classic*, September 1932

CHAPTER TWO

38 Ben Maddox, "Mayfair Charm," *Screenland*, May 1936

39 Herbert Marshall, (as told to Drake Hunt), "An Open Letter to America's Fighting Men," *Hollywood*, March 1943

40 review of *Betty at Bay*, *The Cheltenham Looker-On*, October 19, 1918

41 Norman Fenton, *Shell Shock and its Aftermath*, C.V. Mosby, c. 1926, pg. 162

ENDNOTES

42 Ken Olsen, "Booted After Battle," *The American Legion*, June 2016

43 review of *The Younger Generation*, *New Statesman*, c. 1919, Vol. 12, pg. 399

44 Arnold Bennett, "Introductory Note," J. Drinkwater's *Abraham Lincoln: A Play*, Houghton Mifflin, c. 1919, pg. x

45 "Herbert Marshall: Amputee Movie Star," SAG-AFTRA, Summer 2014, Pg. 46 (original article was posted in *Variety*, February 23, 1966)

46 Brad Richards, "Herbert Marshall: Gentleman," *Films of the Golden Age*, Spring 2002

47 Ben Deacon, "What New York Critics Think of Marie Lohr, Gifted Actress; Poor Play," *Manitoba Free Press*, February 18, 1922

48 "Reprimand for Audiences," *Plays and Players*, Vol. 8, 1960

49 Burns Mantle, "Along Broadway," *Pittsburgh Post-Gazette*, February 5, 1922

50 Joy Carroll, *Pride's Court*, Dell, c. 1980, pg. 17

51 "Herbert Marshall Talks of Favorites," *Ottawa Citizen*, May 11, 1943

52 Tarn, review of *The Young Idea*, *The Spectator*, V. 130, c. 1923

53 Cole Lesley, *Remembered Laughter: The Life of Noel Coward*, Knopf, c. 1976, pg. 69

54 PhilipHoare, *Noel Coward, A Biography*, Sinclair-Stevenson, c. 1995, pg. 509

55 *The Era*, November 9, 1922 (England & Wales Death Index lists Ethel's age as 51, but census records from 1871, and marriage records place her birth at 1868)

56 Percy Falcon Marshall, England & Wales National Probate Calendar, March 31, 1928, pg. 213 (London based researcher David Macleod calculated that the sum would be worth £324,000 ($480,000) in 2016)

57 "The Leg and its Achievements," *Journal of the Royal Medical Army Corps*, Vol. 41, 1923, pg. 214 (a Parliament debate of November 6, 1952, placed the number of WWI amputees at 45,000)

58 Reginald Denham, *Stars in My Hair*, Crown, c. 1958, pg. 111

59 Lewis Sawin, (Clare Sheridan letter to Alfred Sutro), *Alfred Sutro: A Man With a Heart*, University Press of Colorado, c. 1989, pg. 189

60 Tallulah Bankhead, *Tallulah: My Autobiography*, University of Mississippi, c. 1952, pg. 134

61 review of *Neilson*, 'Fiction," *Spectrum*, February 13, 1926

62 Brad Richards, " Herbert Marshall: Gentleman," *Films of the Golden Age*, Spring 2002

CHAPTER THREE

63 E.G., "Edna Best of *These Charming People* Made Pictures in England," *Boston Herald*, January 3, 1926 (Best's London address at the time: 16a John Street, Adelphi)

64 Hubert Griffith, review of *By-Ways*, *Dramatic Critic*, May 22, 1926

65 Noel Coward, *Present Indicative-An Autobiography*, Doubleday, c. 1937

66 John C. Wilson, *Noel, Tallulah, Cole and Me: A Memoir of Broadway's Golden Age*, c. 2015, pg. 34

67 Gladys Hall (as Faith Service), "Why Bart Marshall Gets You!" *Modern Screen*, June 1936

68 Peter Batten, "Footlights and Dressing Rooms," *Sunday Times* (Perth), June 13, 1943

69 Muriel Elwood, *Pauline Frederick - On and Off Stage*, A. Kroch, c. 1940, pg. 1953

70 John Gielgud, *Sir John Gielgud: A Life in Letters*, Arcade, c. 2005, pg. 10

71 Sheridan Morley, *John Gielgud: The Authorized Biography*, Simon and Schuster, c. 2010, pg. 74

72 Basil Dean, *Mind's Eye: An Autobiography*, Hutchinson, c. 1973, pg. 34

73 "Marshall's Disconcerting Charm," *American Weekly*, June 1, 1947

74 "London," *Variety*, April 11, 1928

75 Brad Richards, "Herbert Marshall - Gentleman," *Films of the Golden Age*, Spring 2002

76 "Decree Against Actor," *Derby Daily Telegraph*, April 30, 1928

77 Harriet Menken, review of *The High Road*, *Long Island News & Owl*, September 13, 1928

78 Dixie Tighe, "Obstacle Proved a Stimulus to Herbert Marshall's Success," *Standard Union*, October 23, 1928

79 "Jeanne Eagels, Star of *Rain*, Dies of Liquor," *Lewiston Evening Journal*, October 4, 1929

80 Selina Hastings, *The Secret Lives of Somerset Maugham*, Arcade, c. 2009, pg. 267

81 Selina Hastings, *The Secret Lives of Somerset Maugham*, Arcade, c. 2009, pg. 285

82 Rosa Reilly, "Sound Appeal," *Screenland*, January 1929

83 Michael Barrett, review of *The Letter*, Popmatters.com, July 21, 2011

84 Charles Darnton, "Hollywood's Hold on British Actors," *Screenland*, October 1936

85 "From Accountant to Actor," *Boston Herald*, February 3, 1929

86 Thomas Kiernan, *Olivier: the Life of Laurence Olivier*, Sidgwick & Jackson, c. 1981. pg. 63

87 Ursula Greville, review of *Heat Wave*, *The Sackbut*, January 1930, pg. 142

CHAPTER FOUR

88 Laura Benham, "More About Herbert Marshall," *Screenland*, May 1933

89 Frank Scully, "All Over the Place on One Leg," *Variety*, November 5, 1930

90 Burns Mantel, "On Broadway," *Boston Herald*, June 7, 1931 (In his report, Mantel wrote that Marshall used a "cork" leg)

91 Charlotte Chandler, *It's Only a Movie: Alfred Hitchcock*, Applause, c. 2006, pg. 78

ENDNOTES

92 Sidney Gottlieb, *Alfred Hitchcock: Interviews*, University of Mississippi, c. 2003, pg. 144

93 Francois, Truffaut, *Hitchcock*, Simon & Schuster, c. 1967, pg. 53

94 Chalres Landstone, "Leaves from a theatre note-book," *Jewish Quarterly*, c. 1971, pgs. 172-173

95 Robert Osborne, introducing the film *Murder!* during Marshall all-day tribute, August 16, 2014

96 "Quits Film Lead, Speeds to Husband," *Boston Herald*, February 19, 1931

97 "English Star Will Return to Hollywood With Husband," *Repository*, February 21, 1931

98 "Love Laughs at Locksmiths," *Photoplay*, December 1931

99 Lawrence J. Quirk, *Claudette Colbert-An Illustrated Biography*, Crown Pub., c. 1985, pg.40

100 Burns Mantel, review of *There's Always Juliet*, *Tampa Tribune*, February 28, 1932

101 Dorothy Manners, "Herbert Marshall - Just the Opposite of Gable," *Movie Classic*, September 1932

102 Laura Benham, "More About Herbert Marshall," *Screenland*, May 1933

103 Steven Bach, *Marlene Dietrich: Life and Legend*, William Morrow, c. 1992, pg. 135

104 Jeff Laffel, "Sylvia Sidney," *Films in Review*, September/October 1994

105 Mick LaSalle, *Complicated Women*, St. Martin's Press, c. 2000, pgs. 162-163

106 Maud M. Miller, "Herbert Marshall Tells About Kay Francis," *Film Pictorial*, July 1, 1933

107 "The Screen Parade," *The Tampa Tribune*, October 30, 1932

108 "New Names and Faces of '32," *Variety*, January 3, 1933

109 Leslie Storm, "Kay Francis," *Film Weekly*, April 28, 1933

110 Maud M. Miller, Herbert Marshall Tells About Kay Francis," *Film Pictorial*, July 1, 1933

111 Philip Hoare, *Noel Coward: A Biography of Noel Coward*, Simon and Schuster, c. 1996, pg. 261-262

112 "They Put Mr. Marshall's Name In Lights All Over London," *Brooklyn Daily Eagle*, February 21, 1932

113 Graceann Macleod comments to author, sent August 5, 2016

114 review of *The Faithful Heart*, *The Era*, May 4, 1932

115 "Dubbed English Film Resented by Marshall," *Variety*, September 12, 1933

116 Roy Moseley, *Evergreen: Victor Saville in His Own Words*, SIU Press, c. 2000, pg. 58

CHAPTER FIVE

117 Florence Ross, "The New Love Code," *Picture Play*, March 1934

118 *Hollywood Reporter*, February 7, 1933 (The film was re-titled *Runaway Queen*, with Anna Neagle and Fernand Gravey in the roles intended for MacDonald and Marshall)

119 "'Queen' Postponement Freezes Up at $200,000," *Variety*, July 4, 1933

120 "The Passing Show," *New York Sun*, February 21, 1933 (Article mistakenly notes that Edna was also present. Best was not on the ship manifest when Marshall arrived on February 15. She was listed as his London contact.)

121 Elinor Glyn, "Will He Be the Greatest Screen Lover?" *Modern Screen*, April 1933

122 Victor Saville, Roy Moseley (ed.), *Evergreen: Victor Saville in His Own Words*, Carbondale, c. 2000, pg. 67

123 Laura Wagner, 'Laura's Miscellaneous Musings," (blog), April 28, 2010

124 Anthony Slide, *Fifty Classic British Films, 1932-1982*: A Pictorial Record, Courier Corp., c. 2013, pg. 7

125 Jill Stewart, "Film Actress Madeleine Carroll Dies," *Los Angeles Times*, October 4, 1987

126 Elisabeth Goldbeck, "Can Herbert Marshall Have Sex Appeal, Now That He's a Daddy?" *Movie Classic*, January 1934

127 Lawrence J. Quirk, *Claudette Colbert - An Illustrated Biography*, Crown, c. 1985, pg. 62

128 Mollie Merrick, "Mary Boland Presents Impressions Gained on Set on Visit to Hawaii," *San Francisco Chronicle*, November 18, 1933

129 Ruth Rankin, "Actresses Clamor for *This Man!*" *Photoplay*, July 1934

130 "Was DeMille to Blame?" *Seattle Daily Times*, December 24, 1933

131 "Either Side of the Atlantic is 'Home' to Herbert Marshall," *Dansville Breeze*, December 21, 1933

132 Brad Richards, "Herbert Marshall - Gentleman," *Films of the Golden Age*, Spring 2002

133 Ruth Rankin, "Actresses Clamor for *This Man!*" *Photoplay*, July 1934

134 Ruth Rankin, "Actresses Clamor for *This Man!*" *Photoplay*, July 1934

135 Stephen Michael Shearer, *Gloria Swanson: The Ultimate Star*, St. Martin's, c. 2013, pg. 257 (Swanson's autobiography indicated that she was introduced to Marshall at the home of Richard Barthelmess)

136 Gloria Swanson, *Swanson on Swanson*, Simon & Schuster (Pocket Books), c. 1980, pg. 451

137 Joan Standish, "Edna Best Admits Marital Trouble," *Movie Classic*, July 1934

138 Stephen Michael Shearer, *Gloria Swanson: The Ultimate Star*, St. Martin's, c. 2013, pg. 264

139 Stephen Michael Shearer, *Gloria Swanson: The Ultimate Star*, St. Martin's, c. 2013, pg. 21

ENDNOTES

140 Lawrence J. Quirk, *Norma - The Story of Norma Shearer*, St. Martin's, c. 1988, pgs. 156-157

141 Lawrence J. Quirk, *Norma - The Story of Norma Shearer*, St. Martin's, c. 1988, pgs. 154

142 Mick LaSalle, *Complicated Women*, St. Martin's Press, c. 2000, pg. 199

143 Bob Thomas, "Herbert Marshall Misses Filmland's Good Old Days," *Reading Eagle*, September 8, 1963

144 *Silver Screen* article, June 1934

145 "Good News," *Modern Screen*, June 1934

146 Stephen Michael Shearer, *Gloria Swanson: The Ultimate Star*, St. Martin's, c. 2013, pg. 259 (The letter is archived at The Harry Ransom Center, University of Texas at Austin)

147 Laura Benham, "Two Hearts in Waltz Time," *Picture Play*, August 1934

148 Hedda Hopper, "Many Film Stars Have Pet Roles They Yearn to Do," *Evansville Courier*, October 15, 1941

149 Stephen Michael Shearer, *Gloria Swanson: The Ultimate Star*, St. Martin's, c. 2013, pg. 258

150 Brian Kellow, *The Bennetts: An Acting Family*, University of Kentucky Pr., c. 2004, pg. 184

151 Louella Parsons review, "Outcast Lady," *Los Angeles Examiner*, November 22, 1934

152 J. Eugene Chrisman, "Shearer to Bennett to Garbo," *Screenplay*, September 1934

153 "Marie Antoinette," *Variety*, June 26, 1934

154 Gavin Lambert, *Norma Shearer*, Knopf, c. 1990, pg. 216

155 James Arthur, "I'm Tired of Being a Gentleman," *Picturegoer*, December 8, 1934

156 Otis Wiles, "What It's Like to Work With Garbo," *Photoplay*, November 1934 (Wiles was part of the MGM publicity department, which put a questionable slant on much of his own input into this article)

157 Mollie Merrick, "Hollywood in Person," *Springfield Republican*, October 7, 1934

158 Selina Hastings, *The Secret Lives of Somerset Maugham*, Arcade, c. 2009, pg. (Maugham once stated that Fane was based on the supercilious, steely self-controlled personality of his brother, F.H. Maugham.)

159 Selina Hastings, *The Secret Lives of Somerset Maugham*, Arcade, c. 2009, pg. 253

160 "Edna Best Sought for Staged Maugham Novel," *Plain Dealer*, October 5, 1930

161 Tony Villeco, *Silent Stars Speak - Interviews with Twelve Cinema Pioneers*, McFarland, c. 2001, pg. 80

162 "British Star Takes 'K.O.' In Movie Brawl," *Rochester Democrat and Chronicle*, September 26, 1934

163 "Filmland Writer Scores One-Punch Victory Over English Actor at Party," *State Times Advocate*, September 25, 1934 (Saunders referred to the 1902 novel *The Virginian*, in which the lead character, after being called a son-of-a-bitch, points his gun and says, "When you call me that, *smile!*")

164 Fay Wray, *On the Other Hand: A Life Story*, St. Martin's Press, c. 1989, pg. 162-164

165 Moira Finnie, "John Monk Saunders - Something in the Air," Movie Morlocks.com, February 6, 2008

166 Karen Burroughs Hannsberry, "Margaret Sullavan - The Lonely Rebel," *Films of the Golden Age*, Spring 1997

CHAPTER SIX

167 Mollie Merrick, "Hollywood in Person," *Springfield Republican*, October 7, 1934

168 J.R. Jr., "Notes on the Passing Show," *Dallas Morning News*, August 24, 1935

169 "Marshall Must Work," *Evening Star* (D.C.), January 5, 1935 (As it turned out, Marshall only made one film at Paramount that year, *Accent on Youth*)

170 George Shaffer, "Hollywood in Review," January 5, 1935

171 Brad Richards, "Herbert Marshall - Gentleman," *Films of the Golden Age*, Spring 2002

172 Karen Burroughs Hannsberry, "Margaret Sullavan - The Lonely Rebel," *Films of the Golden Age*, Spring 1997

173 Brad Richards, "Herbert Marshall - Gentleman," *Films of the Golden Age*, Spring 2002

174 "Actress and Husband are Now Living Apart," *Charlotte Observer*, June 7, 1935

175 Jan Herman, *A Talent For Trouble: The Life of Hollywood's Most Acclaimed Director, William Wyler*, Da Capo, c.1997, page 136

176 Jan Herman, *A Talent for Trouble: The Life of Hollywood's Most Acclaimed Director, William Wyler*, Da Capo, c. 1997, pgs. 169-170

177 Jan Herman, *A Talent for Trouble: The Life of Hollywood's Most Acclaimed Director, William Wyler*, Da Capo, c. 1997, pg, 177

178 Elizabeth Yeaman column, *Hollywood Citizen News*, October 30, 1934

179 Herbert Marshall letter to William Wyler, William Wyler Papers, AMPAS Herrick Library, Beverly Hills

180 Mick LaSalle, *Complicated Women*, St. Martin's Pr., c. 2000, pgs. 187-188

181 Matthew Kennedy, *Edmund Goulding's Dark Victory: Hollywood's Genius Bad Boy*, Terrace, c. 2004, pg. 155

182 Philip Hoare, *Noel Coward: A Biography of Noel Coward*, Simon and Schuster, c. 1996, pg. 273. In *The Letters of Noel Coward* (Knopf Doubleday, c. 2008), Coward enthused, "Sugar ... is inundated with film offers. He is signing with Metro Goldwyn and getting ten thousand dollars. It is really lovely for him and we are all very glad."

ENDNOTES

183 "Ann Harding and Ex-Mate Plan Suits," *Los Angeles Times*, December 24, 1934

184 Maurice Savage, review of *The Lady Consents*, *Evening Tribune*, February 18, 1936

185 Mollie Merrick column, *Evening Post* (Chicago), June 4, 1935

186 *International Motion Picture Almanac, 1936-37*, Quigley, c. 1936

187 Gregory J.M. Catsos, "Sylvia Sidney," *Filmfax*, November 1990

188 "Drew Loses Leg," *Variety*, June 19, 1935

189 Ed Sullivan, "Bread Upon the Waters," *Silver Screen*, August 1936

190 Hubbard Keavy column, *The Milwaukee Sentinel*, December 3, 1936

191 Deborah Martinson, *Lillian Hellman: A Life with Foxes and Scoundrels*, Counterpoint, c. 2011, pg. 109

192 Graham Greene, review of *The Dark Angel*, *The Spectator*, October 4, 1935

193 A. Scott Berg, *Goldwyn: A Biography*, Riverhead Books, c. 1998, pg. 258

194 Stephen Michael Shearer, *Gloria Swanson - The Ultimate Star*, St. Martin's Pr., c. 2013, pg. 273

195 "Movie Stars Top Own Bosses on Salary List," *San Diego Union*, January 28, 1937 (This AP report was based on MGM salaries for the year 1935)

196 Gladys Hall (as Faith Service), "Why Bart Marshall Gets You!" *Modern Screen*, June 1936

197 Frank Capra, *The Name Above the Title: An Autobiography*, Da Capo, c. 1997, pg. 218

198 John Howard Reid, *A Risky Business - Crime in the Movies*, Reid Books, c. 2015, pg. 142

199 Brain Taves, email dated April 18, 2017

200 Stephen Michael Shearer, *Gloria Swanson - The Ultimate Star*, St. Martin's Pr., c. 2013, pg. 112

201 Francis Watson, "The Death of George V," *History Today*, December 12, 1986

202 Sada Cowan, "'I'm No Gentleman' - Says Herbert Marshall," *Macon Telegraph*. February 16, 1936

203 Sidney Skolsky, "Hollywood," *Augusta Chronicle*, March 27, 1936

204 George Eells, *Ginger, Loretta and Irene Who?*, Putnam, c. 1976, pg. 220

205 "Salaries," *Variety*, June 17, 1936

206 Ben Maddox, "Mayfair Charm," *Screenland*, May 1936

207 Elizabeth Yeaman, review of *Girl's Dormitory*, *Hollywood Citizen News*, September 17, 1936

208 Florence Fisher Parry, "Hollywood Presents a New Screen Face," *Pittsburgh Press*, August 18, 1936

209 Richard Lamparski, *Whatever Became of ... ?,* Crown, c. 1968, pg. 70-71(Simon's birth year varies, according to her tombstone, passenger lists, and border crossings: 1910, 1911, 1914)

210 Ida Zeitlin, "Most Exciting Newcomer!" *Screenland,* November 1936

211 Franc Dillon, "That Thing Called Temperament," *Modern Screen,* May 1938

212 Sheilah Graham column, *Evening Star,* June 23, 1936

213 Sidney Skolsky, "Hollywood," *Augusta Chronicle,* September 30, 1936 (the biggest donors gave $200 each)

214 "Red Actors," *Dallas Morning News,* September 26, 1936

215 "Herbert Marshall May or May Not Be At His Best," *The Dallas Morning News,* October 22, 1936

216 Sheilah Graham, "Hollywood Today," *Milwaukee Journal,* November 18, 1936

217 "Chit Chat," *The Stage,* October 29, 1936

218 Dixie Tighe, "Herbert Marshall's Reticence (British) Overpowers Press," *New York Post,* November 23, 1936

219 Gladys Hall, "Herbert Marshall's Best Girl," *Motion Picture,* May 1937

220 A.L.B. review of *A Woman Rebels, Times-Picayune,* November 5, 1936

221 Richard B. Jewell and Vernon Harbin, *The RKO Story,* Octopus Books, c. 1982, pg. 100

222 Barbara Leaming, *Katharine Hepburn,* Hal Leonard Corp., c. 2004, pg. 267

223 Anne Edwards, *Katharine Hepburn: A Remarkable Woman,* MacMillan, c. 1985, pg. 74 (*The Animal Kingdom* ran from January-June 1932, at the Broadhurst Theatre)

224 Franc Dillon, "That Thing Called Temperament," *Modern Screen,* May 1938

CHAPTER SEVEN

225 Sheilah Graham, "Hollywood Today," *Milwaukee Journal,* July 10, 1936

226 Franc Dillon, "That Thing Called Temperament," *Modern Screen,* May 1938

227 Jerry Asher, "The Hollywood Reporter," *Macon Telegraph,* July 12, 1936

228 George Shaffer, "Commodores Cruise Gay Event," *Arkansas Gazette,* September 15, 1936

229 Frank S. Nugent, review of *Quality Street, The New York Times,* April 9, 1937

230 Edith Lindeman, "The Virginia Reel," *Richmond Times,* November 19, 1936

231 "Marshall Gives Steed 'Juice,' So Doctor Stitches," *Oregonian,* August 24, 1936

232 Erskine Johnson, "Close-Ups of Celebrities of Movie Town," *Arkansas Gazette,* April 7, 1938

ENDNOTES

233 "Herb Marshall's Hush Money Tax Deduction," *Variety*, August 2, 1939 (the tax claim covered 1933-35)

234 Stephen Michael Shearer, *Gloria Swanson - The Ultimate Star*, St. Martin's, c. 2013, pg. 277

235 Stephen Michael Shearer, *Gloria Swanson - The Ultimate Star*, St. Martin's, c. 2013, pg. 6

236 Gloria Swanson, *Swanson on Swanson*, Random House (Pocket Books), pg. 463

237 Stephen Michael Shearer, *Gloria Swanson - The Ultimate Star*, St. Martin's, c. 2013, pg. 112

238 "Gloria Swanson Files Divorce Suit Against Titled 3rd Husband," *The Boston Herald*, October 22, 1930

239 Stephen Michael Shearer, *Gloria Swanson - The Ultimate Star*, St. Martin's, c. 2013, pg. 4

240 Adela Rogers St. Johns, "Love, Laughter and Tears - The Hollywood Story," *Oregonian*, January 7, 1951

241 Gloria Swanson, *Swanson on Swanson*, Random House (Pocket Books), pg. 462

242 Gloria Swanson, *Swanson on Swanson*, Random House, c. 1980, pg. 456

243 Franc Dillon, "That Thing Called Temperament," *Modern Screen*, May 1938

244 Gloria Swanson, *Swanson on Swanson*, Random House, c. 1980, pg. 453

245 Jonas I. Bromberg, "Alcohol and Chronic Pain," Nat. Inst. on Alcohol Abuse and Alcoholism (January 7, 2011)

246 Edwin Martin, "Cinemania," *Hollywood Citizen News*, February 17, 1937

247 Sheilah Graham interview with Ernst Lubitsch, "Hollywood Today," *Milwaukee Journal*, March 5, 1937

248 Scott Eyman, *Ernst Lubitsch: Laughter in Paradise*, Simon & Schuster, c. 2015, pg. 232

249 Scott Eyman, *Ernst Lubitsch: Laughter in Paradise*, Simon and Schuster, c. 2015, pg.232-23

250 Paul Harrison, "Wanted: Some Tough Luck for Marlene," *Daily Nonpareil*, July 31, 1938

251 James Reid, "We Cover the Studios," *Photoplay*, July 1937

252 Gladys Hall, "Herbert Marshall's Best Girl," *Motion Picture*, May 1937

253 Sara Hamilton, "Roundup of Characters," *Photoplay*, May 1938

254 John Hobart, "A Gentleman From Ladies and Gentleman," *San Francisco Chronicle*, July 16, 1939

255 Edith Lindeman, "Hollywood Has Discovered a Leading Man Can Act Parental," *Richmond Times*, June 5, 1938

256 movie column, *Syracuse Herald*, June 14, 1938

257 "Herbert Marshall's Love Suit," *Los Angeles Evening Herald Express*, April 14, 1938

258 "Sues Film Star For Alienation Of Affections," *Morning Star*, April 15, 1938

259 "Herbert Marshall Denies Settling Love Theft Suit," *Los Angeles Examiner*, May 14, 1938

260 Dan Callahan, *Barbara Stanwyck: The Miracle Woman*," University Pr. of Mississippi, c. 2012, pg. 66

261 Lawrence J. Quirk, *Claudette Colbert: An Illustrated Biography*," Crown Pub., c. 1985, pgs. 103, 106-107

262 Hedda Hopper, "*Zaza* Gains Anew Told On Screen," *Evansville Courier*, January 3, 1939

CHAPTER EIGHT

263 Robert McIlwaine, "Grownup Juvenile," *Modern Screen*, February 1939

264 Harrison Carroll column, *Los Angeles Evening Herald Express*, April 17, 1939

265 Elinor Hughes, "Theater and Screen," *The Boston Herald*, November 13, 1936

266 Drew Pearson, Robert S. Allen, "Washington Merry-Go-Round," *San Francisco Chronicle*, December 24, 1938

267 "Herbert Marshall Bought No Bonds, Gave Callers Tea," *Springfield Republican*, June 22, 1939

268 "Herbert Marshall, Bing's Brother Tells of Spurning Flier in Philippine Bonds," *Omaha World-Herald*, June 22, 1939

269 Hal Burton, "Tell Buckner Courtship of Loretta Young," *Omaha World-Herald*, June 20, 1939

270 John Hobart, "A Gentleman From 'Ladies and Gentlemen,'" *San Francisco Chronicle*, July 16, 1939

271 Maude Cheatham, "Foreign Love Technique," *Silver Screen*, September 1939

272 Harry Mines, "Raves and Raps," *Daily News*, June 30, 1939

273 Ed Sullivan, "Looking at Hollywood," *Chicago Tribune*, July 31, 1939

274 "Edna Best Rushes Departure," *Philadelphia Inquirer*, August 26, 1939

275 Gavin Lambert, *Norma Shearer*, Knopf, c. 1990, pg. 284 (Lambert mistakenly wrote that both Shearer and Raft returned on the *S.S. Normandie*. Ship manifests indicate that Shearer left Le Havre on the *SS Manhattan*, August 31. Raft had left Le Havre on August 23 on the *Normandie*)

276 "Movie Stars in Europe," *San Francisco Chronicle*, August 27, 1939

277 Louella Parsons column, *Lexington Herald*, September 10, 1939

278 "Lorillard Audition," *Broadcasting*, January 1, 1940

279 Richard B. Jewell, *The RKO Story*, Crown, c. 1982, pg. 148

ENDNOTES

280 Dan Van Neste, *The Magnificent Heel: The Life and Films of Ricardo Cortez*, BearManor, c. 2017, pg. 242

281 William Hare, *Hitchcock and the Methods of Suspense*, McFarland, c. 2007, pg. 63

282 Robert McLaughlin, *We'll Always Have the Movies: American Cinema During WWII*, University Press of Kentucky, c. 2006, pg. 53

283 Louella Parsons, "George Brent Refuses Role With Bette Davis In Film," *Sacramento Bee*, May 20, 1940

284 Jan Herman, *A Talent for Trouble: The Life of Hollywood's Most Acclaimed Director, William Wyler*," Da Capo, c. 1997, pg. 208

285 Larry Smith, email, August 18, 2016

286 "Herbert Marshall, Touring for Britain, Likes Northwest," *Seattle Daily Times*, April 26, 1941

287 Registrar's Report, Serial No. U-679, April 25, 1942 (Marshall residing at 716 N. Rexford Dr., Beverly Hills)

288 Jan Herman, *A Talent for Trouble: The Life of Hollywood's Most Acclaimed Director, William Wyler*," Da Capo, c. 1997, pg. 223

289 Christopher Plummer, *In Spite of Myself: A Memoir*, Knopf Doubleday, c. 2008, pgs. 99-100

290 Whitney Stine, *"I'd Love to Kiss You"*: Conversations *with Bette Davis*, Pocket Books, c. 1990, pg. 139

291 Michael Troyan, *A Rose for Mrs. Miniver: The Life of Greer Garson*, Univ. Press of Kentucky, c. 1998, pg. 122

292 "Herbert Marshall Draws Plum Role," *Dallas Morning News*, July 25, 1941

293 Sheilah Graham, "Director, Not Her Mother, Bosses Shirley Now," *Evening Star*, November 8, 1941

CHAPTER NINE

294 Anne Edwards, *Shirley Temple: American Princess*, William Morrow, c. 1988, pg. 133

295 Anne Edwards, *Shirley Temple: American Princess*, William Morrow, c. 1988, pg. 132

296 Shirley Temple Black, *Child Star*, McGraw-Hill, c. 1988, pg. 334

297 "Lovers Out of Love," *Variety*, April 20, 1938

298 1930 U.S. Census (Elizabeth and Irene, living on 32nd Avenue in Queens Co.) April 2, 1930

299 Elizabeth Wilson (a.k.a Liza), "Mrs. Marshall Gives the Lowdown on Bart," *Screenland*, February 1942

300 Kay Francis Diaries, Kay Francis collection, Wesleyan Cinema Archives, Middletown, CT. (May 24, 1942: "Bart, Reggie for drinks.")

301 Louella Parsons column, *San Diego Union*, July 17, 1941

302 Lynn Kear and John Rossman, *Kay Francis - A Passionate Life and Career*, McFarland, c. 2006, pg. 211

303 Quentin Reynolds, "The Story of Dieppe," *New York Post*, April 12, 1943

304 Kevin Bash, email to author in March 2007, (transcription of Marine Corpsman Bob Allen, 1944)

305 Sheilah Graham, column, *Milwaukee Journal-Sentinel*, April 4, 1943

306 Herbert Marshall (told to Drake Hunt), "An Open Letter to Hollywood's Fighting Men," *Hollywood*, March 1943

307 John Chapman, "Chapman's Hollywood," *Boston Traveler*, April 28, 1942

308 Jeffrey Meyers, *Somerset Maugham: A Life*, Knopf Doubleday, c. 2010, pg. xvi

309 Selina Hastings, *The Secret Lives of Somerset Maugham*, Arcade, c. 2009, pg. 208

310 "Mr. Maugham Gives Praise," *Milwaukee Journal-Sentinel*, July 26, 1942

311 "Top Coin Pix Minus Stars," *Variety*, March 10, 1943

312 James Montgomery Flagg, "Flagg Looks at Marshall's Eyes," *Milwaukee Journal-Sentinel*, November 15, 1941

313 "V-Loan Booster Herbert Marshall Is Welcomed Here," *Ottawa-Citizen*, May 11, 1943

314 Kay Francis, diary, February 20, 1943, Kay Francis collection, Wesleyan Cinema Archives, Wesleyan Univ., Middletown, CT.

315 Carole Landis, *Four Jills in a Jeep*, World Pub. Co, c. 1944

316 Elizabeth Wilson (a.k.a Liza), "Mrs. Marshall Gives the Lowdown on Bart," *Screenland*, February 1942

317 Robert L. Calder, *Beware the British Serpent: The Role of Writers in British Propaganda in the United States, 1939-1945*, McGill-Queen's Pr., c. 2004, pg. 257

318 *Variety*, September 17, 1942 (Marshall, Warrick and Smith added to the all-star cast, Frank Lloyd directing)

319 Jimmy Fidler column, *Greensboro Daily News*, April 20, 1943

320 Chip Royal, "Marshall Turns to Cartoons As Best Way to Shoo Blues," *Reading Eagle*, June 27, 1943

321 Janine Basinger, "The World War II Combat Film: Definition," from *The War Film* by Robet T. Eberwein, Rutger's University Pr., c. 2004, pg. 39

322 Myrna Loy, *Myrna Loy-Being and Becoming*, Knopf, c. 1987, pg. 182

323 Robert Francis, "The Theater," *Brooklyn Eagle*, May 19, 1943

ENDNOTES

324 Joseph Egan, re: *Young Ideas*, email dated October 24, 2016

325 Richard Lertzman, William Birnes, *The Life and Times of Mickey Rooney*, Simon & Schuster, c. 2015, pg. 228

326 Sheilah Graham column, *Evening Star*, March 11, 1946

CHAPTER TEN

327 Violet Kochendoerfer, *One Woman's World War II*, Univ. of Kentucky Pr., c. 1994, pg. 149

328 Patty De Roulf, "The Untold Story of Herbert Marshall," *Motion Picture*, June 1945

329 Jay Carmody, column, *Evening Star*, May 30, 1945

330 *Variety*, November 13, 1945

331 Tom Hiney, *Raymond Chandler: A Biography*, Grove Press, c. 1997, pg. 147

332 Tom Weaver, *I Was a Monster Movie Maker: Conversations ...* , McFarland, c.2001, pg. 160

333 Kay Francis Diaries, Kay Francis collection, Wesleyan Cinema Archives, Middletown, CT. (July 4, 1944)

334 Erskine Johnson, "Hollywood," *Advocate*, March 13, 1945

335 "Movie Marshalls Planning Divorce," *Reno Evening Gazette*, October 9, 1945

336 Louella Parsons column, *Philadelphia Inquirer*, October 7, 1946

337 Robert McIlwaine, "Grownup Juvenile," *Modern Screen*, February 1939

338 Gladys Hall, "Herbert Marshall's Best Girl," *Motion Picture*, May 1937

339 Jeremy Paxman, *Great Britain's Great War*, Penguin, c. 2013

340 *Daily Express*, November 3, 1932

341 Lenore Coffee, *Storyline: Recollections of a Hollywood Screenwriter*, Cassell, London, c. 1973, pg. 62

342 Gene Handsaker, "Telescope Trained on British Star," *Union-Sun*, August 10, 1946

343 "Marshall as Maugham in *Razor's Edge*," *Columbus Dispatch*, January 2, 1947

344 Selina Hastings, *The Secret Lives of Somerset Maugham*, Aracade, c. 2009, pg. 473

345 Hector Arce, *The Secret Life of Tyrone Power*, William Morrow, c. 1979, pg. 180

346 Matthew Kennedy, *Edmund Goulding's Dark Victory: Hollywood's Genius Bad Boy*, Terrace, c. 2004, pg. 240

347 Cliff Aliperti, "Herbert Marshall, Biography of the Trouble in Paradise Star," (blog: Immortal Ephemera), August 16, 2014

348 Hedda Hopper column, *Buffalo Courier-Express*, August 10, 1945 (Orson Welles did the narration, uncredited)

349 "Selznick's 'Duel' First for Wounded Vets," *New York Evening Post*, December 20, 1946 (Two days after the premier, the press release was held at the Los Angeles Egyptian, December 31)

350 Roger Manvell, "New Spirit in Continental Films," *Cinema*, July 1947

351 Joan Fontaine, *No Bed of Roses*, William Morrow, c. 1978, pgs. 185-186

352 Murder in Celluloid: http://www.greatdetectives.net/detectives/big-list-shows/casebook-gregory-hood/

353 "Herbert Marshall's Disconcerting Charm," *Oregonian*, June 1, 1947

354 Beverly Linet, *Star-Crossed: The Story of Robert Walker and Jennifer Jones*, Berkley Books, c. 1988, pg. 197

CHAPTER ELEVEN

355 "Actor Marshall to Marry 'Boots,'" *Oregonian*, February 25, 1947

356 "Boots Mallory Drunk Driving Suspect," *Los Angeles Evening Herald Express*, April 28, 1947

357 "Admits to '3 or 4' Scotches," *Kansas City Star*, April 29, 1947

358 "Ex-Follies Girl Is Held For Drunk Driving In Herbert Marshall's Car," *Sacramento Bee*, April 28, 1947

359 "After She Was Cleared," *Times-Picayune*, June 2, 1947

360 "Free Boots Mallory of Drunk Driving Charge," *Register-Republic*, May 28, 1947

361 Gene Handsaker, "Telescope Trained on British Star," *Union Sun*, August 10, 1946

362 "New Movie Studio Ahead of Schedule," *Brooklyn Eagle*, page 10, March 20, 1947

363 C.A., "A Good Movie—Look Who Wrote It," *PM Daily*, December 26, 1947

364 Reynold Humphries, *Hollywood Blacklists: A Political and Cultural History*, Edinburgh Univ. Pr., c. 2008, pg. 83

365 Myrtle Agnes Fiddler, Ivan Trachy Eslava, Mississippi Marriages 1776-1935, March 4, 1912, (The 1900 Census lists Myrtle, age 4, born, May 31, 1896, in Mobile, Alabama)

366 "Husband, 18, Jailed on His Wedding Day," *New Orleans Item*, March 5, 1912

367 1920 Census (Mobile, Alabama), January 27, 1920, lists Lillian (Patricia) age 8

368 Elisabeth Goldbeck, "Boots Mallory—She's a Star After One Picture!" *Movie Classic*, January 1933

369 "Thomson Hill News Notes," *The Daily Star*, August 7, 1931

370 Hubbard Keavy, "Screen Life in Hollywood," *Advocate*, September 2, 1932

371 Walter Winchell, "On Broadway," *Syracuse Journal*, December 6, 1932

ENDNOTES

372 Richard Koszarski, *The Man You Love to Hate: Erich von Stroheim and Hollywood*, Oxford University Pr. c. 1983, pg. 252 (from an interview with Leonard Spigelgass)

373 Cecilia Auger, "Going Places," *Variety*, May 9, 1933

374 "News of the Dailies," *Variety*, September 5, 1933

375 "Actress Denies Legal Wedlock," *Huntsville Times*, March 19, 1933

376 "About New York's Ban on the Common-Law Wife," *San Francisco Chronicle*, June 18, 1933

377 "New York Takes Away the Favorite Implements of its 'Gold-Diggers,'" *Kansas City Star*, May 17, 1933

378 obituary, "Cagney's Brother William; 'Business Brains of Family,'" *Los Angeles Times*, January 5, 1988

379 "Actor's In-Law Signs Slaying Confession," *Omaha World-Herald*, June 27, 1953

380 Inez Wallace, "'Slow Down,' Inez Wallace Warns Herbert Marshall," *Plain Dealer*, September 21, 1947

381 John Douglas Eames, *The MGM Story*, Crown, c. 1982, pg.224

382 Erskine Johnson column, *Trenton Evening Times*, October 10, 1950

383 Roby Heard, "The Real Liberace Story," *Boston Traveler*, March 10, 1954

384 "Sarah Marshall in Footlights Debut," *Boston Traveler*, September 20, 1949

385 Joan Hanauer, "Picked Up Stage Know-How From Parents, Says Actress," *Morning Star*, July 14, 1957

386 Brian Neve, *The Many Lives of Cy Enfield*, University of Wisconsin Pr., c. 2015, pg. 75

387 Brian Neve, *The Many Lives of Cy Enfield*, University of Wisconsin Pr., c. 2015, pg. 70-71

388 George Sanders, *Memoirs of a Professional Cad*, Putnam, c. 1960

389 Marie Torre, "TV-Radio Today," *Democrat and Chronicle*, June 19, 1957 (Francis claimed that injuries prevented her from accepting other acting offers)

390 "Actor Herbert Marshall Reported Critically Ill," *Richmond Times-Dispatch*, May 8, 1951

391 John Lester, "Mystery Clicks, Rated Big TV Hit," *Nassau Review-Star*, November 6, 1951

392 Reruns of the series (1953) were advertised as *Herbert Marshall Presents* and *Times Square Playhouse*

393 Dorothy Manners, "Pick Marshall to Star with Ingrid," *Boston American*, July 26, 1952 (In 1953, Rossellini filmed a variation on the Colette theme, *Journey to Italy*, with George Sanders in role intended for Marshall.)

394 Sheilah Graham column, *Evening Star*, August 3, 1953

395 Harry Heuser, "Avian Flu Threats and 'The Birds' on the Wireless," Broadcastellan blog, October 10, 2005

396 Tom Weaver, *Interviews with B Science Fiction and Horror Movie Makers*, McFarland, c. 2006, pg. 318

397 Louella Parsons column, *Boston American*, September 18, 1954

CHAPTER TWELVE

398 Barbara R. Cooper, *Great Britons of Stage and Screen: In Conversation*, Rowman & Littlefield, c. 2015, pg. 64

399 Richard Todd, *In Camera: An Autobiography Continued*, Hutchinson, c. 1989, pg. 87

400 Ed Sikov, *Dark Victory: The Life of Bette Davis*, MacMillan, c. 2008, pg. 315

401 G.D.B., review of *Wicked as They Come*, Boston Herald, February 14, 1957

402 Jeanine Basinger, *A Woman's View*, Alfred A. Knopf, c. 1993, pg. 68

403 "Judge Defends Dahl Picture," *Advocate*, May 2, 1957

404 James Robert Parish, *Paramount Pretties*, Castle, c. 1972, pgs. 530-531

405 William J. Mann, *Behind The Screen: How Gays and Lesbians Shaped Hollywood 1910-1969*, Viking, c. 2001, pg. 312 (*Confidential* was based in New York. Scott sued in California—a technicality that lost her the case)

406 Frances Herridge, "Curtain Cues," *New York Post*, March 19, 1956

407 Sarah Marshall interview, (c. 2010) http://www.perfectloverthedoc.com/mission.html

408 Sheilah Graham column, *Seattle Daily Times*, January 24, 1958

409 Leonard Lyons, "The Lyons Den," *Boston Herald*, February 15, 1957

410 Christopher Plummer, *In Spite of Myself*, Knopf Doubleday, c. 2008, pg. 228

411 "TV Grows Up and Settles Down, Marshall Finds," *Evening Star*, March 15, 1957 (Marshall was referring to the Alfred Hitchcock episode *A Bottle of Wine*.")

412 Joel Eisner, *The Price of Fear: The Film Career of Vincent Price, in His Own Words*, Black Bed Sheet Books, c. 2013, pg. 77 (Price first made mention of he and Marshall "laughing ourselves sick" in a 1964 interview)

413 "High Tribute to Gracious Colman," *Daily Nonpareil*, May 20, 1958

414 "Feverish Efforts Fail Mrs. Marshall," *Los Angeles Times*, December 2, 1958

415 Hobe Morrison, "Edna Best in Nursing Home," *Tarrytown Daily News*, June 24, 1970

416 David Niven, *Bring on the Empty Horses*, Putnam, c. 1975, pg. 341

417 Brad Richards, "Herbert Marshall: Gentleman," *Films of the Golden Age*, Spring 2002

418 Myrna Loy, James Kotsilibas-Davis, *Myrna Loy-Being and Becoming*, Knopf, c. 1987, pg. 295

419 James Meade, review of *Fever in the Blood*, San Diego Union. January 27, 1961

ENDNOTES

420 Mike Connolly, "TV Topics," June 11, 1961

421 Pat Williams, review of *A Majority of One*, *The Daily Record*, June 15, 1961

422 James Robert Parish, email to author, May 25 and July 5, 2016

423 James Robert Parish, email to author, April 4, 2017 (Parish's meeting with Kay was in Falmouth, August 1963)

424 Jetti Ames conversation and letter, February 18, 2003, April 9, 2003

425 William J. Mann, *Behind the Screen - How Gays and Lesbians Shaped Hollywood 1910-1969*, Viking, c. 2001, pgs. 212-214

426 Glenn Erickson review of *Five Weeks in a Balloon*, DVD Savant (dvdtalk.com), March 17, 2006

427 Glen O. Gabbard, Krin Gabbard, *Psychiatry in the Cinema*, American Psychiatric Assoc., c. 1999, pg. 103

428 Lawrence J. Quirk, *Joan Crawford: The Essential Biography*, University of Kentucky Pr., c.2002, pg. 213

429 Thomas Leitch, Introduction from *John Huston as Adaptor*, State University New York Pr., c. 2017, pg. 14

430 Harry MacArthur review of *The List of Adrian Messenger*, *The Evening Star*, May 29, 1963

431 Bob Thomas, "Herbert Marshall Finds Nostalgia in Old Hollywood," *Times Advocate* September 17, 1963

432 Alex Freeman column, *State Times Advocate*, March 25, 1964

433 Rex Reed, "The Presidents Speak in Familiar Accents," *New York Times*, September 20, 1964

434 "Charles Siebert: An Appreciation," http://charlessiebertappreciation.com/

435 Elizabeth Ashley, Ross Firestone, *Actress: Postcards from the Road*, Fawcett Crest, c. 1979, pg. 48

436 Glenn Erickson, review of *The Third Day*, DVD Savant (dvdtalk.com), 2013

437 "Marshall Rites Held," *Schenectady Gazette*, January 27, 1966 (Boots is also interred at Chapel of the Pines)

438 Henry Mills, "Just an Old Smoothie," *Motion Picture*, November 1940

439 John Rosenfield, "Elegant Prototype Lost to Pictures," *Dallas Morning News*, February 4, 1966

440 Jeffrey Richards, *Visions of Yesterday*, Routledge, c. 2014, pg. 80

441 W. Somerset Maugham, *A Writer's Notebook*, Knopf Doubleday, c. 2012, pg. 365

LEGACY

442 Charles Addams, *Monster Rally*, (Foreword by John O'Hara), Simon & Schuster, c. 1950. pg. vi

443 Hal Eaton, "Hal Eaton on Broadway," *Jersey Journal*, March 21, 1957

444 Chip Royal, "Marshall Turns to Cartoons As Best Way to Shoo Blues," *Reading Eagle*, June 27, 1943

445 "Old Enough," *Omaha World-Herald*, February 23, 1964

446 Sarah Marshall in video portion of Perfect Lover, c. 2015 (http://www.perfectlover-thedoc.com/mission.html)

447 "Miss Marshall Has Taken Over - In Spades," *TV Guide*, July 14, 1962

448 Sheila Weller, "California Dreamgirl," *Vanity Fair*, November 20, 2007

449 Mick Brown, Tearing Down the Wall of Sound: The Rise and Fall of Phil Spector, A&C Black, c. 2012, pg. 359

450 Anjelica Huston, *Watch Me: A Memoir*, Simon & Schuster, c. 2014, pg.11

451 Dennis McDougal, *Five Easy Decades*, John Wiley & Sons, c. 2008. pg. 215

452 Gerald Ayres, *Everywhere Hollywood*, Gerald Ayres, c. 2016, pg. 202

453 Dennis McDougal, *Five Easy Decades*, John Wiley & Sons, c. 2008. pg. 163

454 Ship manifest for *Empress of Australia*, arriving in Liverpool from Montreal, October 10, 1953

455 Hilda Lloyd Marshall, Probate Calendar, London (March 1974)

456 Hobe Morrison, "Edna Best in Nursing Home," Tarrytown Daily News, June 24, 1970

457 "A Conversation with Tim Bourne, Independent Producer," Craig Miller Prod. Vimeo, March 11, 2013

458 Ward Morehouse, "Sarah Marshall Quit School to Act," *Long Island Star-Journal*, April 22, 1959

459 Hilary Cadigan, "From the Apple to the Peach: An Interview with Producer Tim Bourne," *Oz*, May 9, 2016

460 Robert Osborne, Turner Classic Movies' "Summer Under the Stars," August 16, 2014

ACKNOWLEDGEMENTS

461 Mark Alan Vieira, email to author, September 18, 2016

462 W. Somerset Maugham, *The Summing Up*, Doubleday, c. 1938

Paris Bound (1929) Newlyweds Bart and Edna, playing newlyweds, at the Lyric

HERBERT MARSHALL CREDITS

STAGE
(Not all of Marshall's minor roles 1910-1913 are included on this list)

1910:
The Arcadians - by Mark Ambient and Alexander M. Thompson (music by Lionel Monckton and Howard Talbot); D: Robert Courtneidge; Cast: Eric Blore, Herbert Marshall (footman)

Second to None - by Walter Howard; P/D: N. Carter Slaughter; Cast: in bit roles were Herbert Marshall and Ronald Colman

1911:
The Adventure of Lady Ursula - (Opera House, Buxton) by Anthony Hope; Cast: Herbert Marshall (servant)

1912:
Cinderella - (Prince's Theatre) by Newman Maurice; Cast: Elsie Craven, Nora Erskine, Sims Woolley, K. Scott Barrie, Herbert Marshall (Johnny Woggle)

1913:
Brewster's Millions - (Prince's Theatre) by Winchell Smith and Byron Ongley; Cast: Percy Hutchison, Gerald Fitzgerald, Ernest Deans, Herbert Marshall (Tommy Smith)

1913-14:
The Headmaster - (on tour) by Edward Knoblock and Wilfred Coleby; Cast: Cyril Maude, Herbert Marshall (Jack), Mollie Maitland, Frances White

1914-15:
Grumpy - (on tour) by Horace Hodges and T. Wigney Percival; D: Horace Hodges; Cast:

Cyril Maude, Herbert Marshall (Ernest Heron), Margot Kelly

1915-16:
Grumpy - (U.S. and Canada tour) Cast: Cyril Maude, Herbert Marshall (Ernest Heron), John Harwood, Elsie Mackay

1918:
Betty at Bay - (on tour) by Jessie Porter; Cast: Kathleen Sinclair, Herbert Marshall (Dick Fellowes)

1918-19:
Make-Believe - (Lyric) by A. A. Milne; producer: Nigel Playfair; Cast: Rosa Lynd, Kinsey Peile, Herbert Marshall (Baron Bluebeard, Pirate Bill, Red Prince)

1919:
The Younger Generation - (Lyric) by Stanley Houghton; D: Stanley Drewitt; Cast: Nigel Playfair, Ada King, Leslie Banks, Herbert Marshall (Arthur Kennion)

You Never Know, Y'Know - (Criterion) by Martin Henry and Hannaford Bennett (adapted from Georges Feydeau, *La Puce a l'Oreille*) Cast: Fred Eastman, Kitty Barlow, Herbert Marshall (Etienne)

Abraham Lincoln - (Lyric) by John Drinkwater; Cast: William .J. Rea, Harcourt Williams, Mary Raby, Herbert Marshall (Johnson White/Edward Stanton), Reginald Denham

Candida - (Stratford Festival, one performance) by George Bernard Shaw; Cast: Ellen O'Malley, Herbert Marshall (Rev. James Morrell), Nigel Playfair

Riding for a Fall (Royal Court Theatre) by Mrs. Hardy; Cast: Herbert Marshall (Adrian Fitzclarence), Ernest R. Holloway, Leonard Upton, Kinsey Peile

1920:
Merchant of Venice - (Duke of York's Theatre) by William Shakespeare; Cast: Maurice Moscovitch, Edwin Greenwood, Herbert Marshall (Antonio), George Hayes

On the High Road - (St. Martin's Theatre, one performance) by Anton Chekhov; Cast: Harold Scott, Dennis Wyndham, Herbert Marshall (Kusma), Cathleen Nesbitt

John Ferguson - (Lyric) by St. John G. Ervine; Cast: William J. Rea, Marie O'Neill, Herbert Marshall (Andrew Ferguson), Moyna Macgill, J.M. Kerrigan

Defeat - (Lyric, one performance) by John Galsworthy; Cast: Herbert Marshall (officer), Cathleen Nesbitt (girl)

As You Like It - (Lyric) by William Shakespeare; Cast: Ivan Sampson, Herbert Marshall (Jacques), Nigel Playfair, Athene Seyler, George Hayes, William J. Rea

Wurzel-Flummery - (Lyric, one performance) by A. A. Milne; Cast: Nigel Playfair, Herbert Marshall (Richard Meriton), Moyna Magill

CREDITS

Brown Sugar - (Duke of York's Theatre) by Lady Arthur Lever; Cast: Eric Lewis, Martin Walker, Charles Kenyon, Herbert Marshall (Lord Sloane), Edna Best, Henrietta Watson

The Crossing - (Comedy Theatre) by Bertram Forsythe and Algernon Blackwood; Cast: Herbert Marshall (Andrew Grimshaw), Hubert Harben, Halliwell Hobbes, Marjorie Gordon, Irene Rooke

1921:

A Safety Match - (Strand Theatre) by Ian Hay; Cast: Herbert Marshall (Jim Carthew), Franklyn Bellamy, Oswald Roberts

Count "X" - (Garrick) by Horace Vachell; Cast: Herbert Marshall (Colin Rossiter), Leon M. Lion, Moyna Macgill

Mother of Pearl - (Winter Garden, one performance) by Gertrude Jennings; Cast: Herbert Marshall (Ted Harris), Sydney Fairbrother, Marie Lohr

Her Destiny - (Portsmouth Theatre Royal, one performance) by Horace Vachell, adapted from the play *L'Inconnu*, by Louis Verneuil; Cast: Marie Lohr, Herbert Marshall (Saville), Cyril Cunningham, Mollie Maitland

1921-22:

Fedora - (Canada, U.S. tour) by Victorien Sardou; Cast: Marie Lohr, Herbert Marshall (Count Loris Ipanoff), Edmund Gwenn, Hilda Spong

The Voice From the Minaret - (Canada, U.S. tour) by Robert Hichens; Cast: Marie Lohr, Herbert Marshall (Andrew Fabian), Edmund Gwenn

The Marionettes - (Canada, U.S. tour) by Pierre Wolff; Cast: Marie Lohr, Herbert Marshall (Marquis), Herbert Ross, Mollie Maitland

Her Destiny - (Canada, U.S. tour) by Horace Vachell, adapted from the play *L'Inconnu*, by Louis Verneuil; Cast: Marie Lohr, Herbert Marshall (Saville), Helen Haye, Mollie Maitland

1922:

Defeat - (Everyman Theatre) by John Galsworthy; Cast: Herbert Marshall (officer), Mary Merrall (girl)

Windows - (Court Theatre) by John Galsworthy; Cast: Herbert Marshall (Geoffrey March), John Howell, Leslie Banks, Irene Rooke, Mary Odette, Ernest Thesiger, Leon M. Lion

Belinda - (Globe) by A.A. Milne; cast: Irene Vanbrugh, Herbert Marshall (John Tremayne), Dion Boucicault

1922-23:

The Young Idea - (on tour) (Savoy) by Noel Coward; Cast: Herbert Marshall (George Brent), Noel Coward, Leslie Banks, Ann Trevor, Mollie Maitland, Irene Rathbone, Kate Cutler

1923:

The Case for the Prosecution - (Shaftsbury, one performance) by Thomas Sterling Boyd; Cast: Geoffrey Bevan, Herbert Marshall (Alan Carnegie)

Aren't We All? - (Globe) by Frederick Lonsdale; Cast: Marie Lohr, Vivian Reynolds, Herbert Marshall (Willie Tatham), Charles Hickman

The Voice Outside - (Globe) by Gertrude Jennings; Cast: Marie Lohr, Herbert Marshall (Alec Verne)

The Machine-Wreckers - (Kingsway Theater) by Ernst Toller; Cast: Herbert Marshall (Jimmy Cobbett), John H. Moore, George Hayes

The Man Who Ate the Popomack - (Savoy, one performance) by W.J. Turner; D: Reginald Denham; Cast: Herbert Marshall (Lord Belvoir), Isabel Jeans, George Hayes, Reginald Denham, Leo Carroll

1923-1924:

Paddy The Next Best Thing - (Savoy) by Edith Ostlere and Mrs. W. Gayer Mackay; Cast: Josephine Wilson, Peggy O'Neil, Herbert Marshall (Laurence Blake), Brian Aherne, Una O'Connor

1924:

Alice-Sit-by-the-Fire - (Comedy Theatre) by J.M. Barrie; Cast: Herbert Marshall (Steve Rollo), Graham Browne, Marie Tempest, Elizabeth Irving

Far Above Rubies - (Comedy Theatre) by Alfred Sutro; D: Stanley Bell; Cast: Marie Lohr, Ralph Forbes, Herbert Marshall (Constantine Tedcastle), Vivian Reynolds, Marie Tempest

This Marriage - (Comedy Theatre) by Eliot Crawshay-Williams; Cast: Tallulah Bankhead, Herbert Marshall (Christopher Maitland), Tom Reynolds, Cathleen Nesbitt, Auriol Lee

The Ware Case - (Adelphi, one performance) by George Pleydell Bancroft; Cast: Gerald du Maurier, Herbert Marshall (Barrister), Ernest Thesiger, Edmund Gwenn, Jack Buchanan, Leslie Banks, C. Aubrey Smith, Gladys Cooper, Marie Lohr; (In aid for King George's Pension Fund for Actors)

Morals - (Little Theatre) by Jules Eckert Goodman; Cast: Herbert Marshall (Dick), Edna Best, Robert Andrews, Helen Haye

Dear Father - (New Scala, one performance) by Michael Arlen; Cast: Herbert Marshall, Isabel Jeans, Brian Gilmour

The Pelican - (Ambassadors) by Tennyson Jess and H.M. Harwood; Cast: Herbert Marshall (Marcus Heriot), Frederick Kerr, Robert Andrews, Charles Cherry, Elizabeth Pollock

1925:

Nellie - (Prince of Wales, one performance) by Hartley Carrick and Edmund Maurice; Cast: Herbert Marshall (Colonel Hamilton), Owen Roughwood

CREDITS

Reprieved - (Prince of Wales, one performance) by H.C.G. Stevens; Cast: Herbert Marshall (husband), Ian Hunter

The Verdict - (Aldwych Theatre, one performance) by Olive Lethbridge; Cast: Herbert Marshall (Sir John Verney), Walter Butler

Lavender Ladies - (Comedy Theatre) by Daisy Fisher; Cast: Herbert Marshall (Hayward Clear), Arthur W. Holman, Louise Hampton, Elissa Landi, James Raglan

The Pelican - (Times Square Theatre, New York) by Tennyson Jess and H.M. Harwood; D: Frederick Kerr; Cast: Herbert Marshall (Marcus Heriot), Frederick Kerr, Margaret Lawrence, Robert Andrews

1925-1926:
These Charming People - (Gaiety) (U.S. tour) by Michael Arlen; D: Winchell Smith; Cast: Cyril Maude, Edna Best, Herbert Marshall (Geoffrey Allen), Alfred Drayton, Alma Tell

1926:
By-Ways - (Globe) by H.C.M. Hardinge (from his novel *A Bowl of Red Roses*); Cast: Herbert Marshall (Jim Bathurst), Margaret Bannerman, Francis Lister, Cyril Cunningham

Engaged - (Globe) by William Hurlbut; Cast: Herbert Marshall (Tom Harraway), Leonard Upton, Margaret Bannerman, Nina Boucicault

The Queen Was in the Parlour - (St. Martin's, and Duke of York's) by Noel Coward; D: Basil Dean; Cast: Francis Lister, Herbert Marshall (Prince Keri of Zalgar), Madge Titheradge, Viola Tree

The Beautiful White Devil - (Globe, one performance) by Neil MacDonald; Cast: Herbert Marshall (Sir Philip Wroxley), Frank Vosper, Francis Lister

1927:
Interference - (St. James) by Roland Pertwee and Harold Dearden; D: Gerald du Maurier; Cast: Gerald du Maurier, Herbert Marshall (Philip Voaze), Basil Loder, Frank Lawton, Moyna Magill

A Perfect Gentleman - (New Theatre, one performance) by Edgar Wallace; Cast: Gerald du Maurier, Herbert Marshall, Gladys Cooper

I'll Give You a Ring - (Globe, one performance) by G. Carten; P: Herbert Marshall; Cast: Ralph Richardson, Herbert Marshall (Waiter), Bruce Belfrage

1928:
Sexes and Sevens - (Globe, one performance) by Arthur Wimperis; Cast: Ernest Truex, Ronald Squire, Leon Quartermaine, Gerald du Maurier, Herbert Marshall (3rd Waiter), Francis Lister

S.O.S. - (St. James) by Walter Ellis; Cast: Gerald du Maurier, Herbert Marshall (Sir Julian Weir), Gracie Fields

London Pride - (Drury Lane, one performance) by Gladys Unger and A. Neil Lyon; Cast: Edmund Gwenn, Ernest Thesiger, Cedric Hardwicke, George du Maurier, Herbert Marshall (Menzies), Edna Best, Evelyn Laye, Nigel Bruce, Leslie Banks, Viola Tree, Hermione Baddeley, Gertrude Lawrence, Gracie Fields; (Charity matinee for Charing Cross Hospital)

Come With Me - (New Theatre) by Margaret Kennedy and Basil Dean; D: Basil Dean; Cast: Edna Best, Herbert Marshall (Ronald Luckin), Dame May Whitty, Ian Hunter

1928-1929:
The High Road - (Fulton Theatre, New York) by Frederick Lonsdale; D: Frederick Lonsdale; Cast: Herbert Marshall (Duke of Warrington), Edna Best, Frederick Kerr, Hilda Spong, John Williams, Alfred Drayton, Winifred Harris

1929:
Paris Bound - (Lyric) by Phlip Barry; Cast: Edna Best, Herbert Marshall (Jim Hutton), Laurence Olivier, Margaret Turner, Betty Schuster, Henrietta Watson

Looking at You - (London Pavilion, one performance) by Douglas Byng and Lance Lister; Cast: Ernest Thesiger, Herbert Marshall, Edna Best, Sacha Guitry, Sonnie Hale, Stanley Holloway, Alfred Lunt, Lynn Fontanne, Gracie Fields, Sydney Howard, Yvonne Printemps, Tilly Losch, Jessie Mathews

A Bill of Divorcement - (St. Martin's) by Clemence Dane; Cast: Edna Best, Herbert Marshall (Hilary Fairfield), Cathleen Nesbitt

Heat Wave - (St. James) by Roland Pertwee (from a book by Denise Robins); D: Walter Hackett; Cast: Herbert Marshall (Hugh Dawltry), Lawrence Hardman, Ann Todd, Phyllis Nielson-Terry

1930:
Michael and Mary - (St. James) by A. A. Milne; Cast: Herbert Marshall (Michael), Edna Best, Frank Lawton, Elizabeth Allan, Torin Thatcher

The Swan - (St. James) by Ferenc Molnar; E: Gilbert Miller; Cast: Herbert Marshall (Prince Albert), Edna Best, Colin Clive

1931:
Tomorrow and Tomorrow - (Henry Miller's Theatre, New York) by Philip Barry (original title *Hail and Farewell*); D: Gilbert Miller; Cast: Herbert Marshall (Nicolas Hay), Zita Johann, Adele Schuyler, Osgood Perkins, Harvey Stephens

1931-1932:
There's Always Juliet - (Apollo, London) (Empire Theatre, New York) by John van Druten; D: Auriol Lee; Cast: Herbert Marshall (Dwight Houston), Edna Best, Cyril Raymond, Dame May Whitty

CREDITS

1932-1933:
Another Language - (Lyric) by Rose Franken; D: Auriol Lee; cast: Herbert Marshall (Victor Hallam), Edna Best (replaced by Celia Johnson), Mary Jerrold, Louis Hayward, Rex Harrison (understudy to Marshall, before replacing Louis Hayward)

1939:
Ladies and Gentlemen - (Santa Barbara, San Francisco, Los Angeles) by Charles MacArthur, Ben Hecht (original script by Ladislaus Bus-Fekete); P: Gilbert Miller; D: Charles MacArthur, Lewis Allen; Cast: Helen Hayes, Herbert Marshall (Mr. Campbell), Connie Gilchrist, Evelyn Varden, Joseph Sweeney, Robert Keith, Roy Roberts

1940:
Still Life - (El Capitan Theatre, Hollywood) by Noel Coward; one-act play included in Coward's *Tonight at 8:30* (filmed as *Brief Encounter*); Cast: Rosalind Russell, Herbert Marshall (Alec Harvey), Heather Angel, Una O'Connor, Doris Lloyd, Freddie Bartholomew, Edmund Gwenn; (August 1940 benefit for the British War Relief)

1961:
A Majority of One - (on tour June-August) - Playhouse in the Park, Philadelphia, Pa., Pocono Playhouse, Mountain Home, Pa., Lakewood Theater, Skowhegan, Me., Falmouth Playhouse, Ma., Gristmill Playhouse, Andover, N.J., Lake Whalom Playhouse, Fitchburg, Ma., Ogunquit Playhouse, Ogunquit Me., Lakes Region Playhouse, Laconia-Gilford, N.H., Ivoryton Playhouse, Essex, Ct., Cape Playhouse, Dennis, Ma.; D: Elliot Martin; Cast: Herbert Marshall (Mr. Asano), Dora Weissman/Zamah Cunningham, Yoneko Ohashi, Risa Schwartz, Stuart Unger/John Dutra

Trouble in Paradise (1932) Miriam Hopkins, Marshall and Kay Francis (Paramount)

FILM

(In order per AFI release dates; UK films per London premier)

Mumsie (1927) Twickenham (MGM distributor in Australia); P/D: Herbert Wilcox; Cast: Pauline Frederick, Nelson Keys, Herbert Marshall (Col. Armytage)

Pusher-in-the-Face (1929) Paramount; (Story by F. Scott Fitzgerald); D: Robert Florey; Cast: Lester Allen, Raymond, Hitchcock, Estelle Taylor, Lillian Walker, Carol McComas, Reginald Owen, Herbert Marshall (bit), Preston Foster. (Filmed for the Actors' Fund and Authors' League)

The Letter (1929) Paramount; P: Monte Bell; D: Jean De Limur; Cast: Jeanne Eagels, Reginald Owen, Herbert Marshall (Geoffrey Hammond), O.P. Heggie, Irene Brown, Lady Tsen Mei;

Academy Award nomination: Best Actress (Jeanne Eagels)

Murder! (1930) British International; D: Alfred Hitchcock; Cast: Herbert Marshall (Sir John Menier), Norah Baring, Esme Percy, Una O'Connor, Phyllis Konstam, Miles Mander

The House that Shadows Built (1931) Paramount (Documentary celebrating Paramount's 20th anniversary, includes a clip from Marshall's upcoming *Secrets of a Secretary*)

Secrets of a Secretary (1931) Paramount; D: George Abbott; Cast: Claudette Colbert, Herbert Marshall (Lord Paul Danforth), Georges Metaxa, Betty Lawford, Mary Boland, Burton Churchill

The Calendar (1931) (aka *Bachelor's Folly*) Gainsborough, British Lion; P: Michael Balcon; D: T. Hayes Hunter; Cast: Herbert Marshall (Garry Anson), Edna Best, Gordon Harker, Anne Grey, Nigel Bruce, Melville Cooper

Michael and Mary (1931) Gainsborough; P: Michael Balcon; D: Victor Saville; Cast: Herbert Marshall (Michael Rowe), Edna Best (Mary Rowe), Frank Lawton, Elizabeth Allan

The Faithful Heart (1932) (aka *Faithful Hearts*) Gainsborough; P: Michael Balcon; D: Victor Saville; Cast: Herbert Marshall (Waverly Ango), Edna Best, Mignon O'Doherty, Anne Grey

Blonde Venus (1932) Paramount; D: Josef von Sternberg; Cast: Marlene Dietrich, Herbert Marshall (Edward Farady), Cary Grant, Dickie Moore, Gene Morgan, Rita La Roy, Robert Emmett O'Connor, Sidney Toler, Sterling Holloway, Hattie McDaniel, Dennis O'Keefe

Trouble in Paradise (1932) Paramount; P/D: Ernst Lubitsch; Cast: Miriam Hopkins, Kay Francis, Herbert Marshall (Gaston Monescu), Charlie Ruggles, Edward Everett Horton, C. Aubrey Smith, Leonid Kinskey, Luis Alberni

Evenings for Sale (1932) Paramount; D: Stuart Walker; Cast: Herbert Marshall (Count Franz von Degenthal), Sari Maritza, Charlie Ruggles, Mary Boland, George Barbier, Bert Roach

I Was a Spy (1933) Gaumont-British; P: Michael Balcon; D: Victor Saville; Cast: Madeleine Carroll, Conrad Veidt, Herbert Marshall (Stephan), Edmund Gwenn, Sir Gerald Du Maurier, Nigel Bruce, Martita Hunt

The Solitaire Man (1933) MGM; D: Jack Conway; Cast: Herbert Marshall (Oliver Lane), May Robson, Elizabeth Allan, Ralph Forbes, Mary Boland, Lionel Atwill, Lucille Gleason

Four Frightened People (1934) Paramount; D: Cecil B. DeMille; Cast: Claudette Colbert, Herbert Marshall (Arnold Ainger), Mary Boland, William Gargan, Leo Carrillo, Nella Walker

Riptide (1934) MGM; D: Edmund Goulding; Cast: Norma Shearer, Robert Montgomery, Herbert Marshall (Lord Philip Rexford), Mrs. Patrick Campbell, Skeets Gallagher, Ralph Forbes, Lilyan Tashman, George K. Arthur, Halliwell Hobbes, Cora Sue Collins, Arthur Treacher

Outcast Lady (1934) (released in England as *A Woman of the World*) MGM; D: Robert Z. Leonard; Cast: Constance Bennett, Herbert Marshall (Napier), Ralph Forbes, Mrs. Patrick Campbell, Hugh Williams, Elizabeth Allan, Leo Carroll, Henry Stephenson

The Painted Veil (1934) MGM; D: Richard Boleslawski; Cast: Greta Garbo, Herbert Marshall (Walter Fane), George Brent, Warner Oland, Jean Hersholt, Bodil Rosing, Katharine Alexander, Cecilia Parker, Keye Luke, Mary Forbes

The Good Fairy (1935) Universal; D: William Wellman; Cast: Margaret Sullivan, Herbert Marshall (Max Sporum), Frank Morgan, Reginald Owen, Eric Blore, Alan Hale, Beulah Bondi, Cesar Romero, Luis Alberni, Matt McHugh, Gavin Gordon

The Flame Within (1935) MGM; D: Edmund Goulding; Cast: Ann Harding, Herbert Marshall (Gordon Phillips), Maureen O'Sullivan, Louis Hayward, Henry Stephenson

Accent on Youth (1935) Paramount; D: Wesley Ruggles; Cast: Sylvia Sidney, Herbert Marshall (Stephen Gaye), Phillip Reed, Holmes Herbert, Catharine Doucet, Astrid Allwyn, Ernest Cossart, Donald Meek, Lon Chaney Jr., Samuel S. Hinds

The Dark Angel (1935) Samuel Goldwyn (United Artists); P: Samuel Goldwyn; D: Sidney Franklin; Cast: Fredric March, Merle Oberon, Herbert Marshall (Gerald Shannon), Janet Beecher, John Halliday, Henrietta Crossman, Frieda Inescort, Cora Sue Collins

> Academy Award nominations: Best Actress (Merle Oberon), Best Sound Recording, Best Art Direction (won)

If Only You Could Cook (1935) Columbia; D: William A. Seiter; Cast: Herbert Marshall (Jim Buchanan), Jean Arthur, Leo Carrillo, Lionel Stander, Alan Edwards, Frieda Inescort, Gene Morgan, Ralf Harolde, Matt McHugh, Russell Hicks, Bess Flowers

The Lady Consents (1936) RKO; D: Stephen Roberts; Cast: Ann Harding, Herbert Marshall (Mike Talbot), Margaret Lindsay, Walter Abel, Edward Ellis, Hobart Cavanaugh, Ilka Chase

Till We Meet Again (1936) (aka *Reunion*) Paramount; D: Robert Florey; Cast: Herbert Marshall (Alan Barclow), Gertrude Michael, Lionel Atwill, Rod La Rocque, Guy Bates Post, Spencer Charters, Christian Rubb

Forgotten Faces (1936) Paramount; D: E.A. Dupont; Cast: Herbert Marshall (Harry Ashton), Gertrude Michael, James Burke, Robert Cummings, Jane Rhodes, Alan Edwards, Mary Gordon, Bess Flowers, Irving Bacon, Matt McHugh

Girl's Dormitory (1936) 20th Century-Fox; D: Irving Cummings; Cast: Herbert Marshall (Stephen Dominik), Ruth Chatterton, Simone Simon, Constance Collier, J. Edward Bromberg, Dixie Dunbar, John Qualen, Shirley Deane, Tyrone Power Jr., Frank Reicher, Christian Rubb

A Woman Rebels (1936) RKO; D: Mark Sandrich; Cast: Katharine Hepburn, Herbert Marshall (Thomas Lane), Elizabeth Allan, Donald Crisp, Doris Dudley, David Manners, Lucile Watson, Van Heflin, Eily Malyon, Doris Lloyd, Molly Lamont

Make Way for a Lady (1936) RKO; D: David Burton; Cast: Herbert Marshall (Christopher Drew), Anne Shirley, Gertrude Michael, Margot Grahame, Taylor Holmes, Clara Blandick, Frank Coghlan Jr., Willie Best

Breakfast for Two (1937) RKO; D: Alfred Santell; Cast: Barbara Stanwyck, Herbert Marshall (Jonathan Blaire), Glenda Farrell, Eric Blore, Donald Meek, Etienne Girardot, Frank M. Thomas

CREDITS

Angel (1937) Paramount; D: Ernst Lubitsch; Cast: Marlene Dietrich, Herbert Marshall (Sir Frederick Barker), Melvyn Douglas, Edward Everett Horton, Ernest Cossart, Laura Hope Crews

Mad About Music (1938) Universal; P: Joe Pasternak; D: Norman Taurog; Cast: Deanna Durbin, Herbert Marshall (Richard Todd), Gail Patrick, Arthur Treacher, William Frawley, Marcia Mae Jones, Helen Parrish, Jackie Moran, Elizabeth Risdon, Nana Bryant, Christian Rub, Sid Grauman

> **Academy Award nominations:** Best Original Story, Best Cinematography, Best Interior Decoration, Best Score, Special Oscar (Deanna Durbin)

Woman Against Woman (1938) MGM; D: Robert B. Sinclair; Cast: Herbert Marshall (Stephen Holland), Virginia Bruce, Mary Astor, Janet Beecher, Marjorie Rambeau, Juanita Quigley, Zeffie Tilbury, Sarah Padden, Marie Blake

Always Goodbye (1938) 20th Century-Fox; D: Sidney Lanfield; Cast: Barbara Stanwyck, Herbert Marshall (Jim Howard), Ian Hunter, Cesar Romero, Lynn Bari, Binnie Barnes, John Russell, Mary Forbes, Franklyn Pangborn

Zaza (1939) Paramount; D: George Cukor; Cast: Claudette Colbert, Herbert Marshall (Dufresne), Bert Lahr, Helen Westley, Constance Collier, Genevieve Tobin, Walter Catlett, Rex O'Malley, Rex Evans, Ann Todd, Monty Woolley

A Bill of Divorcement (1940) RKO; D: John Farrow; Cast: Maureen O'Hara, Adolphe Menjou, Fay Bainter, Herbert Marshall (Gray Meredith), Dame May Whitty, Patrick Knowles, C. Aubrey Smith, Ernest Cossart

Foreign Correspondent (1940) United Artists; P: Walter Wanger; D: Alfred Hitchcock; Cast: Joel McCrea, Laraine Day, Herbert Marshall (Stephen Fisher), George Sanders, Albert Basserman, Robert Benchley, Edmund Gwenn, Eduardo Cianelli, Harry Davenport

> **Academy Award nominations:** Best Supporting Actor (Albert Basserman), Best Art Direction, Best Cinematography, Best Special Effects, Best Sound, Best Original Screenplay

The Letter (1940) Warner Bros.; D: William Wyler; Cast: Bette Davis, Herbert Marshall (Robert Crosbie), James Stephenson, Frieda Inescort, Gale Sondergaard, Bruce Lester, Doris Lloyd, Willie Fung

> **Academy Award nominations:** Best Picture, Best Director, Best Actress (Bette Davis), Best Supporting Actor (James Stephenson), Best Editing, Best Original Score, Best B&W Cinematography

Adventure in Washington (1941) Columbia; D: Alfred E. Green; Cast: Herbert Marshall (John Coleridge), Virginia Bruce, Gene Reynolds, Samuel S. Hinds, Ralph Morgan, Bess Flowers, Pierre Watkin, James Flavin

The Little Foxes (1941) Samuel Goldwyn Prod. (RKO distributor) P: Samuel Goldwyn; D: William Wyler; Cast: Bette Davis, Herbert Marshall (Horace Giddens), Teresa Wright, Richard Carlson, Dan Duryea, Patricia Collinge, Charles Dingle, Carl Benton Reid, Russell Hicks

> **Academy Award nominations:** Best Picture, Best Director, Best Actress (Bette Davis), Best Supporting Actress (for both Teresa Wright and Patricia Collinge), Best Screenplay, Best Music Scoring of a Dramatic Picture, Best Film Editing, Best Art Direction

When Ladies Meet (1941) MGM; D: Robert Z. Leonard; Cast: Joan Crawford, Robert Taylor, Greer Garson, Herbert Marshall (Rogers Woodruff), Spring Byington, Rafael Storm

> **Academy Award nomination:** Best Art Direction

Kathleen (1942) MGM; D: Harold S. Bucquet; Cast: Shirley Temple, Herbert Marshall (John Davis), Laraine Day, Gail Patrick, Felix Bressart, Nella Walker, James Flavin

The Moon and Sixpence (1942) United Artists; D: Albert Lewin; Cast: George Sanders, Herbert Marshall (Geoffrey Wolfe), Doris Dudley, Eric Blore, Steven Geray, Albert Basserman, Florence Bates

> **Academy Award nomination:** Best Score

Forever and a Day (1943) RKO; D: Rene Clair, Edmund Goulding, Cedric Hardwicke, Frank Lloyd, Victor Saville, Robert Stevenson, Herbert Wilcox; Cast: Brian Aherne, Robert Cummings, Charles Laughton, Ida Lupino, Herbert Marshall (curate), Ray Milland, Anna Neagle, Merle Oberon, Gladys Cooper, Cedric Hardwicke, Ian Hunter, Buster Keaton, Elsa Lanchester, Eric Blore, Jessie Mathews, Claude Rains, C. Aubrey Smith, Kent Smith, Ruth Warwick, Dame May Whitty, Roland Young, Victor McLaglan, Edmund Gwenn (and others)

Flight for Freedom (1943) RKO; D: Lothar Mendes; Cast: Rosalind Russell, Fred MacMurray, Herbert Marshall (Paul Turner), Eduardo Ciannelli, Walter Kingsford, Hugh Beaumont

> **Academy Award nomination:** Best Art Direction and Interior Decoration

Young Ideas (1943) MGM; D: Jules Dassin; Cast: Susan Peters, Herbert Marshall (Michael Kingsley), Mary Astor, Elliot Reid, Richard Carlson, Allyn Joslyn, Frances Rafferty, Frank Faylen, Ava Gardner, Noel Neill

Andy Hardy's Blonde Trouble (1944) MGM; D: George B. Seitz; Cast: Lewis Stone, Mickey Rooney, Fay Holden, Sara Haden, Herbert Marshall (Dr. Standish), Bonita Granville, Jean Porter, Keye Luke

The Enchanted Cottage (1945) RKO; D: John Cromwell; Cast: Dorothy McGuire, Robert Young, Herbert Marshall (John Hillgrove), Mildred Natwick, Spring Byington, Hillary Brooke

CREDITS

Academy Award nomination: Best Score

The Unseen (1945) Paramount; D: Lewis Allen; Cast: Joel McCrea, Gail Russell, Herbert Marshall (Dr. Charles Evans), Phyllis Brooks, Isobel Elsom, Norman Lloyd

Academy Award nomination: Best Sound

Crack-Up (1946) RKO; D: Irving Reis; Cast: Pat O'Brien, Claire Trevor, Herbert Marshall (Traybin), Ray Collins, Wallace Ford

The Razor's Edge (1946) 20th Century-Fox; D: Edmund Goulding; Cast: Tyrone Power, Gene Tierney, John Payne, Anne Baxter, Clifton Webb, Herbert Marshall (W. Somerset Maugham), Lucille Watson, Frank Latimore, Elsa Lanchester, Bess Flowers

Academy Award nominations: Best Picture, Best Art Direction, Best Supporting Actor (Clifton Webb), Best Supporting Actress (Anne Baxter - won)

Duel in the Sun (1946) Selznick Studio; D: King Vidor; Cast: Jennifer Jones, Joseph Cotton, Gregory Peck, Lionel Barrymore, Herbert Marshall (Scott Chavez), Lillian Gish, Walter Huston, Charles Bickford, Harry Carey, Tilly Losch, Butterfly McQueen

Academy Award nominations: Best Actress (Jennifer Jones), Best Supporting Actress (Lillian Gish)

Ivy (1947) Universal; D: Sam Wood; Cast: Joan Fontaine, Patrick Knowles, Herbert Marshall (Miles Rushworth), Richard Ney, Sir Cedric Hardwicke, Lucile Watson, Sara Allgood, Henry Stephenson, Molly Lamont, Una O'Connor, Bess Flowers

High Wall (1947) MGM; D: Curtis Bernhardt; Cast: Robert Taylor, Audrey Totter, Herbert Marshall (Willard Whitcombe), Dorothy Patrick, H.B. Warner, Warner Anderson, Moroni Olsen

The Secret Garden (1949) MGM; D: Fred M. Wilcox; Cast: Margaret O'Brien, Herbert Marshall (Archibald Craven), Dean Stockwell, Gladys Cooper, Elsa Lanchester, Brian Roper, Reginald Owen

The Underworld Story (1950) United Artists; D: Cy Enfield; Cast: Dan Duryea, Herbert Marshall (E.J. Stanton), Gale Storm, Howard Da Silva, Michael O'Shea, Mary Anderson, Gar Moore, Frieda Inescort, Harry Shannon, Alan Hale Jr.

Black Jack (1950) (U.S. release 1952, as *Captain Blackjack*) Classic Pictures; D: Julien Duvivier; Cast: George Sanders, Herbert Marshall (Dr. Curtis), Agnes Moorehead, Patricia Roc

Anne of the Indies (1951) 20th Century-Fox; D: Jacques Tourneur; Cast: Jean Peters, Louis Jourdan, Debra Paget, Herbert Marshall (Dr. Jameson), Thomas Gomez

Angel Face (1953) RKO; D: Otto Preminger; Cast: Robert Mitchum, Jean Simmons, Mona Freeman, Herbert Marshall (Charles Tremayne), Leon Ames, Barbara O'Neil, Bess Flowers

Riders to the Stars (1954) United Artists; D: Richard Carlson; Cast: William Lundigan, Herbert Marshall (Dr. Donald Stanton), Richard Carlson, Martha Hyer, Dawn Addams

Gog (1954) United Artists; D: Herbert L. Strock; Cast: Richard Egan, Constance Dowling, Herbert Marshall (Dr. Van Ness)

The Black Shield of Falworth (1954) Universal; D: Rudolph Mate; Cast: Tony Curtis, Janet Leigh, David Farrar, Barbara Rush, Herbert Marshall (William, Earl of Macworth), Torin Thatcher, Daniel O'Herlihy, Patrick O'Neal, Ian Keith, Doris Lloyd, Rhys Williams

The Virgin Queen (1955) 20th Century-Fox; D: Henry Koster; Cast: Bette Davis, Richard Todd, Joan Collins, Jay Robinson, Herbert Marshall (Robert Dudley, Earl of Leicester), Dan O'Herlihy

Academy Award nomination: Best Costume Design

Wicked As They Come (1956) (U.S. release 1957, as *Portrait in Smoke*) Columbia; D: Ken Hughes; Cast: Arlene Dahl, Phil Carey, Herbert Marshall (Stephen Collins), Michael Goodliffe, Ralph Truman, Faith Brook

The Weapon (1956) (U.S. release 1957) Republic; D: Val Guest; Cast: Steve Cochram, Lizbeth Scott, Herbert Marshall (Inspector MacKenzie), Nicole Maurey, John Whiteley, George Cole

Stage Struck (1958) RKO; D: Sidney Lumet; Cast: Henry Fonda, Susan Strasberg, Joan Greenwood, Herbert Marshall (Robert Harley Hedges), Christopher Plummer

The Fly (1958) 20th Century-Fox; D: Kurt Neumann; Cast: Al Hedison, Patricia Owens, Vincent Price, Herbert Marshall (Inspector Charas), Kathleen Freeman, Charles Herbert

College Confidential (1960) Universal; D: Albert Zugsmith; Cast: Steve Allen, Jayne Meadows, Walter Winchell, Mamie Van Doren, Mickey Shaughnessy, Cathy Crosby, Herbert Marshall (Henry Addison), Conway Twitty

Midnight Lace (1960) Universal-International; D: David Miller; Cast: Doris Day, Rex Harrison, John Gavin, Myrna Loy, Roddy McDowell, Herbert Marshall (Charles Manning), Natasha Parry, Hermoine Baddeley, John Williams, Richard Ney, Rhys Williams, Doris Lloyd

Academy Award nomination: Best Costume Design

A Fever in the Blood (1961) Warner Bros.; D: Vincent Sherman; Cast: Efrem Zimbalist Jr., Angie Dickinsen, Jack Kelly, Don Ameche, Ray Danton, Herbert Marshall (Governor Thornwall), Carroll O'Connor

Five Weeks in a Balloon (1962) 20th Century-Fox; D: Irwin Allen; Cast: Red Buttons, Fabian, Barbara Eden, Cedric Hardwicke, Peter Lorre, Richard Hayden, Barbara Luna, Billy Gilbert, Herbert Marshall (Prime Minster), Reginald Owen, Henry Daniell, Mike Mazurki

The List of Adrian Messenger (1963) Universal; D: John Huston; Cast: George C. Scott, Dana Wynter, Clive Brook, Herbert Marshall (Sir Wilfred Lucas), Gladys Cooper, John

Merivale Cameos: Kirk Douglas, John Huston, Frank Sinatra, Robert Mitchum, Burt Lancaster, Tony Curtis

The Caretakers (1963) UA; D: Hall Bartlett; Cast: Robert Stack, Polly Bergen, Joan Crawford, Janis Paige, Diane McBain, Van Williams, Constance Ford, Sharon Hugueny, Herbert Marshall (Dr. Jubal Harrington), Barbara Barrie, Robert Vaughn, Ellen Corby

Academy Award Nomination: Best Cinematography

The Third Day (1965) Warner Bros.; D: Jack Smight; Cast: George Peppard, Elizabeth Ashley, Roddy McDowell, Arthur O'Connell, Mona Washbourne, Herbert Marshall (Austin Parsons), Sally Kellerman, Arte Johnson

DOCUMENTARIES & SHORTS:

Mr. Herbert Marshall Appeals (1932) UK charity appeal; Herbert Marshall (presenter)

Hollywood on Parade (1934) Paramount; 11 minute short featuring: Herbert Marshall, Norma Shearer, Clive Brook, Dolores del Rio, Marie Dressler, Will Rogers, Clark Gable, Leslie Howard, Gene Raymond, Diana Wynyard

20th Century Fox (1936) Reporter James Fidler takes viewers on a tour of the newly organized 20th Century-Fox studio. Among those seen are: Herbert Marshall, Alice Faye, Ruth Chatterton, Shirley Temple, Myrna Loy, Loretta Young, Warner Baxter, Janet Gaynor

The Shining Future (1944) (aka *Road to Victory*) Warner Bros.; D: LeRoy Prinz; Cast: Herbert Marshall (himself), Charlie Ruggles, Jimmy Lydon, Jack Carson, Frank Sinatra, Deanna Durbin, Cary Grant, Dennis Morgan, Irene Manning, Bing Crosby. (20 minute short to promote the Canadian War Bond Drive. *Road to Victory* was a 10 minute version distributed in the U.S.)

Monuments of the Past (1946) Produced and distributed by Carl Junghans; Narrator: Herbert Marshall; 12 minute Technicolor tribute to the Navajo cliff-dwellers of the Grand Canyon.

The Love Goddesses (1965) Paramount; D: Saul J. Turell; Archive footage that featured Herbert Marshall, Claudette Colbert, Mae West, Jeanette MacDonald, Maurice Chevalier, Clara Bow, Louise Brooks, Clive Brook, Myrna Loy, Dorothy Lamour, Dick Powell, Barbara Stanwyck, Ricardo Cortez, Gloria Swanson

Queer Icon - The Cult of Bette Davis (2009) **Black Summers Prod.** D: Mike Black; Interviews with Matthew Martin, Matthew Kennedy, Allan R. Ellenberger, Scott O'Brien, Ed Sikov, Anthony Slide, et. al; (includes scenes from *The Little Foxes*)

January 26, 1941 - Good times with Humphrey Bogart and Alice Faye during a broadcast of *If You Could Only Cook* for Screen Guild Theater (CBS)

RADIO

1931:
Five Arts (**NBC**) March 12 - HM (guest speaker)

1934:
Louella Parsons (**CBS**) March 14 - Scene from *Riptide* - HM, Norma Shearer
Preview of Riptide (**ABC**) March 29 - HM, Norma Shearer
California Melodies (**ABC**) April 10 - HM, Mills Brothers
Hall of Fame (**NBC**) July 1- *The Romantic Lady* by Michael Arlen; HM, Miriam Hopkins

1935:
Hollywood Hotel (**CBS**) April 19 - Scene from *The Flame Within* - HM, Ann Harding, Louis Hayward; May Robson, Edmund Goulding, Dick Powell, Louella Parsons (host for this series)

CREDITS

1936:

Hollywood Hotel (**CBS**) January 10 - Scene from *The Lady Consents* - HM, Ann Harding; Dick Powell, Frances Langford

Shell Chateau (**NBC**) January 25 - HM, Cab Calloway; Al Jolson (host)

Lux Radio Theatre (**CBS**) June 22 - *The Dark Angel* - HM, Merle Oberon, Rod La Rocque, Cecil B. DeMille (host for this series)

Camel Caravan (**CBS**) September 22 - *Michael and Mary* by A.A. Milne - HM, Madeleine Carroll; Alice Faye, Benny Goodman

Lux Radio Theatre (**CBS**) December 28 - *Cavalcade* by Noel Coward - HM, Madeleine Carroll, Una O'Connor, David Niven, Noel Coward (host)

1937:

Lux Radio Theatre (**CBS**) February 22 - *Captain Blood* - Errol Flynn, Olivia de Havilland, Basil Rathbone, Donald Crisp, HM (host)

Lux Radio Theatre (**CBS**) March 15 - *Desire* - HM, Marlene Dietrich, Otto Kruger, Ernst Lubitsch (guest)

Lux Radio Theatre (**CBS**) May 24 - *Under Two Flags* - HM, Olivia de Havilland, Lupe Velez, Lionel Atwill

Chase and Sanborn Hour (**NBC**) September 19 - HM (host), Nelson Eddy

Chase and Sanborn Hour (**NBC**) September 26 - HM (host), Claudette Colbert (dramatic sketch with HM), Nelson Eddy, Dorothy Lamour, W.C. Fields, Edgar Bergen

Chase and Sanborn Hour (**NBC**) October 3 - HM (host), Sally Eilers, Nelson Eddy, Dorothy Lamour, Edgar Bergen, W.C. Fields

Lux Radio Theatre (**CBS**) November 22 - *The Petrified Forest* by Robert E. Sherwood; HM, Margaret Sullavan, Eduardo Ciannelli, Donald Meek

Your Hollywood Parade (**NBC**) December 22 - HM, Rosemary Lane, Billy Halop, Leo Gorcey, Billy and Bobby Mauch, Dick Powell (host)

1938:

Lux Radio Theatre (**CBS**) February 21 - *Romance* by Edward Sheldon - HM, Madeleine Carroll

Easter Service from Hollywood Bowl (**Mutual**) April 17 - HM (reads "Salutation to the Dawn")

Lux Radio Theatre (**CBS**) April 17 - *Mad About Music* - HM, Deanna Durbin, Gail Patrick, Walter Huston (host)

Hollywood Hotel (**CBS**) June 24 - preview of *Always Goodbye* - HM, Barbara Stanwyck, Caesar Romero; Frances Langford

Lux Radio Theatre (**CBS**) July 4 - *I Found Stella Parish* - HM, George Brent, Constance Bennett, Lucile Watson

Hollywood Hotel (**CBS**) September 9 - October 14 (HM hosted Friday evenings and acted in dramatic segments) September 9: *Dark Angel* - HM, Claudette Colbert; September 16: *Bulldog Drummond* - HM, Charles Butterworth. H. B. Warner, Frieda Inescort; September 23: *Big Softie* - HM, Josephine Hutchison; September 30: *History is Made at Night* - HM, Joan Bennett, Thomas Mitchell; October 7: *I Met Him in Paris* - HM, Ginger Rogers, David Niven; October 14: *Berkeley Square* - HM, Heather Angel, Charles Butterworth

Lux Radio Theatre (**CBS**) November 28 - *Interference* - HM, Leslie Howard, Mary Astor, Gail Patrick

Texaco Star Theater (**CBS**) November 30 - *Lend Me Your Eyes* - HM, Andrea Leeds, John Barrymore (host)

Christmas for One-Third of the Nation (**NBC**) - December 24 - HM, Virginia Bruce, Henry Fonda, Miriam Hopkins, Eddie Cantor, Melvyn Douglas, Edward G. Robinson, Charles Boyer, Sally Eilers, Gene Autry, Helen Gahagan, Billy and Bobby Mauch, Marie Wilson

1939:

Screen Guild Theater (**CBS**) January 15 - *Miss Brown of Worcester* - HM, Loretta Young, Fred Astaire, Franklin Pangborn; Ernst Lubitsch, George Murphy (host)

Texaco Star Theater (**CBS**) February 1 - *Manhattan Masquerade* - HM, Frances Langford

Silver Theater (**ABC**) February 27 - *Dear Victim* - HM, Maureen O'Sullivan, Conrad Nagel (host)

Rudy Vallee Show (**NBC**) May 4 - HM, Bert Lahr, Rudy Vallee

Hollywood Playhouse (**NBC**) May 7 - HM presents Charles Boyer with British Federation of Actors and Authors Medal

Tribute to King George and Queen Elizabeth (**NBC**) June 11 - Farewell scene from *Romeo & Juliet* - HM, Judith Anderson; also on broadcast: Ronald Colman, Greer Garson, Nigel Bruce, C. Aubrey Smith, Gertrude Lawrence, Leslie Howard, Basil Rathbone, Vivien Leigh, Laurence Olivier, Freddie Bartholomew, Errol Flynn, Edna Best, George Sanders, Madeleine Carroll

Hollywood Playhouse (**NBC**) October 4 - November 15 (HM hosted and acted in drama presentations) October 4: *Michael and Mary* - HM, Madeleine Carroll; October 11 - *If You Could Only Cook* - HM, Ginger Rogers; October 18 - *Let's Live Tonight* - HM, Kay Francis; October 25 - *There's Always Juliet* - HM, Edna Best; November 1 - *Between Ships* - HM, Gail Patrick; November 8 - *For All Our Lives* - HM, Anne Shirley; November 15 - *She Married an Artist* - HM, Kay Francis

Screen Guild Theater (**CBS**) December 3 - *Accent on Youth* - HM, Gertrude Lawrence

1940:

Lux Radio Theatre (**CBS**) January 1 - *Sorrell and Son* - HM, Karen Morley, Richard Carlson

CREDITS

Lux Radio Theatre (**CBS**) January 29 - *Intermezzo* - HM, Ingrid Bergman, Gail Patrick

Silver Theater (**ABC**) February 18 - *Heaven is Like That* - HM, Conrad Nagel (host)

Lux Radio Theatre (**CBS**) May 27 - *Vigil in the Night* - HM, Olivia de Havilland, Helen Chandler

Suspense (**CBS**) July 21 - *The Lodger* - HM, Edmund Gwenn, Lurene Tuttle

Canadian Red Cross (**CBC**) September 29 - British War Relief - HM, Reginald Gardiner, Dionne Quintuplets, Alan Mowbray, Anna Neagle, Gloria Jean, Mary Pickford, Vivien Leigh, Laurence Olivier, Madeleine Carroll, Merle Oberon, C. Aubrey Smith

Kraft Music Hall (**NBC**) October 10 - HM, Dorothy Lamour, Bob Burns

Campbell Playhouse (**CBS**) December 6 - *Kind Lady* - HM, Gladys George

Friendship Bridge (**WRUL**) December 11 - *The Night Before You Marry Her* by Frederic Lonsdale; HM, Jessica Tandy, Romney Brent

Information Please (**NBC**) December 20 - HM, Louis Bromfield

Christmas Greeting to England (**KGO**) December 25 - HM, Bette Davis, Spencer Tracy, Bob Hope, Madeleine Carroll, Charles Laughton, Elsa Lanchester, Charles Boyer

1941:

Screen Guild Theater (**CBS**) January 26 - *If You Could Only Cook* - HM, Alice Faye, Humphrey Bogart

Jack Benny Show (**NBC**) February 1 - HM (guest host), Mary Livingston, Don Wilson

Jack Benny Show (**NBC**) February 8 - HM, Jack Benny, Mary Livingston, Don Wilson

Celebration for Jack Benny (**NBC**) May 9 - HM, Claudette Colbert, Eddie Cantor, Ed Sullivan,

Eddie "Rochester" Anderson, Mary Livingston, Jack Benny

Lux Radio Theatre (**CBS**) May 12 - *Craig's Wife* - HM, Rosalind Russell

Hollywood Premier (**WHEC**) July 11 - scenes from *Adventure in Washington*; HM, Gene Reynolds, Louella Parsons (host)

Kraft Music Hall (**NBC**) October 16 - HM, Joan Bennett, Don Ameche

Community Chest (**KGO**) October 17 - HM

Eddie Cantor Show (**NBC**) October 29 - HM, Eddie Cantor

The New Old Gold Show (**NBC**) weekly November 3, 1941- April 24, 1942; HM (host), Merry Macs, Bert Wheeler; guests included: Virginia Bruce, Mary Astor, Lucille Ball, Constance Bennett, Ilona Massey, Marlene Dietrich, Janet Gaynor, Maureen O'Hara, Edward Everett Horton

1942:

Screen Guild Theater (**CBS**) January 11 - *Love Affair* - HM, Myrna Loy, Roger Pryor (host/director)

Kraft Music Hall (**NBC**) May 14 - HM, Gene Tierney, Bing Crosby, Bob Crosby
Armstrong's Theater of Today (**CBS**) October 31 - HM
Stage Door Canteen (**CBS**) November 5 - HM, Ralph Edwards, Hildegarde
Philip Morris Playhouse (**CBS**) November 6 - *Rebecca* - HM, Edna Best
Abbott and Costello (**NBC**) November 26 - HM, Bud Abbott, Lou Costello
Burns and Allen (**CBS**) December 15 - HM, George Burns, Gracie Allen

1943:
Over Here (**Blue Network**) January 9 - HM, Joan Bennett, Groucho Marx, James Melton
Eddie Cantor (**NBC**) February 17 - HM, Eddie Cantor, Janet Blair, Dinah Shore
Screen Guild Theater (**CBS**) March 1 - *This Above All* - HM, Virginia Bruce
Radio's Reader Digest (**ABC**) May 16 - *The Cargo of Innocence* - HM, Conrad Nagel
Duffy's Tavern (**NBC**) May 18 - HM, Shirley Booth
Philip Morris Playhouse (**CBS**) May 21 - *The Thirty-Nine Steps* - HM, Madeleine Carroll
Broadway Bandbox September 21- HM (reads OWI message), Frank Sinatra
Soldiers With Wings September 30 - HM, Cass Daley
Eddie Cantor (**NBC**) October 6 - HM (sings "Pistol Packin' Mama"), Eddie Cantor
Screen Guild Theater (**CBS**) October 11, *Love Affair* - HM, Virginia Bruce
Sealtest Village Store (**NBC**) November 18 - HM, Joan Davis, Jack Haley
Command Performance (**AFRS**) November 27 - HM, Virginia O'Brien, Frances Langford, Tommy Cook
Silver Theater (**ABC**) December 5 - *Help Wanted* - HM, Virginia Bruce
Sealtest Village Store (**NBC**) December 16 - HM, Joan Davis, Jack Haley
Duffy's Tavern (**NBC**) December 21 - HM, Dinah Shore
Lux Radio Theatre (**CBS**) December 27 - *Kathleen* - HM, Shirley Temple

1944:
Soldiers With Wings (**Mutual**) January 19 - HM, Kay Francis
Eddie Cantor (**NBC**) January 26 - HM, Eddie Cantor
Lux Radio Theatre (**CBS**) March 6 - *The Letter* - HM, Bette Davis, Vincent Price
Jack Carson Show (**CBS**) April 5 - HM, Jack Carson, Dale Evans
Globe Theater (**CBS**) April 9 - *Strange Victory* - HM (host), Kay Francis, Walter Pidgeon
Burns and Allen (**CBS**) April 11 - HM, George Burns, Gracie Allen
Silver Theater (**ABC**) April 23 - *The Woman I Killed* - HM
Dinah Shore Show May 18 - HM, Dinah Shore
Silver Theater (**ABC**) May 21 - *The Guardsman* - HM, Ingrid Bergman, Nigel Bruce

CREDITS

Screen Guild Theater (**CBS**) June 3 - *My Son, My Son* - HM, Freddie Bartholomew, Heather Angel

Cavalcade of America (**NBC**) June 26, 1944 - *What Price Freedom?* - HM, Herbert Rawlinson

Mail Call (**AFRS**) June 28 - HM, Marjorie Main, Andrews Sisters, Gloria DeHaven

The Man Called X (**CBS**) (**NBC**) July 10, 1944-May 20, 1952 - HM as Ken Thurston/"Mr. X"

Suspense (**CBS**) July 17 - *The Beast Must Die* - HM

Atlantic Spotlight (**NBC**) September 16 - HM, "Battle of Britain Day" - HM (narrator), Ronald Colman, Nigel Bruce, Greer Garson, C. Aubrey Smith, Basil Rathbone, Merle Oberon

Screen Guild Theater (**CBS**) October 16 - *Mad About Music* - HM, Gloria Jean, Eric Blore

Dunninger (**NBC**) November 1 - HM, Gloria Blondell

Old Gold Comedy Theater (**NBC**) December 17 - *Lucky Partners* - HM, Jane Wyman, Sheldon Leonard, Harold Lloyd (host)

Christmas on the Blue (**NBC**) December 25 - HM, Gracie Fields, Andrews Sisters, Charlotte Greenwood, Ed Wynn, Keenan Wynn, Joe E. Brown

1945:

Cavalcade of America (**NBC**) February 19 - *Washington and the Traitor* - HM, Walter Huston (host)

Command Performance (**AFRS**) March 15 - HM, Humphrey Bogart, Lauren Bacall, Jimmy Durante, Edward Arnold, Sons of the Pioneers

This is My Best (**CBS**) May 1 - *The Snow Goose* - HM

Suspense (**CBS**) May 24 - *My Own Murderer* - HM

Bob Hope Show (**NBC**) May 29 - HM, Bob Hope, Frances Langford, Bing Crosby

Seventh War Loan (**ABC**) June 27 - *Rebecca* - HM, Joan Fontaine, Agnes Moorehead (*Variety*: "*Rebecca* ... has been done before on the air, but ... never with such skill as by this threesome.")

Screen Guild Theater (**CBS**) August 20 - *Laura* - HM, Gene Tierney, Dana Andrews, Clifton Webb

Screen Guild Theater (**CBS**) September 10 - *Private Worlds* - HM, Claudette Colbert, Isabel Jewel, Frank Albertson

This is My Best (**CBS**) September 18 - *Turnip's Blood* - HM, Rosemary DeCamp

Request Performance (**CBS**) November 18 - HM, Judy Canova, Lauritz Melchior

Sealtest Village Store (**NBC**) December 6 - HM, Jack Haley, Eve Arden

1946:

Theater of Romance (**CBS**) February 26 - *The Enchanted Cottage* - HM, Robert Young, Lurene Tuttle

Hollywood Star Time (**CBS**) August 31 - *Lost Horizon* - HM

Cavalcade of America (**NBC**) September 2 - *With Cradle and Clock* - HM

Hollywood Star Time (**CBS**) October 5 - *Intermezzo* - HM (Marshall takes over as host, and starred in numerous broadcasts) October 19 - *Ball of Fire* - HM, Lucille Ball; October 26 - *Bedella* - HM, Gene Tierney; November 2 - *Holy Matrimony* - HM, Frank Morgan; November 9 - *One Way Passage* - HM, Teresa Wright; November 23 - *Woman in the Window* - HM, Joan Bennett; December 14 - *Mad About Music* - HM, Ann Blyth; December 21 - *Three Wise Guys* - HM, James Dunn; December 28 - *A Star is Born* - HM, Diana Lynn

Screen Guild Theater (**CBS**) October 21 - *Michael and Mary* - HM, Ann Todd

Sealtest Village Store (**NBC**) November 14 - HM, Jack Haley, Eve Arden

1947:

Hollywood Star Time (**CBS**) January 10 - *It's a Date* - HM, Mary Astor, Vanessa Brown; February 1 - *Hired Wife* - HM, Jane Wyman; February 8 - *The Letter* - HM, Ann Todd, Vincent Price; February 15 - *Talk of the Town* - HM, Cary Grant, Marguerite Chapman; February 22 - *Journey into Fear* - HM; March 8 - *My Name is Julia Ross* - HM, Ann Todd, Dame May Whitty; March 15 - *The Petrified Forest* - HM, Anne Baxter; March 27 - *Love is News* - HM, Bob Hope

Sealtest Village Store (**NBC**) February 27 - HM, Jack Haley, Eve Arden

Bob Hope Show (**NBC**) April 22 - HM, Bob Hope, Martha Tilton

Screen Guild Theater (**CBS**) May 12 - *Brief Encounter* - HM, Lilli Palmer

Hollywood Star Preview (**NBC**) October 12 - *Naked City* - HM, Dorothy Hart

The Constant Invader (**Various stations**) Fall of 1947 - 13-week series of dramatizations on tuberculosis control - HM (narrator)

1948:

Bob Hope Show (**NBC**) January 13 - HM, Bob Hope, Jerry Colonna, Vera Vague

Screen Guild Theater (**CBS**) January 26 - *Brief Encounter* - HM, Irene Dunne

Hollywood Theatre of Stars (**NBC**) October 15 - *The Silver Teapot* - HM

Electric Theater (**CBS**) October 24 - *The Admirable Crichton* - HM

Suspense (**CBS**) December 23 - *Holiday Story* (also known as *Rich Man, Poor Man*) - HM

Hallmark Playhouse (**CBS**) December 30 - *Lost Horizon* - HM

CREDITS

1949:
Hollywood Star Theater (**NBC**) April 8 - HM, June Lockhart
Screen Guild Theater (**CBS**) May 12 - *Temptation Harbor* - HM, Signe Hasso
Screen Guild Theater (**CBS**) June 23 - *Stairway to Heaven* - HM, David Niven, Diana Lynn
University Theater (**NBC**) July 9 - *Goodbye Mr. Chips* - HM
Family Hour of Stars (**CBS**) July 31 - *To Mary, With Love* - HM

1950:
Tomorrow for Two (**United Nations Radio-NBC**) March 19 - HM
MGM Theater of the Air (**WMGM**) April 12 - *They Met in Bombay* - HM
Screen Guild Theater (**CBS**) June 8 - *My Son, My Son* - HM, Angela Lansbury, Roddy McDowell
Hollywood Star Playhouse (**CBS**) August 28 - *Flute in the Night* - HM
Screen Guild Theater (**CBS**) October 26 - *Michael and Mary* - HM, Joan Fontaine
Suspense (**CBS**) November 2 - *The Victoria Cross* - HM

1951:
Suspense (**CBS**) October 8 - *Betrayal in Vienna* - HM
Hollywood Sound Stage (**CBS**) December 20 - *Brief Encounter* - HM, Joan Fontaine
Suspense (**CBS**) December 31 - *Rogue Male* - HM

1952:
Suspense (**CBS**) March 3 - *The Thirty-Nine Steps* - HM
Screen Guild Theater (**CBS**) March 20 - *Michael and Mary* - HM, Deborah Kerr
Suspense (**CBS**) April 21 - *Diary of Captain Scott* - HM
Hollywood Star Playhouse (**CBS**) May 11 - *Drury Bones* - HM
Suspense (**CBS**) November 3 - *Frankenstein* - HM
Theater of Romance (**CBS**) December 4 - *Red* by W. Somerset Maugham - HM
Theater of Romance (**CBS**) December 25 - *The Cave* - HM

1953:
Suspense (**CBS**) January 5 & 12 - *The Mystery of Edwin Drood* (two parts) - HM
Suspense (**CBS**) March 9 - *The Dead Alive* - HM
Suspense (**CBS**) April 27 - *The Man Within* - HM
Lux Radio Theater (**CBS**) July 20 - *The Birds* - HM
Suspense (**CBS**) October 5 - *Action* - HM

1954:
Hallmark Hall of Fame (**CBS**) January 24 - *The Story of Lord Baden-Powell* - HM, Lionel Barrymore (host)

Suspense (**CBS**) February 22 - *Murder by Jury* - HM

Hallmark Hall of Fame (**CBS**) March 21 - *The Story of Edmund Burke* - HM

Hallmark Hall of Fame (**CBS**) November 7 - *The Man Who Saved the King* - HM

Biography in Sound (**NBC**) November 28 - *His Finest Hour: Winston Churchill* - HM, Laurence Olivier

Biography in Sound (**NBC**) December 19 - *Meet Ernest Hemingway* - HM, Laurence Oliver

1955:
Sunday Playhouse (**CBS**) April 10 - *Captain Huckabee's Beard* - HM

Amos and Andy Music Hall (**NBC**) October 28 - HM

1956:
Biography in Sound (**NBC**) May 11 - *The Wonderful World of Robert Brenchley* - HM, Jimmy Durante, Irving Berlin

Suspense (**CBS**) December 23 - *Back for Christmas* - HM

1957:
Suspense (**CBS**) July 14 - *Flood on the Goodwyns* - HM, Hans Conried

Radio Workshop (**CBS**) April 21 - *The Son of Man* - HM, Raymond Massey, Robert Young, Victor Jory, Vincent Price

1958:
Suspense (**CBS**) February 9 - *The Long Shot* - HM

Suspense (**CBS**) September 7 - *The Man Who Won the War* - HM

American Foundation for the Blind - two, half-hour public service broadcasts by HM

1959:
Suspense (**CBS**) March 1 - *The Waxwork* - HM

1960:
The Search (**CBS**) December 11 - *The Search* - HM, Lurene Tuttle

November 1960 - Colonel Cat episode of *Hong Kong* (ABC) with daughter Sarah Marshall

TV

1950:
Ken Murray Show (October 7, 1950) HM (guest star), Alan Young, Darla Hood; Marshall in drama segment *Thicker Than Water*

Airflyte Theater (October 26, 1950) *Municipal Report* by O. Henry; D: Marc Daniels; Cast: HM, Frederick O'Neal, Dorothea Duckworth, Joe Silver, William Gaxton

Showtime USA (October 29, 1950) HM and Gertrude Lawrence in a scene from *Susan and God*

1951:
Kate Smith Evening Hour (October 24, 1951) HM (guest star), Kay Thompson, Williams Brothers, Jackie Gleason; Marshall in drama sketch *In The Fog*

Robert Montgomery Presents (November 5, 1951) *An Inspector Calls* by J. B. Priestley; Cast: HM, Sarah Marshall, Faith Brook, Isobel Elsom

1952:
The Unexpected (March-December 1952) anthology series, 39 episodes; Host: HM; (rebroadcast later as *Times Square Playhouse* and *Herbert Marshall Presents*)

Ford Television Theatre (October 30, 1952) *Girl in the Park* based on a story by Rachel Maddux; D: Robert Stevenson; Cast: HM, Joan Caulfield

1954:
Lux Video Theatre (April 22, 1954) *Gavin's Darling* by Richard P. McDonagh; D: Buzz Kulik; Cast: HM, Barbara Rush, Rex Reason

What's My Line (November 28, 1954) HM (mystery guest)

The Best of Broadway (December 8, 1954) *The Philadelphia Story* by Philip Barry; D: Sidney Lumet; Cast: Dorothy McGuire, John Payne, HM (Seth Lord), Mary Astor, Richard Carlson, Dick Foran, Charles Winninger

The Elgin Hour (December 14, 1954) *Yesterday's Magic* based on the play by Luigi Pirandello; D: Don Richardson; Cast: HM, Judith Anderson, Roddy McDowall, Francis Lederer, Rex O'Malley

1955:
Lux Video Theatre (April 7, 1955) *The Browning Version* by Terence Rattigan; D: Earl Eby; Cast: HM (Andrew Crocker-Harris), Judith Evelyn, Paul Cavanagh, Rod Taylor

December Bride (November 6, 1955) *The Laundromat Show*; Cast: HM (guest star), Spring Byington, Verna Felton, Harry Morgan

Celebrity Playhouse (December 20, 1955) *The Hoax* by Irving Wallace; D: Gerald Freedman; Cast: HM, Paul Henreid

CREDITS

1956:

Lux Video Theatre (October 4, 1956) *Now Voyager* from the novel by Olive Higgins Prouty; D: James P. Yarbrough; Cast: Laraine Day, Herbert Marshall (Dr. Jacquith), Richard Carlson, Gordon MacRae (host), William Holden (guest)

The George Gobel Show (December 15, 1956) HM (guest star)

1957:

Alfred Hitchcock Presents (February 10, 1957) *A Bottle of Wine* by Borden Deal; D: Herschel Daugherty; Cast; HM (Judge Harley Gordon), Jarma Lewis, Robert Horton

I've Got a Secret (February 27, 1957) HM (guest star), Garry Moore (host)

The Loretta Young Show (March 10, 1957) *Louise* by Marian Spitzer; D: Norman Foster; Cast: HM (Bo Barrett), Viveca Lindfors, Norma Varden, Loretta Young (host)

Playhouse 90 (October 24,1957) *The Mystery of Thirteen* (adapted from *They Hanged My Saintly Billy* by Robert Graves); D: Robert Mulligan; Cast: Jack Lemmon, Margaret O'Brien, Herbert Marshall (Dr. Knight), Gladys Cooper, Henry Jones, Romney Brent, John Baragrey, Vincent Price (host)

1958:

The Art Linkletter Show (January 24, 1958) HM (guest star)

Studio One (January 27, 1958) *Balance of Terror* play by Peter Shaffer; D: Jack Smight; Cast: Corinne Calvert, Louis Hayward, HM (Colonel Beaumont), June Lockhart, Leonid Kinskey, Hugh Marlowe

Alfred Hitchcock Presents (June 29, 1958) *Little White Frock* by Stacy Aumonier; D: Herschel Daugherty; Cast: HM (Colin Bragner), Julie Adams, Tom Helmore

1960:

Adventure in Paradise (January 18, 1960) *Nightmare on Napuka*; D: Josef Leytes; Cast: Gardner McKay, HM (Dr. Morgan), Martin Landau

Adventure in Paradise (March 14, 1960) *There Is An Island*; D:James Neilson; Cast: Gardner McKay, HM (Judge)

Hong Kong (November 16, 1960) *Colonel Cat* by Robert Buckner; D: Budd Boetticher; Cast: Rod Taylor, Lloyd Bochner, HM (Sir John Dalman), Sarah Marshall, Jack Kruschen

1961:

Michael Shayne (January 13, 1961) *Spotlight on a Corpse* by Brett Halliday; D: Sidney Salkow; Cast: Richard Denning, HM (Collier Davis), Robert Lansing, Constance Moore, Ruta Lee

Zane Grey Theater (April 6, 1961) *The Atoner* by Howard Dimsdale (as Arthur Dales); D: Laslo Benedek; Cast: Dick Powell (host), HM (Simon Baker), Virginia Gregg, Scotty Morrow

1963:
Hollywood Without Makeup (June 1963) Compilation of home-movies taken by Ken Murray (Clip of HM, Norma Shearer and Clark Gable at the 1934 Academy Awards)

77 Sunset Strip (September 20, 1963) *"5"* by Harry Essex (five episodes); D: William Conrad; Cast: Efrem Zimbalist Jr., Richard Conte, HM (Father Anthony), Wally Cox, Peter Lorre, Diane McBain, Burgess Meredith, Joseph Schildkraut, William Shatner, Ed Wynn

1964:
The Presidency: A Splendid History (September 23, 1964) P: Richard Siemanowski; D: Joseph K. Chomyn; Cast: Fredric March (host/narrator), Dana Andrews, HM, Robert Ryan, Jason Robards, Ed Begley, Macdonald Carey

RECORDINGS

1936:
Cavalcade (by Noel Coward) Cast: HM (Robert Marryot), Madeleine Carroll, David Niven, Una O'Connor, Noel Coward (host) (Recording of 1936 radio broadcast, released in 1996 on AEI)

1942:
The Count of Monte Cristo (by Alexander Dumas) Cast: Herbert Marshall (Edmond Dantes), Pedro de Cordorba, Victor Young Orchestra (DECCA)

1945:
The Snow Goose (by Paul Gallico) Cast: Herbert Marshall (Phillip Rhayader), Joan Loring, Victor Young Orchestra (DECCA)

1956:
Sermons and Meditations of John Donne (by John Donne) Herbert Marshall (narrator) (CAEDMON)

1957:
The Book of Job (condensed Biblical reading) Cast: Herbert Marshall (Job), Martin Balsam, Clarence Derwent, Joseph Holland (CAEDMON)

INDEX

A

A Majority of One 281-*282*, 283-284
A Woman Rebels 144, 148-150
Accent on Youth 127-128
Adventure in Washington 186-*187*
Aherne, Brian 16, 145
Allen, Steve *278*-279
Always Goodbye 163-*164*, 165
Andy Hardy's Blonde Trouble 212-213
Angel 155-*156*, 157
Angel Face 259-*260*
Anne of the Indies 257
Another Language 84-85
Arthur, Jean *132*-133
Ashley, Elizabeth *289*
As You Like It 20-21
Astor, Mary *161*-162, 170-*171*, *211*, 256

B

Ball, Lucille 184
Bainter, Fay *177*
Bankhead, Tallulah 34
Baxter, Anne 228-*229*, 230
Bennett, Constance 108-*109*, 110-111
Benny, Jack 184
Bergman, Ingrid 184, 260
Best, Edna *22*-23, 29, 34, 36, *38*-41, 43, *47*-48, 49-51, 56-57, 60-*61*, 63, *65*, 68, 70-*74*, 79, 84-*88*, 93-*94*, 98, 101-104, 106-107, 111, 119, 145-*146*, 174-*176*, 177, 179, 235, 251, *259*, 270, 276, 298-299

marriages 23, 49, *55*
children *38*, 41, 49, 95, 175-176
Betty at Bay 18
Bill of Divorcement, A (play) 57-58, 177
Bill of Divorcement, A (1940) *177*-178
Black Jack 253-*254*, 255
Black Shield of Falworth, The 265-*266*
Blonde Venus 75-*77*, 78-79
Blore, Eric *6*-7, 120, 151, 157-*158*, 159, 204, 248, 276, 286
Bogart, Humphrey 184, *344*
Boland, Mary 72, 83-*84*, *96*, 98
Bourne, Timothy Marshall 263, *299*-301
Breakfast for Two 157-*158*
Brent, George 30, 112-113, 170, 182-183, 256
Brook, Clive 75-76, 163, 268
Bruce,. Nigel 242, 286
Bruce, Virginia *161*-162, 171, 186-*187*, 188

C

Calendar, The (aka *Bachelor's Folly*) 73
Caretakers, The 284-*285*
Carroll, Madeleine *92*-93, 154, 217
Cavalcade 154
Chandler, Raymond 222
Chatterton, Ruth 50, 69, 140-*142*, 190
Clive, Colin 63, 107
Cochran, Steve 269
Colbert, Claudette *71*-73, *96*-97, 98-*100*, 101, 165-166

Cole, Lester 242
College Confidential 277-*278*, 279
Collins, Joan 267
Colman, Ronald 7, 15, 73, 75, 83, 93, 140, 147, 151-152, 169, 172, 199, *218*, 235, 276, 286
Coward, Noel *28*-30, 41-43, 50, 56-58, 85, 93, 106, 125, 131, 154, 208, 270
Crack-Up 223-225
Crawford, Joan 190-*191*, 192, 284-*285*, 286
Curtis, Tony 265-*266*, 286
Cukor, George 57, 165-166, 178, 229-230

D

Dahl, Arlene 268
Dark Angel, The 127, 129-*130*, 131
Davis, Bette 91, 122, 124, *182*-183, 188-*189*, 190, *266*-267, 271, 281, 286
Day, Doris 277, *279*-281
Day, Laraine 179, 195-196
DeMille, Cecil B. 96-*100*, 103
Dean, Basil 42-43, 48
Dietrich, Marlene 75-*77*, 78, 83, 126-127, *155*-156, 157
Douglas, Melvyn *155*-156, 157, 171, 188
du Maurier, Gerald 43-*44*, 45, 57, 66
Duel in the Sun 214, 230-*231*, 232-*233*, 234
Durbin, Deanna 159-*160*, 165
Duryea, Dan *252*-253
Duvivier, Julien 251, 253, 255

E

Eagels, Jeanne 51-*52*, 53
Egan, Richard *262*-263
Enchanted Cottage, The 214, 219-*220*
Evenings for Sale 83-84

F

Faithful Heart, The 86-88
Fairbanks Jr., Doug 172, 188, 248, 304
Faye, Alice 184, 200, *344*
Fever in the Blood 281
Fields, W.C. *139*
Five Weeks in a Balloon 284
Flagg, James Montgomery 205-206
Flame Within, The 123-125
Flight for Freedom 209-210
Florey, Robert 54, 133-*134*, 135-136, 305
Fly, The 274-*275*
Fonda, Henry 273
Fontaine, Joan 234-*235*, 293
Forgotten Faces 137-138, 139
Foreign Correspondent 179-*180*, 181, 195, 303
Forever and a Day 206-*207*, 303
Four Frightened People 96-*97*, 98-*100*
Francis, Kay 79-*82*, 83, 91, 102, 122, 139-140, 177,*199*-201, 206, 213, 222, 257, 283, 305, *336*

G

Gabor, Zsa Zsa 253-255
Gable, Clark *101*, 119
Garbo, Greta 30, 70, 91, *111*-113, 126, 197, 293
Gardiner, Reginald 199, *223*, 277, 290
Gargan, William 98-*99*
Garson, Greer 190-191
Gielgud, John 43, 47-48
Gilbert, John 68, 70
Girl's Dormitory 140-*142*
Gish, Lillian 176, 232-233
Glyn, Elinor 91-92, 102
Gog 262-263
Good Fairy, The 116, *118*, 120-122, 124
Goulding, Edmund 102, 104-*105*, 106, *123*-124, 136, *152*, 198, 230, 277, 288
Grant, Cary 77-78, 172
Grumpy 8-11
Gwenn, Edmund 24

INDEX

H

Harding, Ann 57, *123*-125, *126*, 163, 191
Harrison, Rex 85, *279*-280
Hayes, Helen 171, *173*-174
Hayward, Louis 85, *123*-125
Hellman, Lillian 130, 188, 190
Hepburn, Katharine 57, 91, 142, *144*, 148-150, 178, 272
High Road, The 49-50, 53, 55-56
High Wall 236, 240-*241*, 242
Hitchcock, Alfred 65-68, 111, 178-179, 181, 262, 271, 293
Hopkins, Miriam 79-80, 82, 172, *336*
Howard, Leslie 32, 45, 131, 140, 149, 170-*171*, 174
Hunter, Ian 49, 164
Huston, John 232, 286

I

I Was a Spy 92-93
If Only You Could Cook 127, *132*-133, 184
Interference 43-*45*, 170-*171*
Ivy 234-*235*

J

Jones, Jennifer 214, 231-*233*, 236

K

Kahmann, Dee Anne Cummings 277-*278*, 298-*299*
Kathleen 192, 195-*196*

L

La Rocque, Rod *134*, 135, *146*, *152*-153, 179, 199
Ladies and Gentlemen 171, *173*-174
Lady Consents, The 125-*126*
Lanchester, Elsa 250
Landi, Elissa 36
Lawrence, Gertrude 40, 50, 56
Letter, The (1929) 51-*52*, 53-55
Letter, The (1940) 54, 124, *182*-183, 190
Liberace 251

Lillie, Beatrice 40, 50, 56
List of Adrian Messenger, The 286
Little Foxes, The 124, 188-*189*, 190
Lohr, Marie 24-*26*, 27, 31, 33, 206
Lombard, Carole 83, 129
Lonsdale, Fredrick 56
Loy, Myrna 129, 184, 192, 210-211, *279-280*, 281
Lubitsch, Ernst 79-*82*, 91, 93, 114, *155*-157
Lundigan, William *261*

M

MacColl, James 208
MacDonald, Jeanette 91, 250
MacMurray, Fred *209*
Mad About Music 159-*160*, 174
Maitland, Molly (Hilda Lloyd Bosley) 8-*9*, 11, 14, 23-24, 29, 36, 49, 298
Make Way for a Lady 150-*151*, 195
Mallory, Boots 214, 222, *223*, 236, 238-240, 242, *243*-244, *245*, 246-247, 249-251, 253-256, 258, 268, 274, 276
March, Fredric 57, 93, 129-*130*, 131, 135, 288
Marshall, Ann 200, 206, *215*, 249, 283-284, 287, *296-297*, 299
Marshall, Ethel May Turner 1-5, 22, 30
Marshall, Herbert Brough Falcon
    childhood 2-5
    WWI 7-8, 11-16
    Injury/amputation/phantom pain 13-16, 31, 154
    marriages 8, 55, 178-179, 242
    volunteer work 184-186, 200-201, 206, 210-211, 213, 217-219, 240
Marshall, Percy Falcon 1-5, 22, 30, 47-48
Marshall, Sarah Lynn 79, 85-*86*, 93-*94*, 95, 102, 104, 119, 147-148, 159, 174-*175*, 176, 179, 192, 195, 200, *215*, 235, 251, 258-*259*, 263, 270, 272, 279, 281, 287, *294-295*, 296, *299*, 304, *353*

Maude, Cyril 8-*10*, 11, 39
Maugham, W. Somerset 30, 51-53, 103, 112-113, 182, 202, 204-205, *215*, 225-*226*, 227-230, 258, 291, 295
McCrea, Joel 179, 181, *221*-222
McGuire, Dorothy 219-220, 256
Meredith, Burgess 150
Michael and Mary (play) 59-60, 63
Michael and Mary (film) 60-*61*
Michael, Gertrude 133-*134*, 135, *137*-138, 150
Midnight Lace 277, *279-280*, 281
Miller, Gilbert 43, 68, 171, 270
Milne, A.A. 19, 59, *61*
Mitchum, Robert 259-260, 286
Montgomery, Robert 102, 104, 106, 176, 258
Moon and Sixpence, The 202-*203*, 204-204
Moore, Dickie 77
Moorehead, Agnes *254*-255
Morgan, Frank *118*, 120-121, 172, 191, 305
Mumsie 46-*47*
Murder 66-*67*, 68

N
Nesbitt, Cathleen 20, 34
Niven, David 147,151, 277

O
O'Brien, Margaret *249*-250
O'Brien, Pat 224-225
Oberon, Merle 129-*130*, 131, 136
Olivier, Laurence 57
Osborne, Robert 68, 183, 301
Outcast Lady 108-*109*, 110-111
Owen, Reginald 51, 54, *118*, 120-121

P
Painted Veil, The 30, *111*-113, 198
Paris Bound 57
Parish, James Robert 269, 282-283, 303-304

Payne, John 228-*229*
Peck, Gregory 232
Peppard, George 288-*289*
Peters, Jean *257*
Playfair, Nigel 19, 21
Plummer, Christopher 190, 273
Powell, William 83, 107
Power, Tyrone 110, 141, 176, 228-*229*, 230
Preminger, Otto 259-260
Price, Vincent *274*-275

R
Rains, Claude 15, 271
Rathbone, Basil 15, 50, 71, 136
Razor's Edge, The 205, *215*, 227-*229*, 230, 235
Reynolds, Gene 186-*187*
Riders to the Stars 261
Riptide 102, 104-*105*, 106-107, 154
Rooney, Mickey *212*-213
Roper, Brian *249*-250
Ruggles, Wesley 127-128,
Russell, Gail *221*
Russell, Lee 155, 161-*163*, 167, 172, *176*-177, *178*-179, 192-*193*, *194*, 197-199, 206, 211, 214, 222, 236, 239, 249, 298
Russell, Rosalind 184, 197, *209*
Ryan, Robert 287-288

S
Sanders, George 179, 202-*203*, 204, 253-*254*, 255
Saunders, John Monk 114, 116, 137
Saville, Victor 60-*61*, 88, 92-93
Scott, Lizabeth 268-*269*
Secret Garden, The 249-251
Secrets of a Secretary 71-73, 101
Selznick, David O. 174, 214, 230
Shearer, Norma 70, 91, *101*-102, 104-*106*, 110, 176, 206
Shirley, Anne 150-*151*

INDEX

Sidney, Sylvia 76, 122, *127-128*, 133
Simmons, Jean 259-*260*
Simon, Simone 140-*142*
Slaughter, N. Carter 7, 17, 19
Smith, C. Aubrey 50, 136, 248, 272, 286
Solitaire Man, The 93, 95-*96*
Stage Struck 272-*273*
Stallings, Laurence 16, 51
Stanwyck, Barbara 91, 157-*158*, 163-*164*, 165, 206
Strachey, Lytton 226
Stockwell, Dean *249*-250
Strasberg, Susan 272-*273*
Sturges, Preston 120
Sullavan, Margaret 116, *118*, 120-122, 124
Swan, The 63-*65*, 120
Swanson, Gloria 88, *90*, 97, 102-103, 106-108, 110-111, 113-*115*, 116, 119, 124-125, 127, 131, 135, 138-139, 151-*152*, 153-154, 165, 179, 198, 305

T

Taylor, Robert 191, 241-242
Temple, Shirley 192, 195-*196*
Thalberg, Irving 102, 104-105, 107, 110
The Man Called X 194, 213-214, 248, 258
There's Always Juliet 74-75, 177
These Charming People 39-41
Third Day, The 288-*289*
Tierney, Gene 228-*229*, 230
Till We Meet Again 133-*134*, 135-*136*
Todd, Richard 267
Tomorrow and Tomorrow 68-69
Totter, Audrey 241
Tracy, Spencer 185
Trouble in Paradise 79-*82*, 174, 248
Trevor, Claire 224-225

U

Underworld Story, The 251-*252*, 253
Unseen, The 214, *221*-222

V

Virgin Queen, The 266-267
von Sternberg, Josef 75-76, 83, 116
von Stroheim, Erich 244-245

W

Warwick, Ruth *207*-208
Weapon, The 268-*269*
Webb, Clifton 228-*229*, 230
When Ladies Meet 190-*191*, 192
Whitty, Dame May 49, 74, 248
Wicked as They Come 268
Wilde, Oscar 1, 212, 225
Woman Against Woman 161-162
Wright, Teresa *189*
Wray, Fay 114, 116
Wyler, William 116, 120-122, 124, 178, 182-183, 188-190, 200, 202

Y

Young, Loretta 172-173
Young, Robert 192, 219
Young, Roland 199
Young Idea, The 28-30
Young Ideas 211

Z

Zanuck, Darryl 140, 169, 227
Zaza 144, 165-*167*, 171

PHOTO CREDITS

Every effort has been made to trace the copyright holders of photographs in this book; if any have been inadvertently overlooked, the author and publisher will be pleased to make the necessary changes.

All Warner Bros. © Warner Bros. Entertainment Inc. Co. All Rights Reserved

All MGM © Metro-Goldwyn-Mayer Studios Inc. All Rights Reserved

All 20th Century-Fox photos © 20th Century-Fox Film Corp. All Rights Reserved

All Paramount photos © Paramount Pictures. All Rights Reserved

All Columbia photos Columbia Pictures-Sony Entertainment. All Rights Reserved

All Universal photos © Universal Studios. All Rights Reserved

All RKO photos © RKO Pictures LLC. All Rights Reserved

All Allied Artists photos, c. Allied Artists Int. Inc. All Rights Reserved

All other photos, unless otherwise noted, are from the author's collection. The author thanks Brian Taves for access to photos from the Robert Florey estate.

Back cover: *Trouble in Paradise* with Kay Francis (Paramount); *The Little Foxes* with Bette Davis (Warner Bros.); *Riptide* with Norma Shearer (MGM)

ABOUT THE AUTHOR

Scott O'Brien paid tribute to six cinema legends who never had full-fledged biographies written: Kay Francis, Virginia Bruce, Ann Harding, Ruth Chatterton, George Brent and Sylvia Sidney. Scott contributes numerous articles for publications such as *Films of the Golden Age*, *Classic Images* and *Filmfax*. Guest appearances include the San Francisco Silent Film Festival, Cinecon, KRCB's *Outbeat Radio* and *A Novel Idea*, as well as Jan Wahl's "Inside Entertainment," for the Bay Area KRON-TV. Scott has introduced film classics *Trouble in Paradise* (1932) and *Double Harness* (1933) at the Library of Congress' Packard Theater in Culpeper, Va. Scott appeared in two documentaries: *Queer Icon: The Cult of Bette Davis* (2009), and *Reabhloidithe Hollywood* (2013) for Irish television, chronicling the career of George Brent, a former dispatcher for the IRA. Scott lives with his spouse Joel Bellagio in Sonoma County. (website:www.scottobrienauthor.com)

www.ingramcontent.com/pod-product-compliance
Lightning Source LLC
Chambersburg PA
CBHW071951220426
43662CB00009B/1081